RESEARCH SYNTHESIS AND META-ANALYSIS

4th Edition

APPLIED SOCIAL RESEARCH
METHODS SERIES

Series Editors

LEONARD BICKMAN, Peabody College, Vanderbilt University, Nashville
DEBRA J. ROG, Vanderbilt University, Washington, DC

RESEARCH SYNTHESIS AND META-ANALYSIS

A Step-by-Step Approach

4th Edition

Harris Cooper
Duke University

APPLIED SOCIAL RESEARCH METHODS SERIES

Volume 2

SAGE

Los Angeles | London | New Delhi
Singapore | Washington DC

For information:

SAGE Publications, Inc.
2455 Teller Road
Thousand Oaks, California 91320
E-mail: order@sagepub.com

SAGE Publications India Pvt. Ltd.
B 1/I 1 Mohan Cooperative
  Industrial Area
Mathura Road, New Delhi 110 044
India

SAGE Publications Ltd.
1 Oliver's Yard
55 City Road
London EC1Y 1SP
United Kingdom

SAGE Publications Asia-Pacific
  Pte. Ltd.
33 Pekin Street #02-01
Far East Square
Singapore 048763

Printed in the United States of America

Library of Congress Cataloging-in-Publication Data

Cooper, Harris M.
  Research synthesis and meta-analysis : a step-by-step approach /
Harris M. Cooper.—4th ed.
    p. cm.—(Applied social research methods series; 2)
  Rev. ed. of: Synthesizing research. 3rd ed. c1998.
  Includes bibliographical references and index.
  ISBN 978-1-4129-3705-4 (pbk.)
    1. Social sciences—Research. I. Cooper, Harris M. Synthesizing research. II. Title.

H62.C5859 2009
300.72—dc22   2008044920

This book is printed on acid-free paper.

9   10   11   12   13   10   9   8   7   6   5   4   3   2   1

Acquisitions Editor:	Vicki Knight
Associate Editor:	Sean Connelly
Editorial Assistant:	Lauren Habib
Production Editor:	Catherine M. Chilton
Copy Editor:	Brenda Weight
Typesetter:	C&M Digitals (P) Ltd.
Proofreader:	Doris Hus
Indexer:	Diggs Publication Services
Cover Designer:	Arup Giri
Marketing Manager:	Stephanie Adams

Contents

Preface to the Fourth Edition

Every scientific investigation begins with the researcher examining reports of previous studies related to the topic of interest. Without this step, researchers cannot expect their efforts to contribute to an integrated, comprehensive picture of the world. They cannot achieve the progress that comes from building on the efforts of others. Also, investigators working in isolation are doomed to repeat the mistakes made by their predecessors.

Until recently, little guidance was available for how to conduct a research synthesis—how to find research already conducted on a particular topic, gather information from research reports, evaluate the quality of research, integrate results, interpret the cumulative findings, and present a comprehensive and coherent report of the synthesis' findings. This book presents the basic steps in carrying out a research synthesis. It is intended for use by social and behavioral scientists who are unfamiliar with research synthesis and meta-analysis but who possess an introductory background in basic research methods and statistics.

The approach to research synthesis presented in this book represents a significant departure from how reviews were conducted just 30 years ago. Instead of a subjective, narrative approach, this book presents an objective, systematic approach. Herein, you will learn how to carry out an integration of research according to the principles of good science. The intended result is a research synthesis that can be replicated by others, can create consensus among scholars, and can lead to constructive debate on unresolved issues. Equally important, users of this approach should complete their research synthesis feeling knowledgeable and confident that their future primary research can make a contribution to the field.

The scientific approach to research synthesis has rapidly gained acceptance. In the years between its four editions, the procedures outlined in this book have changed from being controversial practices to being accepted ones. Indeed, in many fields the approach outlined herein is now obligatory. The years have also brought improvements in synthesis techniques. The technology surrounding literature searching has changed dramatically. The statistical underpinnings of meta-analysis—the quantitative combination of study results—have been developed and the application of these procedures has become more accessible. Many techniques have been devised to help research synthesists present their results in a fashion that will be meaningful to their audience. Methodologists have proposed ways to make syntheses more resistant to criticism. This fourth edition incorporates these changes.

Several institutions and individuals have been instrumental in the preparation of the different editions of this book. First, the United States Department of Education provided research support while the first and third editions of the manuscript were prepared. Special thanks go to numerous former and current graduate students: Kathryn Anderson, Brad Bushman, Vicki Conn, Amy Dent, Maureen Findley, Pamela Hazelrigg, Ken Ottenbacher, Erika Patall, Georgianne Robinson, David Tom, and Julie Yu. Each performed a research review in his or her area of interest under my supervision. Each has had their work serve as an example in the book, and four of their efforts are used in the current edition to illustrate the different synthesis techniques. Jeff Valentine, also a former student of mine, was a collaborator on the work regarding the evaluation of research discussed in Chapter 5. Four reference librarians, Kathleen Connors, Jolene Ezell, Jeanmarie Fraser, and Judy Pallardy, helped with the chapter on literature searching. Larry Hedges and Terri Pigott have examined my exposition of statistical techniques. Three more graduate students, Ashley Bates Allen, Cyndi Kernahan, and Laura Muhlenbruck, read and reacted to chapters in various editions. Angela Clinton, Cathy Luebbering, and Pat Shanks have typed, retyped, and proofread my manuscripts. My sincerest thanks to these friends and colleagues.

Harris Cooper
Durham, North Carolina

Acknowledgments

SAGE Publications would like to thank the following reviewers:

Jeffrey S. Berman
University of Memphis

Kathaleen C. Bloom
University of North Florida

Douglas D. Perkins
Vanderbilt University

About the Author

Harris M. Cooper is Professor in the Department of Psychology and Neuroscience at Duke University. He earned his doctorate degree in social psychology from the University of Connecticut. His research interests include research synthesis, applications of social and developmental psychology to educational policy issues, homework, school calendars, and afterschool programs.

To Elizabeth

1

Introduction

This chapter describes

- A justification for why attention to research synthesis methods is important
- The goals of this book
- A definition of the terms *research synthesis* and *meta-analysis*
- A comparison of traditional narrative methods of research synthesis and methods based on scientific principles
- A brief history of the development of the methods presented in this book
- A seven-step model for the research synthesis process
- An introduction to four research syntheses that will serve as practical examples in the chapters that follow

Science is a cooperative, interdependent enterprise. The hundreds of hours you might spend conducting a study ultimately contribute just one piece to a much larger puzzle. The value of your study will be determined as much by how it fits with previous work and what questions it leaves for future research as from its own findings. Although it is true that some studies receive more attention than others, this is typically because the piece of the puzzle they solve (or the new puzzle they introduce) is extremely important, not because they are puzzle solutions in and of themselves.

THE NEED FOR ATTENTION
TO RESEARCH SYNTHESIS

Given that science is a cooperative enterprise, trustworthy accounts that accumulate past research are a necessary condition for orderly knowledge building. Yet, until just over a quarter century ago, social scientists paid little attention

1

to how investigators located, evaluated, summarized, and interpreted past research. This omission in methods became glaring after huge increases in the amount of social science research—accompanying the explosion in the number of social researchers that occurred in the 1960s and 1970s—put the lack of systematic synthesis procedures in bold relief. As the amount of research grew, so did the need for credible ways to integrate their findings.

Access to social science scholarship also has changed dramatically. In particular, the ability to find other people's completed research has been facilitated by online reference databases and the Internet. Developing a list of research articles on a topic that interests you used to involve the lengthy and tedious scrutiny of printed compendia. Today, such lists can be generated, scrutinized, and revised with a few keystrokes. In the past, if you found some article abstracts of interest, communication with other researchers could take weeks. Now, with electronic mail and file transfer, documents can be shared in seconds with the press of a button.

The need for trustworthy accounts of past research has also been heightened by growing specialization within the social sciences. Today, time constraints make it impossible for most social scientists to keep up with primary research except within a few topic areas of special interest to them. Four decades ago, Garvey and Griffith (1971) wrote,

> The individual scientist is being overloaded with scientific information. Perhaps the alarm over an "information crisis" arose because sometime in the last information doubling period, the individual psychologist became overburdened and could no longer keep up with and assimilate all the information being produced that was related to his primary specialty. (p. 350)

What was true in 1971 is even truer today.

And finally, the call for use of evidence-based decision making has placed a new emphasis on the importance of understanding how research was conducted, what it found, and what the cumulative evidence suggests is best practice (American Psychological Association's Presidential Task Force on Evidence-Based Practice, 2006). For example, in medicine there exists an international consortium of researchers (Cochrane Collaboration, 2008) producing thousands of papers examining the cumulative evidence on everything from public health initiatives to surgical procedures. In public policy, a consortium similar to that in medicine now exists (Campbell Collaboration, 2008), as do organizations meant to promote government policy making based on rigorous evidence of program effectiveness (e.g., Coalition for Evidence-Based Policy, 2008). Each of these efforts, and many others, relies on research syntheses to assist practitioners and policy makers in making critical decisions meant to improve human welfare.

GOALS AND PREMISES OF THE BOOK

This book is meant to serve as an introductory methods text on how to conduct a research synthesis and meta-analysis in the social and behavioral sciences. The approach I will take applies the basic tenets of sound data gathering to the task of producing a comprehensive integration of past research on a topic. I will assume that you agree with me that the rules of rigorous, systematic social science inquiry are the same whether the inquirer is conducting a new data collection (a primary study) or a research synthesis. However, the two types of inquiry require techniques specific to their purpose.

There is one critical premise underlying the methods described in this text. It is that *integrating separate research projects into a coherent whole involves inferences as central to the validity of knowledge as the inferences involved in drawing conclusions from primary data analysis.* When you read a research synthesis, you cannot take for granted the validity of its conclusions; its validity must be evaluated against scientific standards. Social scientists performing a research synthesis make numerous decisions that affect the outcomes of their work. Each choice may bolster or threaten the trustworthiness of those outcomes. Therefore, if social science knowledge contained in research syntheses is to be trustworthy, *research synthesists must be required to meet the same rigorous methodological standards that are applied to primary researchers.*

Judging the validity of primary research in the social sciences gained its modern foothold with the publication of Campbell and Stanley's (1963) monograph *Experimental and Quasi-Experimental Designs for Research,* and a lineage of subsequent work refined this approach (e.g., Bracht & Glass, 1968; Campbell, 1969; Cook & Campbell, 1979; Shadish, Cook, & Campbell, 2002). However, it was not until 15 years after Campbell and Stanley's pioneering work that social scientists realized they also needed a way to think about research syntheses that provided systematic guidelines for evaluating the validity of their outcomes as well. This book describes (a) an organizing scheme for judging the validity of research syntheses and (b) the techniques you can use to maximize the validity of conclusions drawn in syntheses you might conduct yourself.

DEFINITIONS OF LITERATURE REVIEWS

There are many terms that are used interchangeably to label the activities described in this book. These terms include *literature review, research review, systematic review, research synthesis,* and *meta-analysis.* In fact, some of these terms should be viewed as interchangeable, whereas some have broader or narrower meanings than others.

The broadest term is *literature review*. Literature reviews typically appear as detailed independent works or as brief introductions to reports of new primary data. When a literature review appears independent of new data, it can serve many different purposes. It can have numerous different focuses, goals, perspectives, coverage strategies, organizations, and audiences (see Table 1.1; Cooper, 1988). For instance, literature reviews can focus on research outcomes, research methods, theories, and/or applications. Literature reviews can attempt (a) to integrate what others have done and said, (b) to criticize previous scholarly works, (c) to build bridges between related topic areas, and/or (d) to identify the central issues in a field. The scope of a literature review that introduces a new primary study typically is quite narrow. It will be restricted to those theoretical works and empirical studies pertinent to the specific issue addressed by the new study.

Literature reviews combining two specific sets of focuses and goals appear most frequently in the scientific literature. This type of literature review, and the focus of this book, has been alternately called a research synthesis, a research review, or a systematic review. *Research syntheses focus on empirical studies and seek to summarize past research by drawing overall conclusions from many separate investigations that address related or identical hypotheses. The research synthesist's goal is to present the state of knowledge concerning the relation(s) of interest and to highlight important issues that research has left unresolved.* From the reader's viewpoint, a research synthesis is intended to "replace those earlier papers that have been lost from sight behind the research front" (Price, 1965, p. 513) and to direct future research so that it yields a maximum amount of new information.

The second kind of literature review is a theoretical review. Here, the reviewer hopes to present the theories offered to explain a particular phenomenon and to compare them in breadth, internal consistency, and the nature of their predictions. Theoretical reviews will typically contain (a) descriptions of critical experiments already conducted or suggested, (b) assessments of which theory is most powerful and consistent with known relations, and sometimes (c) reformulations and/or integrations of abstract notions from different theories.

Often, a comprehensive literature review will address several of these sets of issues. Research syntheses are most common, however, and theoretical reviews will typically contain some synthesis of research. It is also not unusual for research syntheses to address multiple, related hypotheses. A synthesis might examine the relation between several different independent or predictor variables and a single dependent or criterion variable. For example, Brown (1996) summarized research on several types of antecedents to job involvement, including personality variables, job characteristics, supervisory variables, and role perceptions. Or a synthesis might try to summarize research

Table 1.1 Taxonomy of Literature Reviews

Characteristic	Categories
Focus	Research findings
	Research methods
	Theories
	Practices or applications
Goal	Integration
	generalization
	conflict resolution
	linguistic bridge building
	Criticism
	Identification of central issues
Perspective	Neutral representation
	Espousal of position
Coverage	Exhaustive
	Exhaustive with selective citation
	Representative
	Central or pivotal
Organization	Historical
	Conceptual
	Methodological
Audience	Specialized scholars
	General scholars
	Practitioners or policymakers
	General public

SOURCE: Cooper (1988, p. 109). Copyright © 1988, Transaction Publishers. Reprinted by permission.

related to a series of temporally linked hypotheses. Harris and Rosenthal (1985) studied the mediation of interpersonal expectancy effects by first synthesizing research on how expectancies affect the behavior of the person who holds the expectation and then on how this behavior influenced the behavior of the target.

This book is about research synthesis. Not only is this the most frequent kind of literature review in the social sciences, but it also contains many, if not most, of the decision points present in other types of reviews—and some unique ones as well. I have chosen to favor the label *research synthesis* over other labels for this type of literature review because the labels *research review* and *systematic review* occasionally cause confusion as they can also be applied to the process of research report reviewing, that is, critically evaluating a single study that has been submitted for publication in a scientific journal. Thus, a journal editor may ask a scholar to provide a research review or a systematic review of a manuscript. The term research synthesis avoids this confusion and puts the synthesis activity front and center. Also, this label is used by *The Handbook of Research Synthesis and Meta-Analysis* (Cooper, Hedges, & Valentine, 2009), a text that describes approaches consistent with those presented here but in a more advanced manner.

The term *meta-analysis* is often used as a synonym for *research synthesis*, *research review*, or *systematic review*. In this book, *meta-analysis* will be employed solely to denote the quantitative procedures used to statistically combine the results of studies (these procedures are described in Chapter 5).

WHY WE NEED RESEARCH
SYNTHESES BASED ON SCIENTIFIC PRINCIPLES

Before the methods described in this book were available, most social scientists developed summaries of empirical research using a process in which multiple studies investigating the same topics were collected and described in a narrative fashion. These synthesists would describe one study after another, often arranged temporally, and then would draw a conclusion about the research findings based on their interpretation of what was found in the literature as a whole.

Research syntheses conducted in the traditional narrative manner have been much criticized. Opponents of the traditional research synthesis have suggested that this method—and its resulting conclusions—is imprecise in both process and outcome. In particular, traditional narrative research syntheses lack explicit standards of proof. Readers and users of these syntheses do not know what standard of evidence was used to decide whether a set of studies supported its conclusion (Johnson & Eagly, 2000). The combining rules used by traditional synthesists are rarely known to anyone but the synthesists themselves, if even they are consciously aware of what is guiding their inferences.

Three other disadvantages to traditional research syntheses, at least as they were carried out in the past, have often been leveled against this approach. First, traditional research syntheses rarely involve systematic techniques to ensure that (a) all the relevant research was located and included in the synthesis and (b) information from each study was gathered accurately. Traditional literature searches often stopped after the synthesists had gathered the studies they were already aware of or located through a search of a single reference database. Second, traditional narrative syntheses were prone to use post hoc criteria to decide whether individual studies met an acceptable threshold for methodological quality. This lack of explicit use of a priori quality standards led Glass (1976) to write,

> A common method of integrating several studies with inconsistent findings is to carp on the design or analysis deficiencies of all but a few studies—those remaining frequently being one's own work or that of one's students or friends—and then advance the one or two "acceptable" studies as the truth of the matter. (p. 3)

Finally, traditional narrative syntheses, by their very nature, fail to result in statements regarding the overall magnitude of the relationship under investigation. They cannot answer the questions, "What was the size of the relationship between the variables of interest?" or "How much change was caused by the intervention?" or "Was this relationship or intervention effect larger or smaller than that between other variables of interest or other interventions?"

Concern about the potential for error and imprecision in traditional narrative syntheses encouraged social science methodologists to develop the more rigorous and transparent alternatives described in this book. Today, state-of-the-art research syntheses use a collection of methodological and statistical techniques meant to standardize and make explicit the procedures used to collect, catalog, and combine primary research. For example, literature searching strategies are designed to minimize differences between the results of retrieved studies and studies that could not be found. Before the literature search begins, the criteria for deciding whether a study was conducted well enough to be included in the synthesis are explicitly stated. These criteria then are consistently applied to all studies, regardless of whether the results support or refute the hypothesis under investigation. Data from the research report are recorded using prespecified coding categories by coders trained to maximize interjudge agreement. Meta-analytic statistical methods are applied to summarize the data and provide a quantitative description of the cumulative research findings. Thus, research synthesis and the statistical integration of study results are conducted with the same structure and rigor as is data analysis in primary scientific studies.

One example of how using state-of-the-art research synthesis methods can change cumulative findings was provided by a study conducted by Robert Rosenthal and me (Cooper & Rosenthal, 1980). In this study, graduate students and university faculty members were asked to evaluate a literature on a simple hypothesis: Are there sex differences in task persistence? All the participants in our study synthesized the same set of persistence studies but half of them used quantitative procedures and half used whatever criteria appealed to them, in other words, their own mental inference test. We found statistical synthesists thought there was more support for the sex-difference hypothesis and a larger relationship between variables than did the other synthesists. Statistical synthesists also tended to view future replications as less necessary than other synthesists, although the difference between statistical and other synthesists did not reach statistical significance.

Principal Outcomes of a Research Synthesis

In addition to using a rigorous and systematic approach to cumulating the research, a state-of-the-art research synthesis is expected to provide information on several types of findings relating to the cumulative results of the research it covers. First, if a theoretical proposition is under scrutiny, readers of research syntheses will expect you to give them an overall estimate of the support for the hypothesis, both in terms of whether the null hypothesis can be rejected and the hypothesis' explanatory power. Or if an applied proposition is under scrutiny, readers will expect you to estimate the effectiveness of the intervention or impact of the policy. But you cannot stop there. Your audience also will expect to see tests of whether this relationship or effectiveness estimate is influenced by variations in context suggested by the theory or intervention, how the study was carried out, and who the participants were. Readers expect to be told whether study results systematically varied according to characteristics of the manipulations or interventions (if these were used), the settings and times at which the studies were conducted, differences between participants, characteristics of the measuring instruments, and so on.

A BRIEF HISTORY OF
RESEARCH SYNTHESIS AND META-ANALYSIS

In the previous section, I pointed out that the increase in social science research coupled with the new information technologies and the desire for trustworthy research syntheses in policy domains gave impetus to development of the methods described in this book. In the following, I provide a brief history of people and events that have contributed to these techniques (see Cooper, Patall, & Lindsay, 2009, for a similar history).

Karl Pearson (1904) is credited with publishing what is believed to be the first meta-analysis (Shadish & Haddock, 2009). Pearson gathered data from 11 studies testing the effectiveness of a vaccine against typhoid and calculated for each a statistic he had recently developed, called the correlation coefficient. Based on the average correlations, Pearson concluded that other vaccines were more effective than the new one.

In 1932, Ronald Fisher, in his classic text *Statistical Methods for Research Workers*, wrote, "It sometimes happens that although few or [no statistical tests] can be claimed individually as significant, yet the aggregate gives an impression that the probabilities are lower than would have been obtained by chance" (p. 99). Fisher was noting that statistical tests often fail to reject the null hypothesis because they lack statistical power. However, if the "under-powered" tests were combined, their cumulative power would be greater. Fisher presented a technique for combining the p-values that came from statistically independent tests of the same hypothesis.

Fisher's work would be followed by more than a dozen methodological papers published prior to 1960 (see Olkin, 1990), but the techniques were rarely put to use in research syntheses. Gene Glass (1976) introduced the term meta-analysis to mean the statistical analysis of results from individual studies "for purposes of integrating the findings" (p. 3). Also, Glass (1977) wrote, "The accumulated findings of . . . studies should be regarded as complex data points, no more comprehensible without statistical analysis than hundreds of data points in a single study" (p. 352).

By the mid-1970s, several high-profile applications of quantitative synthesis techniques focused the spotlight squarely on meta-analysis. Each of these research teams concluded that the traditional research synthesis simply would not suffice. Largely independently, they rediscovered and reinvented Pearson's and Fisher's solutions to their problem. In clinical psychology, Smith and Glass (1977) assessed the effectiveness of psychotherapy by combining 833 tests of treatment. In social psychology, Rosenthal and Rubin (1978) presented a research synthesis of 345 studies on the effects of interpersonal expectations on behavior. In education, Glass and Smith (1979) conducted a synthesis of the relation between class size and academic achievement covering 725 estimates of the relation based on data from nearly 900,000 students. In personnel psychology, Hunter, Schmidt, and Hunter (1979) uncovered 866 comparisons of the differential validity of employment tests for black and white workers.

Independent of the meta-analysis movement but at about the same time, several attempts were made to draw research synthesis into a broad scientific context. In 1971, Feldman published an article titled "Using the Work of Others: Some Observations on Reviewing and Integrating," in which he wrote, "Systematically reviewing and integrating . . . the literature of a field may be considered a type of research in its own right—one using a characteristic set of research techniques and methods" (p. 86). In the same year, Light and Smith (1971) argued that if treated properly, the variation in outcomes among related studies could be a valuable source of information, rather than a source of consternation, as it appeared to be when treated with traditional synthesis methods. Taveggia (1974) described six common activities in literature syntheses: selecting research; retrieving, indexing, and coding studies; analyzing the comparability of findings; accumulating comparable findings; analyzing the resulting distributions; and reporting the results.

Two articles that appeared in the *Review of Educational Research* in the early 1980s brought the meta-analytic and synthesis-as-research perspectives together. First, Jackson (1980) proposed six synthesis tasks "analogous to those performed during primary research" (p. 441). In 1982, I took the analogy between research synthesis and primary research to its logical conclusion and presented the five-stage model with accompanying threats to validity that was the precursor of the first edition of this book (Cooper, 1982).

Also in the 1980s, five books appeared that were devoted primarily to meta-analytic methods. Glass, McGaw, and Smith (1981) presented meta-analysis as a new application of analysis of variance and multiple regression procedures, with effect sizes treated as the dependent variable. Hunter, Schmidt, and Jackson (1982) introduced meta-analytic procedures that focused on (a) comparing the observed variation in study outcomes to that expected by chance and (b) correcting observed correlations and their variance for known sources of bias (e.g., sampling errors, range restrictions, unreliability of measurements). Rosenthal (1984) presented a compendium of meta-analytic methods covering, among other topics, the combining of significance levels, effect size estimation, and the analysis of variation in effect sizes. Rosenthal's procedures for testing moderators of effect size estimates were not based on traditional inferential statistics, but on a new set of techniques involving assumptions tailored specifically for the analysis of study outcomes. Light and Pillemer (1984) presented an approach that placed special emphasis on the importance of meshing both numbers and narrative for the effective interpretation and communication of synthesis results. Finally, in 1985, with the publication of *Statistical Methods for Meta-Analysis,* Hedges and Olkin helped elevate the quantitative synthesis of research to an independent specialty within the statistical sciences. This book summarized and expanded nearly a decade of programmatic developments by the authors and established the procedures' legitimacy by presenting rigorous statistical proofs.

Since the mid-1980s, several other books have appeared on meta-analysis. Some of these treat the topic generally (e.g., this text; Hunter & Schmidt, 2004; Lipsey & Wilson, 2001; Roberts & Petticrew, 2006), some treat it from the perspective of particular research design conceptualizations (e.g., Eddy, Hassleblad, & Schachter, 1992; Mullen, 1989), and some are tied to particular software packages (e.g., Johnson, 1993; Wang & Bushman, 1999). Other texts have looked to the future of research synthesis as a scientific endeavor (e.g., Cook et al., 1992; Wachter & Straf, 1990). In 1994, the first edition of *The Handbook of Research Synthesis* was published, and the second edition appeared in 2009 (Cooper, Hedges, & Valentine, 2009).

THE STAGES OF RESEARCH SYNTHESIS

Textbooks on social research methodology present research projects as a sequenced set of activities. Although methodologists differ somewhat in their definitions of research stages, the most important distinctions in stages can be identified with a high degree of consensus.

As noted previously, I argued in 1982 that similar to primary research, a research synthesis involved five stages (Cooper, 1982). The stages presented the principal tasks that need to be undertaken so that the synthesists produce an unbiased description of the cumulative state of evidence on a research problem or hypothesis. For each stage, I codified the research question asked, its primary function in the synthesis, and the procedural differences that might cause variation in conclusions. For example, in both primary research and research synthesis, the problem formulation stage involves defining the variables of interest and the data collection stage involves gathering the evidence. Synthesists, like primary data collectors, can make different choices about how to carry out their inquiries, and differences in methodologies can create differences in their conclusions.

Most importantly, each methodological decision at each stage of a synthesis may enhance or undermine the trustworthiness of its conclusion or, in common social science terms, can create a threat to the validity of its conclusions. (A formal definition of *validity* appears in Chapter 4.) In my 1982 article and earlier editions of this book, I applied the notion of threats-to-inferential-validity to research synthesis. I identified 10 threats to validity that might undermine the trustworthiness of the finding contained in a research synthesis. I focused primarily on validity threats that arise from the procedures used to cumulate studies, for example, conducting a literature search that missed relevant studies. This threats-to-validity approach was subsequently applied to research synthesis by Matt and Cook (1994, revised in 2009), who identified over 20 threats, and Shadish, Cook, and Campbell (2002), who expanded this list to nearly 30 threats. In each case, the authors described threats related to potential biases caused by the process of research synthesis itself as well as to deficiencies in the primary research that made up the evidence base of the synthesis, for example, the lack of representation of important participant populations in the primary studies.

Table 1.2 summarizes a modification of the model that appeared in earlier editions of this book. In the new model (Cooper, 2007a, presented a six-step model), the process of research synthesis is divided into seven steps:

- Step 1: Formulating the problem
- Step 2: Searching the literature
- Step 3: Gathering information from studies
- Step 4: Evaluating the quality of studies
- Step 5: Analyzing and integrating the outcomes of studies
- Step 6: Interpreting the evidence
- Step 7: Presenting the results

These seven steps will provide the framework for the remainder of this book. Different from my earlier conceptualization, the new model separates two of the earlier stages into four separate stages. First, the literature search and the process of extracting information from research reports are now treated as two separate stages. Second, the processes of (a) summarizing and integrating the evidence from individual studies and (b) interpreting the cumulative findings that arise from these analyses are treated separately. These revisions are based on much recent work that suggests these activities are best thought of as independent. Synthesists can thoroughly or cursorily search a literature. Then they can code much or little information from each report, in a reliable or unreliable manner. Similarly, synthesists can correctly or incorrectly summarize and integrate the evidence from the individual studies and then, even if correctly summarized, interpret what these cumulative findings mean either accurately or inaccurately.

Step 1: Formulating the Problem

The first step in any research endeavor is to formulate the problem. During problem formulation, the variables involved in the inquiry are given both abstract and concrete definitions. At this stage you ask, "What are the concepts I want to study?" and "What operations are expressions of these concepts?" In answering these questions, you determine what research evidence will be relevant (and irrelevant) to the problem or hypothesis of interest. Also, during problem formulation, you decide whether you are interested in simply describing the variable(s) of interest to you or you want to investigate a relationship between two or more variables, and whether this relationship is associational or causal in nature.

In Chapter 2, I examine the decision points you will encounter during the problem formulation stage. These decision points relate first and foremost to the breadth of the concepts involved in the relations of interest and how these correspond to the operations used to study them. They also relate to the types of research designs used in the primary research and how these correspond to the inferences you wish to make.

Step 2: Searching the Literature

The data collection stage of research involves making a choice about the population of elements that will be the target of the study. In primary social science research, the target will typically include individuals or groups. In research synthesis, identifying target populations is complicated by the fact that you want to make inferences about two targets. First, you want the cumulative result to reflect the results of all previous research on the problem. Second, you hope that the included studies will allow generalizations to the individuals or groups that are the focus of the topic area.

In Chapter 3, I present a discussion of methods for locating studies. The discussion includes a listing of the sources of studies available to social scientists, how to access and use the most important sources, and what biases may be present in the information contained in each source.

Step 3: Gathering Information From Studies

The study coding stage requires that researchers consider what information they want to gather from each research unit. In primary research, the data-gathering instruments might include questionnaires, behavior observations, and/or physiological measures. In research synthesis, this involves the information about each study that you have decided is relevant to the problem of interest. This information will include not only characteristics of the study that are derived from theoretical questions—that is, about the nature of the independent and dependent variables—but also about how the study was conducted and its research design, implementation, and statistical results. Beyond deciding what information to collect and giving this clear definition, this stage requires researchers to develop a procedure for training the people who will gather the information and ensuring that they do so in a reliable and interpretable manner.

Table 1.2 Research Synthesis Conceptualized as a Research Project

Step in Research Synthesis	Research Question Asked at This Stage of the Synthesis	Primary Function Served in the Synthesis	Procedural Variation That Might Produce Differences in Conclusions
Formulating the Problem	What research evidence will be relevant to the problem or hypothesis of interest in the synthesis?	Define the (a) variables and (b) relationships of interest so that relevant and irrelevant studies can be distinguished	Variation in the conceptual breadth and detail of definitions might lead to differences in the research operations (a) deemed relevant and/or (b) tested as moderating influences
Searching the Literature	What procedures should be used to find relevant research?	Identify (a) sources (e.g., reference databases, journals) and (b) terms used to search for relevant research	Variation in searched sources might lead to systematic differences in the retrieved research
Gathering Information From Studies	What information about each study is relevant to the problem or hypothesis of interest?	Collect relevant information about studies in a reliable manner	Variation (a) in information gathered might lead to differences in what is tested as an influence on cumulative results, (b) in coder training might lead to differences in entries on coding sheets, and/or (c) in rules for deciding what study results are viewed as independent might lead to differences in the amount and specificity of data used to draw cumulative conclusions

Evaluating the Quality of Studies	What research should be included in the synthesis based on (a) the suitability of the methods for studying the synthesis question and/or (b) problems in research implementation?	Identify and apply criteria that separate studies conducted in ways that correspond with the research question from studies that do not	Variation in criteria for decisions about study inclusion might lead to systematic differences in which studies remain in the synthesis
Analyzing and Integrating the Outcomes of Studies	What procedures should be used to condense and combine the research results?	Identify and apply procedures for (a) combining results across studies and (b) testing for differences in results between studies	Variation in procedures used to analyze results of individual studies (e.g., narrative, vote count, averaged effect sizes) can lead to differences in cumulative results
Interpreting the Evidence	What conclusions can be drawn about the cumulative state of the research evidence?	Summarize the cumulative research evidence with regard to its strength, generality, and limitations	Variation in (a) criteria for labeling results as important and (b) attention to details of studies might lead to differences in interpretation of findings
Presenting the Results	What information should be included in the report of the synthesis?	Identify and apply editorial guidelines and judgment to determine aspects of methods and results readers of the report will need to know	Variation in reporting might (a) lead readers to place more or less trust in synthesis outcomes and (b) influence others' ability to replicate results

Chapter 4 will present some concrete recommendations about what information you should collect from empirical studies that have been judged relevant to your problem. It also introduces the steps that need to be taken to properly train the people who will act as study coders. Also, Chapter 4 contains some recommendations concerning what you can do when research reports are unavailable or when obtained reports do not have the information you need in them.

Step 4: Evaluating the Quality of Studies

After data are collected, the researcher makes critical judgments about the "quality" of data, or its correspondence to the question that is motivating the research. Each data point is examined in light of surrounding evidence to determine whether it is too contaminated by factors irrelevant to the problem under consideration to be of value. If it is, the bad data must be discarded or given little credibility. For example, primary researchers examine how closely the research protocol was followed when each participant took part in the study. Research synthesists evaluate the methodology of studies to determine if the manner in which the data were collected might make it inappropriate for addressing the problem at hand.

In Chapter 2, I discuss how research designs (e.g., associational or causal) correspond to different research problems, and in Chapter 5, I discuss how to evaluate the quality of research. I also look at biases in quality judgments and make some suggestions concerning the assessment of interjudge reliability.

Step 5: Analyzing and Integrating the Outcomes of Studies

During data analysis, the separate data points collected by the researcher are summarized and integrated into a unified picture. Data analysis demands that the researcher distinguish systematic data patterns from "noise" or chance fluctuation. In both primary research and research synthesis, this process typically involves the application of statistical procedures.

In Chapter 6, I explain some methods for combining the results of separate studies, or methods of meta-analysis. Also, I show how to estimate the magnitude of a relationship or the impact of an intervention. Finally, I illustrate some techniques for analyzing why different studies find different relationship strengths.

Step 6: Interpreting the Evidence

Next, the researcher interprets the cumulative evidence and determines what conclusions are warranted by the data. These conclusions can relate to the evidence with regard to whether the relation(s) of interest are supported by the data and, if so, with what certainty. They can also relate to the generality (or specificity) of the findings over different types of units, treatments, outcomes, and situations.

In Chapter 7, I examine some of the decision rules you should apply as you make assertions about what your research synthesis says. This includes some ideas about interpreting the strength and generality of conclusions as well as the magnitude of relationships and intervention effects.

Step 7: Presenting the Results

Creating a public document that describes the investigation is the task that completes a research endeavor. In Chapter 8, I offer some concrete guidelines for what information needs to be reported regarding how the other six stages of the research synthesis were carried out.

Unlike the earlier editions of this text, I will hold the discussion regarding threats to validity until the final summary chapter, Chapter 9. Instead, I will frame the discussion of the stages of research synthesis by referring to 20 questions producers and consumers of research syntheses might ask that relate to the validity of conclusions. In my teaching, I have found this approach is simpler to follow and helps students keep the big picture in mind as they move through the process. Each question is phrased so that an affirmative response would mean confidence could be placed in the conclusions of the synthesis. The relevant questions will be presented at the beginning of the discussion of each stage and will be followed by the related procedural variations that might enhance or compromise the trustworthiness of conclusions—in other words, what needs to be done to answer the question "yes." Although the 20 questions are not an exhaustive list of those that might be asked, most of the threats to validity identified in earlier works find expression in the questions. A list of the questions appears in Table 1.3.

FOUR EXAMPLES OF RESEARCH SYNTHESIS

I have chosen four research syntheses to illustrate the practical aspects of conducting rigorous summaries of research. The topics of the four syntheses represent a broad spectrum of social science research, encompassing research from social and developmental psychology, clinical/community psychology, educational psychology, and health psychology. They involve diverse conceptual and operational variables. Even though the topics are very different, they are also general enough that readers in any discipline should find all four topics instructive and easy to follow without a large amount of

Table 1.3 A Checklist of Questions Concerning the Validity of Research Synthesis
Conclusions

Step 1: Formulating the problem

1. Are the variables of interest given clear conceptual definitions?
2. Do the operations that empirically define each variable of interest correspond to the variable's conceptual definition?
3. Is the problem stated so that the research designs and evidence needed to address it can be specified clearly?
4. Is the problem placed in a meaningful theoretical, historical, and/or practical context?

Step 2: Searching the literature

5. Were proper and exhaustive terms used in searches and queries of reference databases and research registries?
6. Were complementary searching strategies used to find relevant studies?

Step 3: Gathering information from studies

7. Were procedures employed to ensure the unbiased and reliable (a) application of criteria to determine the substantive relevance of studies and (b) retrieval of information from study reports?

Step 4: Evaluating the quality of studies

8. If studies were excluded from the synthesis because of design and implementation considerations, were these considerations (a) explicitly and operationally defined and (b) consistently applied to all studies?
9. Were studies categorized so that important distinctions could be made among them regarding their research design and implementation?

Step 5: Analyzing and integrating the outcomes of studies

10. Was an appropriate method used to combine and compare results across studies?
11. If a meta-analysis was performed, was an appropriate effect size metric used?
12. If a meta-analysis was performed, (a) were average effect sizes and confidence intervals reported and (b) was an appropriate model used to estimate the independent effects and the error in effect sizes?
13. If a meta-analysis was performed, was the homogeneity of effect sizes tested?
14. Were (a) study design and implementation features (as suggested by Question 8 above) along with (b) other critical features of studies, including historical, theoretical, and practical variables (as suggested by Question 4 above) tested as potential moderators of study outcomes?

Step 6: Interpreting the evidence

15. Were analyses carried out that tested whether results were sensitive to statistical assumptions and, if so, were these analyses used to help interpret the evidence?

16. Did the research synthesists (a) discuss the extent of missing data in the evidence base and (b) examine its potential impact on the synthesis' findings?

17. Did the research synthesists discuss the generality and limitations of the synthesis' findings?

18. Did the synthesists make the appropriate distinction between study-generated and synthesis-generated evidence when interpreting the synthesis' results?

19. If a meta-analysis was performed, did the synthesists (a) contrast the magnitude of effects with other related effect sizes and/or (b) present a practical interpretation of the significance of the effects?

Step 7: Presenting the results

20. Were the procedures and results of the research synthesis clearly and completely documented?

SOURCE: Adapted from Cooper, H. (2007a). *Evaluating and Interpreting Research Syntheses in Adult Learning and Literacy.* Boston, MA: National Center for the Study of Adult Learning and Literacy, World Education, Inc., p. 52.

background in the separate research areas. However, a brief introduction to each topic will be helpful.

The Effects of Choice on Intrinsic Motivation (Patall, Cooper, & Robinson, 2008)

The ability to make personal choices—be they between courses of action, products, or candidates for political office, to name just a few—is central to Western culture. Not surprisingly, then, many psychological theories posit that providing individuals with choices between tasks will improve their motivation to engage in the chosen activity. In this research synthesis, we examined the role of choice in motivation and behavior. First, we examined the overall effect of choice on intrinsic motivation and related outcomes. We also examined whether the effect of choice was enhanced or diminished by a number of theoretically derived moderators including the type of choice, the number of options in the choice, and the total number of choices made, among others. In this synthesis, the studies primarily used experimental designs and were conducted in social psychology laboratories.

The Effect of Homework on Academic
Achievement (Cooper, Robinson, & Patall, 2006)

Requiring students to carry out academic tasks during nonschool hours is a practice as old as formal schooling itself. However, the effectiveness of homework is still a source of controversy. Public opinion about homework fluctuated throughout the 20th century, and the controversy continues today. This synthesis focused on answering a simple question reflected in the article's title: "Does homework improve academic achievement?" We also looked at moderators of homework's effects, including the student's grade level and the subject matter. This research synthesis involved summarizing results from a few experimental studies conducted in actual classrooms, several studies that applied statistical models (multiple regressions, path analyses, structural equation models) to large databases, and many studies that simply correlated the time a student spent on homework with a measure of academic achievement.

Individual Differences in Attitudes
Toward Rape (Anderson, Cooper, & Okamura, 1997)

Rape is a serious social problem. Every day, many women are forced by men to have sex without the woman's consent. This research synthesis examined the demographic, cognitive, experiential, affective, and personality correlates of attitudes toward rape. We found research that looked at the attitudes of both men and women. Demographic correlates of attitudes toward rape included age, ethnicity, and socioeconomic status. Experiential correlates included involvement in previous rapes, knowing others who had been in a rape, and use of violent pornography. Personality correlates included the need for power and self-esteem. What value is there in summarizing research on rape attitudes? We hoped our synthesis would be used to help improve programs meant to prevent rape by helping identify people who would benefit most from rape prevention interventions. These studies were all correlational in nature.

Increasing Physical Activity Among
Aging Adults (Conn, Valentine, & Cooper, 2002)

Despite its known health benefits, physical activity among older adults remains low. In recent years, many interventions have been developed that attempt to get older people more active. This research synthesis focused on studies that evaluated the impact of these interventions. We were interested in the interventions' general success as well as in whether different types of interventions were more or less effective and with what types of participants. These evaluations included some studies that randomly assigned participants to a treatment or no-treatment condition, whereas other studies had the same participants in both the treatment and control conditions, that is, activity levels measured before the intervention were compared with activity levels after the intervention.

EXERCISE

The best exercise while reading this book is to plan and conduct a research synthesis in an area of interest to you. The synthesis should attempt to apply the guidelines outlined in the chapters that follow. If this is not possible, you should try to conduct the more discrete exercises that appear at the end of each chapter. Often, these exercises can be further simplified by dividing the work among members of your class.

2

Step 1

Formulating the Problem

What research evidence will be relevant to the problem or hypothesis of interest in the synthesis?

Primary Function Served in the Synthesis

To define the (a) variables and (b) relationships of interest so that relevant and irrelevant studies can be distinguished from one another

Procedural Variation That Might Produce Differences in Synthesis Conclusions

Variation in the conceptual breadth and detail of definitions might lead to differences in the research operations (a) deemed relevant and/or (b) tested as moderating influences

Questions to Ask When Evaluating the Formulation
for a Problem in a Research Synthesis

1. Are the variables of interest given clear conceptual definitions?

2. Do the operations that empirically define each variable of interest correspond to the variable's conceptual definition?

3. Is the problem stated so the research designs and evidence needed to address it can be specified clearly?

4. Is the problem placed in a meaningful theoretical, historical, and/or practical context?

This chapter describes

- The relationship between concepts and operations in research synthesis
- How to judge the relevance of primary research to a research synthesis problem
- The correspondence between research designs and research synthesis problems
- The distinction between study-generated and synthesis-generated evidence
- The treatment of main effects and interactions in research synthesis
- Approaches to establishing the value of a new research synthesis
- The role of previous syntheses in new synthesis efforts

All empirical work begins with a careful consideration of the research problem. In its most basic form, the research problem includes the definition of two variables and the rationale for studying their association. One rationale can be that a theory predicts a particular association between the variables, be it a causal relationship or a simple association, positive or negative. For example, self-determination theory (Deci, 1980) predicts that providing people with choices in what task to perform or how to perform it will have a positive causal effect on people's intrinsic motivation to do the task and persist at it. So manipulating choice, then measuring intrinsic motivation, will provide evidence on the veracity of the theory. Or a different rationale can be that some practical consideration suggests that any discovered relation might be important. For example, discovering the individual differences that correlate with attitudes about rape, even if there is little theory to guide us about what relationships to expect, might suggest ways to improve programs meant to prevent rape by helping identify people who would benefit most from different types of prevention interventions. Either rationale can be used for undertaking primary research or research syntheses.

The choice of a problem to study in primary research is influenced by your interests and the social conditions that surround you. This holds true as well for your choice of topics in research synthesis, with one important difference. When you do primary research, you are limited in your topic choice only by your imagination. When you conduct a research synthesis, you must study topics that already appear in the literature. In fact, a topic is probably not suitable for research synthesis unless it already has created sufficient interest within a discipline or disciplines to have inspired enough research to merit an effort at bringing it all together.

The fact that syntheses are tied to only those problems that have generated previous research does not mean research synthesis is less creative than primary data collection. Rather, your creativity will be used in different ways in research synthesis. Creativity enters a research synthesis when you must propose overarching schemes that help make sense of many related, but not identical, studies. The variation in methods across studies is always much greater than the variation in procedures used in any single study. For example, studies of choice and intrinsic motivation vary in the types of choices they allow, some involving choices among tasks (e.g., anagrams versus number games) and others involving choices among the circumstances under which the task will be performed (e.g., the color of the stimuli, whether to use a pen or pencil), to name just two types of variations. As a synthesist, you may find no guidance about how these variations should be meaningfully grouped to determine if they affect the relationship between choice and motivation (will grouping the choice manipulations depending on whether they are task relevant versus task irrelevant lead to an important discovery?). Or theories may suggest meaningful groupings, but it will be up to you to discover what these theoretical predictions are (what does self-determination theory say the effect of task relevance should be on how the ability to choose affects motivation?). Defining meaningful groupings of studies and justifying their use will be up to you. Your capacity for uncovering variables that explain why results differ in different studies and your ability to generate explanations for these relationships are creative and challenging aspects of the research synthesis process.

DEFINITION OF VARIABLES
IN SOCIAL SCIENCE RESEARCH

Similarities in Concepts and Operations
in Primary Research and Research Synthesis

The variables involved in any social science study must be defined in two ways. First, the variables must be given *conceptual definitions*. Conceptual definitions describe qualities of the variable that are independent of time and space and can be used to distinguish events that are and are not relevant to the concept. For instance, a conceptual definition of "achievement" might be "a person's level of knowledge in academic domains." "Homework" might be conceptually defined as "tasks assigned by teachers meant to be carried out during nonschool hours."

Conceptual definitions can differ in breadth, that is, in the number of events to which they refer. Thus, if "achievement" is defined as "something gained through effort or exertion," the concept is broader than it is if you use the definition in the paragraph above, relating solely to academics. The second definition would consider as "achievement" effort exerted in social, physical, and political spheres, as well as academic ones. When concepts are broader, we also can say they are more abstract.

Both primary researchers and research synthesists must choose a conceptual definition and a degree of breadth for their problem variables. Both must decide how likely it is that an event represents an instance of the variable of interest. Although it is sometimes not obvious, even very concrete variables, such as homework, require conceptual definitions. So, the first question to ask yourself about how you have formulated the problem for your research synthesis is,

Are the variables of interest given clear conceptual definitions?

In order to relate concepts to concrete events, a variable must also be operationally defined. An *operational definition* is a description of observable characteristics that determine if the event represents an occurrence of the conceptual variable. Put differently, a concept is operationally defined "when the procedures used to produce and measure it are clearly specified" (Elmes, Kantowitz, & Roediger, 2005). For example, an operational definition of the concept "intrinsic motivation" might include "the amount of time a person spends on a task during a free-time period." Again, both primary researchers and research synthesists must specify the operations included in their conceptual definitions.

Differences in Concepts and Operations in Primary Research and Research Synthesis

Differences in how variables are defined can also be found between the two types of research. Primary researchers have little choice but to define their concepts operationally before they begin their studies. They cannot start collecting data until the variables in the study have been given an empirical reality. Primary researchers studying "choice" must define how "choice" will be manipulated or measured before they can run their first participant.

On the other hand, research synthesists need not be quite so operationally precise, at least not initially. For them, the literature search can begin with only a conceptual definition and a few known operations relevant to it. Then, the associated operations can be filled out as they become more familiar with the research. For example, you might know that the interventions meant to increase physical activity among aging adults include providing participants with tangible rewards for exercising and having them enter into written contracts specifying that they exercise more. Once you begin the literature search, you might also find types of interventions you were unaware existed, such as self-monitoring (keeping a diary of physical activity), social modeling (watching others exercise), and providing a health-risk appraisal. As a research synthesist, you have the comparative luxury of being able to evaluate the conceptual relevance of different operations as you find them in the literature.

Of course, some a priori specification of operations is necessary, and you need to begin your synthesis with at least a few empirical realizations in mind. However, during a literature search, it is not unusual to come across operations that you did not know existed but are relevant to the construct you are studying. In sum, primary researchers must know exactly what events will constitute the domain to be sampled in their studies before they begin collecting data. Research synthesists may discover unanticipated operations that fit into the relevant domain along the way.

Another distinction between the two types of inquiry is that primary studies typically involve only one or a few operational definitions of the same construct. In contrast, research syntheses usually involve many empirical realizations for each variable of interest. Although no two participants[1] are treated exactly alike in any single study, this variation will ordinarily be small compared to variation introduced by the differences in the way participants are treated and outcomes are measured in separate studies. For example, a single study of choice and motivation might involve giving participants a choice to do either anagrams or sudokus. However, the synthesists looking at all the choice studies that have been conducted might find manipulations using anagrams, crosswords, sudokus, word finds, cryptograms, video games, and so on. Add to this the fact that research synthesists will also find much greater variation in the location in which studies were conducted (different geographical regions, labs, classrooms, or the workplace) and in sampled populations (college students, children, or workers). The multiple operations contained in research syntheses introduce a set of unique issues that need to be examined carefully.

---

[1] Here, I use the term "participant" in the broader sense, meaning the participant might be an individual person or animal, or a group of such units. For ease of exposition, I will continue to use participant in place of the more cumbersome "units under study."

MULTIPLE OPERATIONS IN RESEARCH SYNTHESIS

Research synthesists must be aware of two potential incongruities that can arise because of the variety of operations they encounter in the literature. First, you might begin a literature search with broad conceptual definitions. However, you may discover that the operations used in previous relevant research have been narrower than your concepts imply. For instance, a synthesis of research on rape attitudes might begin with a broad definition of rape, including any instance of unwanted sexual relations, including women forcing sex upon men. However, the literature search might reveal that past research dealt only with men as the perpetrators of rape. When such a circumstance arises, you must narrow the conceptual underpinnings of the synthesis to be more congruent with existing operations. Otherwise, its conclusions might appear more general than warranted by the data.

The opposite problem, starting with narrow concepts but then encountering operational definitions that suggest the concepts of interest should be broadened, can also confront a synthesist. Our example regarding the definition of "achievement" illustrates this problem. Synthesists might begin a search for studies on homework and achievement expecting to define achievement as relating solely to academic material. However, in perusing the literature, they might encounter studies of homework in classes on music and industrial arts, for example. These studies fit the definition of "homework" (i.e., tasks assigned by teachers meant to be carried out during nonschool hours), but the outcome variables might not fit the definition of achievement because it is not academic. Should these studies be included? It would be fine to do so but you would have to make it clear that your definition of achievement now included performance in nonacademic domains.

When conducting a research synthesis, *as your literature search proceeds, it is very important that you take care to reevaluate the correspondence between the breadth of the definitions of the concepts of interest and the variation in operations that primary researchers have used to define them.* Thus, the next question to ask yourself as you evaluate how well you have specified the problem for your research synthesis is,

---

Do the operations that empirically define each variable of interest correspond to the variable's conceptual definition?

Make certain that your decisions to include certain studies have not broadened your definitions or that operations missing in the literature do not suggest that the conceptual definitions need to be narrowed. In primary research, this redefinition of a problem as a study proceeds is frowned upon. In research synthesis, it appears that some flexibility may be necessary, indeed beneficial.

Multiple Operationism and Concept-to-Operation Correspondence

Webb, Campbell, Schwartz, Sechrest, and Grove (1981) presented strong arguments for the value of having multiple operations to define the same underlying construct. They define *multiple operationism* as the use of many measures that share a conceptual definition "but have different patterns of irrelevant components" (p. 35). Having multiple operations of a construct has positive consequences because

> once a proposition has been confirmed by two or more independent measurement processes, the uncertainty of its interpretation is greatly reduced. . . . If a proposition can survive the onslaught of a series of imperfect measures, with all their irrelevant error, confidence should be placed in it. Of course, this confidence is increased by minimizing error in each instrument and by a reasonable belief in the different and divergent effects of the sources of error. (Webb et al., p. 35)

While Webb and colleagues hold out the potential for strengthened inferences when a variety of operations exists, as happens in a research synthesis, their parting qualification must also be reiterated. Multiple operations can enhance *concept-to-operation correspondence* if the operations encompassed in your research synthesis are individually at least minimally related to the construct. This reasoning is akin to the reasoning applied in classical measurement theory. Small correlations between individual items on a multi-item test, say the items on an achievement test, and a participant's "true" achievement score can add up to a reliable indicator of achievement *if* a sufficient number of minimally valid items are present. Likewise, the conclusions of a research synthesis will not be valid if the operations in the covered studies bear no correspondence to the underlying concept or if the operations share a different concept to a greater degree than they share the intended one. This is true regardless of how many operations are included.

For example, it is easy to see the value of multiple operations when thinking about outcome variables. We are confident that homework affects the broad conceptual variable "achievement" when we have measures of achievement that include unit tests, class grades, and standardized achievement tests, and the relationship between homework and achievement is in the same direction regardless of the achievement measure. We are less confident that the relationship exists if only class grades are used as outcomes. If only class grades are used, it may be that teachers include grades on homework assignments in the class grade and this explains the relationship, whereas homework might have no effect if unit tests or standardized tests serve as measures. These tests do not share the same source of "error." But unit tests are highly aligned with the content of assignments, whereas standardized achievement tests typically are not. Thus, when multiple operations provide similar results, they suggest the operations converge on the same construct, and our confidence grows in the conclusions. If the different operations do not lead to similar results, differences between the operations can give us clues about limitations to our conclusions. For example, if we find homework influences unit tests but not standardized tests, we might speculate that homework influences achievement only when the content of assignments and measures of achievement are highly aligned.

The value of multiple operations of independent variables (ones manipulated in experiments meant to test theories) or intervention variables (treatments in applied settings) also can increase our confidence in conclusions. For example, if experimental studies of homework were all conducted by having high school teachers give one class homework and another class no homework, we know that the teachers also provide all other forms of instruction. Therefore, knowingly or not, the teacher could treat the students in two classes differently in ways other than whether or not they assigned homework; they might have higher expectations for the homework classes and attempt to teach them more during class. So, the rival hypothesis that "differences in how students were treated in ways other than homework might account for achievement differences" could not be ruled out, no matter how many studies had been conducted. However, if there are studies in which homework was manipulated within the same class, these studies would make this rival explanation less plausible. Better yet would be to also have a third type of study in which many different teachers taught a class that was either given homework or had no homework, and which condition the class was in was randomly decided.

In sum then, the existence of a variety of operations in research literatures presents the potential benefit of allowing stronger inferences if the results allow you to rule out irrelevant sources of influence. If results are inconsistent across operations, it allows you to speculate on what the important differences between operations might be.

The use of operations not originally related to the concept. Literature searches can sometimes uncover research that has been cast in a conceptual framework different from the one you want to study but which includes operational measures or manipulations relevant to the concepts of interest to you. For instance, there are several concepts similar to "job burnout" that appear in the research literature, such as "occupational stress" and "job fatigue." It is important to consider whether the operations associated with these different constructs are relevant to your synthesis, even if they have been labeled differently. When relevant operations associated with different abstract constructs are identified, they most certainly should be considered for inclusion in your synthesis. In fact, different concepts and theories behind similar operations can often be used to demonstrate the robustness of results. There probably is no better way to ensure that operations contain different patterns of error than to have different researchers with different theoretical backgrounds perform related investigations.

Substituting new concepts for old ones. Sometimes you will find that social scientists introduce new concepts (and theories) to explain old findings. For example, in a classic social psychology experiment, the notion of "cognitive dissonance" was used to explain why an individual who is paid $1 to voice a counterattitudinal argument subsequently experiences greater attitude change than another person paid $25 to perform the same activity (Festinger & Carlsmith, 1959). Dissonance theory suggests that because the amount of money is not sufficient to justify the espousal of the counterattitudinal argument, the person feels discomfort that can be reduced only through a shift in attitude. However, Bem (1967) recast the results of this experiment by proposing a self-perception theory. Briefly, he speculated that participants who observed themselves espousing counterattitudinal arguments inferred their opinions the same way as an observer: If participants see themselves making an argument for $1, they assume that because they are performing the behavior with little justification, they must feel positive toward the attitude in question.

No matter how many replications of the $1/$25 experiment you uncovered, you could not use the results to evaluate the correctness of the two theories. You must take care to differentiate concepts and theories that predict similar and different results for the same set of operations. If predictions are different, the cumulative evidence can be used to evaluate the correctness of one theory or another, or the different circumstances in which each theory is correct. However, if the theories make identical predictions, no comparative judgment based on research outcomes is possible.

The effects of multiple operations on synthesis outcomes. Multiple operations do more than introduce the potential for more nuanced inferences about conceptual variables. They are also the most important source of variance in the conclusions of different syntheses meant to address the same topic. A variety of operations can affect synthesis outcomes in two ways:

1. *Differences in the included operational definitions.* The operational definitions used in two research syntheses on the same topic can be different from one another. Two synthesists using an identical label for an abstract concept can use very different operational definitions. Each definition may contain some operations excluded by the other, or one definition may completely contain the other.

2. *Differences in operational detail.* Multiple operations also affect outcomes by leading to variation in the attention synthesists pay to methodological distinctions in the literature. This effect is attributable to differences in the way study operations are treated *after* the literature has been searched. At this point, research synthesists become detectives who search for "distinctive clues about why two variables are related differently under different conditions" (Cook et al., 1992, p. 22). They use the observed data patterns as clues for generating explanations that specify the conditions under which a positive, null, or negative relationship will be found between two variables.

Synthesists differ in how much detective work they undertake. Some pay careful attention to study operations. They decide to identify meticulously the operational distinctions among retrieved studies. Other synthesists feel that method- or participant-dependent relations are unlikely or may simply use less care in identifying these.

DEFINING THE RELATIONSHIP OF INTEREST

Whether you are doing primary research or research synthesis, in addition to defining the concepts, you must also decide what type of relationship between the variables is of interest to you. While your conceptual definition of the variables will determine the relevance of different operations, it is the type of relationship that will determine the relevance of different research designs. In order to be able to determine the appropriateness of different research designs, there are three questions that need to be asked about the problem that motivates your research synthesis (see Cooper, 2006, for a more complete discussion of these issues):

1. Should the results of the research be expressed in numbers or narrative?

2. Is the problem you are studying a description of an event, an association between events, or a causal explanation of an event?

3. Does the problem or hypothesis seek to understand (a) how a process unfolds *within* an individual participant over time, or (b) what is associated with or explains variation *between* participants or groups of participants?

Quantitative or Qualitative Research?

With regard to the question, "Should the results of the research be expressed in numbers or narrative?" it should be clear that for the type of research synthesis I am focusing on here, the answer is "numbers." However, this does not mean that narrative or qualitative research will play no role in quantitative research syntheses. For example, in our synthesis of homework research, qualitative studies were used to help compile a list of possible effects of homework, both good and bad. In fact, even opinion pieces were used, such as complaints about homework ("it creates too much stress for children") that appeared in newspaper articles. Qualitative research also was used to help identify possible moderators and mediators of homework's effects. For example, the homework literature search uncovered a survey and interview study (Younger & Warrington, 1996) that suggested girls generally hold more positive attitudes than boys toward homework and expend greater effort on doing homework. This study suggested that this individual difference among students might moderate relationships between homework and achievement. A case study of six families by Xu and Corno (1998) involved both interviews and home videotaping to examine how parents structure the homework environment and help children cope with distractions so they can pay attention to the homework assignment. This study clearly argued for the importance of parents as mediators in the homework process.

Of course, the results of qualitative research can also be the central focus of a research synthesis, not just an aid to quantitative synthesis. Discussions of how to carry out such reviews have occupied the thoughts of scholars much better versed in qualitative research than me. If you are interested in this type of research synthesis, you might examine Noblit and Hare (1988); Paterson, Thorne, Canam, and Jillings (2001); and/or Pope, Mays, and Popay (2007) for detailed examinations of approaches to synthesizing qualitative research.

Description, Association, or Causal Relationship?

Descriptive research. The second question, "Is the problem you are studying a description of an event, an association between events, or a causal explanation of an event?" divides research problems into three groups. First, a research problem might be largely descriptive and take the general form "What is happening?" Here, you might be interested in obtaining an accurate portrayal of some event or other phenomena. In primary research, this might lead you to conduct a survey (Fowler, 2002). For example, older adults might be asked questions about the frequency of their physical activity. Your conclusion might be that "X% of adults over the age of Y routinely engage in physical activity." In research synthesis, you would collect all the surveys that asked a particular question and, perhaps, average the estimates of frequency in order to get a more precise estimate. Or you might examine moderators and mediators of survey results. For example, the average age of participants in the surveys could be used to test the hypothesis that physical activity deceases with age: "Studies with an average participant age of Y revealed more frequent activity than studies with an average participant age of Z."

It is rare to see this kind of descriptive research synthesis in the scholarly social science literature. However, a similar procedure does appear on the nightly news during the weeks leading up to an election, when a news anchor will report the cumulative findings of numerous polls of voters asking about support for candidates or ballot issues. Part of the problem with synthesizing descriptive statistics across the types of studies that appear in social science journals is that the studies often use different scales to operationalize the same variable. For example, it would be difficult to synthesize the levels of activity found in intervention studies because some studies might measure activity by giving participants a pedometer and counting their miles walked. Other studies might measure activity by gauging lung capacity. Measuring time spent on homework would produce less difficulty. Metrics for measuring time should be consistent across studies or easily convertible one to another (e.g., hours to minutes). Measures of achievement would likely be difficult because sometimes it will be measured as unit tests, sometimes as grades, and sometimes as scores on standardized achievement tests.[2]

Another problem with aggregating descriptive statistics is that it is rarely clear what population the resulting averages refer to. Unlike the polls that precede elections, social scientists writing for scholarly outlets often use convenience samples. While we might be able to identify the population (often very narrow) from which the participants of each study have been drawn, it is rarely possible to say what population an amalgamation of such convenience samples is drawn from.

Associational research. A second type of descriptive research problem might be, "What events or phenomena happen together?" Here, researchers take their descriptions a step further and ask whether variables co-occur, or correlate, with one another. Several instances of interest in co-occurrence

---

[2] The problem of nonstandard measurements is lessened when study characteristics are tested as *third* variables because the bivariate relationships *within* the studies can be transformed into standardized effect size estimates, thus controlling for different scales (see Chapter 6).

appear in our synthesis examples. The synthesis of correlates of attitudes toward rape focused exclusively on simple correlations. The synthesis about homework also looked at simple correlations between the amount of time spent on homework reported by students and achievement.

Causal research. The third research problem seeks an explanation for the event: "What events cause other events to happen?" In this case, a study is conducted to isolate and draw a direct *productive* link between one event (the cause) and another (the effect). What constitutes good evidence of causal production is a complex question that I will return to in Chapter 5. In practice, three types of research designs are used most often to help make causal inferences. I will call the first *modeling research.* It takes correlational research a step further by examining co-occurrence in a multivariate framework (Kline, 1998). For example, the synthesis on homework looked at studies that built complex models (using multiple regression, path analysis, or structural equation modeling) to describe the co-occurrence of many variables, one being homework, and academic achievement.

The second approach to discovering causes is called *quasi-experimental research.* Here, unlike the modeling approach, the researcher (or some other external agent) controls the introduction of an intervention or event but does not control precisely who may be exposed to it (see Shadish, Cook, & Campbell, 2002, for an extended discussion of these research designs). For example, in the synthesis on physical activity, some studies looked at groups of older adults that decided on their own to join an exercise intervention (or did so because their physician told them to). Then the researchers tried to match, on preexisting differences, these adults with others who did not exercise; they then calculated the "effect" of exercise. The homework synthesis also included some quasi-experiments.

A unique type of quasi-experiment (often call "preexperimental") involves a *pretest-posttest design* in which participants serve as their own control by being compared on the outcome variable before and after the intervention is introduced. If these appear frequently in a research literature (as they did in the physical activity literature), it is important to remember that whereas such designs equate groups on lots of differences (after all, they are the same people), these study's results are open to all sorts of alternative interpretations. These interpretations are related to the passage of time, including change in participants that would have occurred regardless of the introduction of the intervention (would you expect activity to decrease as people get older?), as well as other interventions or general historical events that happened during the time between the pretest and posttest.

Finally, in *experimental research*, both the introduction of the event *and* who is exposed to it are controlled by the researchers (or other external agents), who then leave treatment assignment to chance (Boruch, 1997). This approach minimizes average preexisting differences between the assigned participants so that we can be most confident that any differences between participants are caused by the variable that was manipulated. Of course, there are numerous other aspects of the design that must be attended to for a strong inference about causality to be made, but for our current purposes, this unique feature of experimental research will suffice, until Chapter 5.

In the synthesis example about choice and motivation, all the included studies involved an experimental manipulation of choice and the random assignment of participants to choice and no-choice conditions. Also, both the homework and physical activity research syntheses include some experimental studies.

Within-Participant or Between-Participant Processes?

Finally, the third question you must ask about the posited relationship is, "Does the problem or hypothesis seek to understand (a) how a process unfolds within an individual participant over time or (b) what is associated with, or explains variation between, participants or groups of participants?" All the designs I have introduced relate to the latter, the differences between participants on a characteristic of interest. The former problem—the problem of change within a participant—would best be studied using the various forms of *single-case* or *time series designs*, research designs in which single participants are tested at multiple times, typically at equal time intervals, during the course of a study. As with between-participants differences, within-participant processes can be studied using designs that are purely descriptive (simple time series), that reveal associations between two processes over time (concomitant time series), or that assess the causal impact of an intervention in the process (interrupted time series). Syntheses of time series research are still rare and the methodology is still quite new. So, the remainder of this book focuses on syntheses of between-participants research. All our synthesis examples involve research that attempted to discover relations involving variation between participants. Still, this makes it no less important to ask whether the research question concerns processes within participants or differences between participants and to understand that the answer will dictate what research designs and synthesis methods will be appropriate for answering the question. If you are interested in within-participant processes, you can consult Shadish and Rinskopf (2007) for a discussion of synthesis of single-case research.

Simple and Complex Relationships

The problems that motivate most research synthesists begin by posing questions about a simple two-variable relationship. Does choice affect motivation? Does homework cause improvements in achievement? The explanation for this is simple: Bivariate relationships have typically been tested more often than more complex relationships. That said, it is rare, if not unheard of, for a synthesis to have only one operation of each of the two variables. For example, 20 subtypes of interventions were included in the activity synthesis and 16 of these were tested separately for their effect on older adults. In the choice synthesis, four different outcome variables were collected that related to the participants' motivation to engage in the task (i.e., tasks engaged in during free time, enjoyment or liking of the task, interest in the task, willingness to engage in the task again) and were tested for whether the different measures revealed different results. In fact, all the example syntheses examined potential influences on the bivariate relationships, as do almost all syntheses, including not just third variables created because of how variables were defined but also variations created by differences in how the study was carried out. These will include design variations (e.g., experiments compared to quasi-experiments) and implementation variations (e.g., setting, time).

Although some specific hypotheses about three-variable relationships—that is, interactions—in the social sciences have generated enough interest to suggest that a research synthesis would be informative, for the vast majority of topics, the initial problem formulation will involve a two-variable question. Again, however, your initial undertaking of the synthesis to establish the existence of a bivariate relationship should in no way diminish the attention you pay to discovering interacting or moderating influences. Indeed, discovering that a two-variable relationship exists quite often would be viewed as a trivial contribution by the research community. However, if bivariate relationships are found to be moderated by third variables, these findings are viewed as a step forward and are given inferential priority. Even when an interaction is the primary focus of a synthesis, the search for higher-order interactions should continue. More will be said on the relationships between variables in Chapter 6, when I discuss how main effects and interactions are interpreted in research synthesis.

Summary

In sum then, in addition to asking whether your research synthesis has (a) provided clear conceptual definitions of the variables of interest and

(b) included operations that are truly correspondent to those conceptual definitions, you must also ask,

> *Is the problem stated so that the research designs and evidence needed to address it can be specified clearly?*

Figure 2.1 summarizes the differences that can arise between research syntheses due to variations in how concepts are defined, operationalized, and related to one another. In the top portion of the figure we see that two synthesists might use conceptual definitions of different breadth. The definitions will affect how many operations will be deemed relevant to the concepts. So, a synthesist who defines homework as "academic work done outside school" will include more operations—for example, tutoring would fit this definition—than a synthesist who defines homework as "tasks assigned by teachers meant to be carried out during nonschool hours." Further, it is also possible that

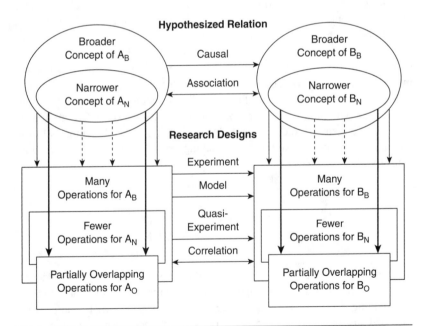

Figure 2.1 Differences Between Research Syntheses Due to Differences in Conceptual Definitions, Relevant Operations, and Variable Relationships

regardless of the breadth of the concepts, the synthesists might differ concerning their decisions about whether certain operations are relevant. For example, one synthesist might include music and industrial arts grades as measures of achievement whereas another might not.

Also, the synthesists might differ in whether they are interested in research that studies an association or a causal link between the variables. This will influence the type of research designs that are deemed relevant and/or how the results of research using different designs are interpreted with regard to their ability to shed light on the relation of interest. So, synthesists who ask the question, "Is homework related to achievement?" would include both correlational and experimental research, while synthesists who ask the question, "Does homework cause improved achievement?" might restrict their synthesis to only experiments and perhaps quasi-experiments. Or, if correlational research is included, it would need to be carefully interpreted as less than optimal for answering this question (a concern we will return to in Chapter 5).

And finally, it is important to remember that some variables in a synthesis can be relatively narrowly defined, whereas others are broadly defined. For example, in our synthesis concerning attitudes toward rape, the term "rape" was defined relatively narrowly as sexual intercourse between a man and a woman without the woman's consent. Still, our literature search uncovered 17 different measures of rape attitudes, but only 5 were used with much frequency. On the other hand, the concept used to define predictors of rape attitudes, "individual differences," was extremely broad. We identified 74 distinct individual difference variables that could be clustered into broader groupings (but narrower than "individual differences") consisting of demographic, cognitive, experiential, affective, and personality measures. As noted previously, much of the creative challenge and reward in doing research synthesis lies in identifying groupings like these and making sense of their different relationships to other variables.

JUDGING THE CONCEPTUAL
RELEVANCE OF STUDIES

It can always be the case that researchers disagree about the conceptual definition of a variable or about the operations relevant to it. In fact, many disputes surrounding research syntheses refer to differences in what studies were included and excluded based on their relevance. Readers who are knowledgeable about the research area will say, "Hey, how come this study wasn't included?" or "How come this study was?" For example, many homework scholars would have objected if our research synthesis included studies that involved students receiving tutoring at the recommendation of the teacher even though including them would have met a strict interpretation of the conceptual definition. Likely, had tutoring studies been included, these scholars would have suggested that the definition of homework, as most people understand it, involves assignments given to the entire class of students. They would have argued that the definition of homework needed to be more precise.

Beyond the breadth or narrowness of the conceptual definition, some research has examined other contextual factors that might affect whether a study is deemed relevant to a research problem. For example, judgments about the relevance of studies to a literature search appear to be related to the searcher's open-mindedness and expertise in the area (Davidson, 1977), whether the decision is based on titles or abstracts (Cooper & Ribble, 1989), and even the amount of time the searcher has for making relevance decisions (Cuadra & Katter, 1967). Thus, while the conceptual definition and level of abstractness that synthesists choose for a problem are certainly two influences on which studies are deemed relevant, a multitude of other factors also affect this screening of studies.

You should begin your literature search with the broadest conceptual definition in mind. In determining the acceptability of operations for inclusion within the broad concept, you should remain as open in your interpretation as possible. At later stages of the synthesis, notably during data evaluation, it is possible to exclude particular operations due to their lack of relevance. However, *in the problem formulation and literature search stages, decisions about the relevance of studies should err on the side of being overly inclusive*, just as primary researchers collect some data that might not later be used in analysis. It is very distressing to find out *after* studies have been retrieved and catalogued that available pieces of the puzzle were passed over and a new search must be conducted. An initially broad conceptual search also will help you think more carefully about the boundaries of your concepts, leading to a more precise definition once the search is completed. So, if studies of tutoring are retrieved because an expansive interpretation of the concept of homework is used ("tasks assigned by teachers meant to be carried out during nonschool hours"), and it is later decided that these ought not be included, it could lead to a refinement of the definition ("tasks assigned to all students").

It is also good practice to *have the initial decision about the potential relevance of a study made by more than one person*. Here, the purpose of having multiple screeners is not only to see if the conceptual definitions lead to agreement among screeners but also to flag for further screening any study that is deemed potentially relevant by any one screener. Often, the initial decision about relevance will be made on limited information about the study, such as the study's abstract. When this is the case, it is even more important to have at least two screeners judge each study and take a second look at studies even if just one screener thought it might be relevant.

Table 2.1 provides an example of a coding sheet to screen for research studying physical activity interventions for older adults. The most critical code is the second, which places each document into one of four categories depending on what the screener thinks it contains. Note that in addition to categories that identify documents as possibly containing data relevant to exercise interventions, the initial screening question includes a category for documents that might not include data for a meta-analysis but that might provide other important information or insights about the topic, perhaps for use in the introduction or discussion of the synthesis results, perhaps identifying possible influences on the impact of the intervention on adult activity. The rest of the information

Table 2.1   Initial Screening Coding Guide

Initial Screening for Relevance	
1. What is the Report ID number?	__ __ __

2. What type of information is contained in this document?
 	
   1 = Background
   2 = Empirical evidence
   3 = Both
   4 = This document is irrelevant
	__

3. If empirical, what type of empirical evidence does this document contain?
 	
   1 = Descriptive
   2 = Evaluation of an intervention
   3 = Both
   4 = Other (specify) _____
	__

If background, what type of background information does this document contain? (Place a 1 in each column that applies, 0 otherwise)
 	
   a. Descriptions of program variations
   b. Issues in program implementation
   c. Arguments for and/or against
   d. Review of previous research
   e. Other (specify) _____
	__
	__
	__
	__
	__

on the sheet relates to characteristics of the document and its producers. This information is typically found in the document records contained in most computerized reference databases, so it typically is not necessary for the screener to examine the full document to find it. When a literature search requires the screening of large numbers of documents (a search of the ERIC database for the mention of the term "homework" in the abstract retrieves over 3200 documents), this is the level at which the initial screening will occur.

STUDY-GENERATED AND SYNTHESIS-GENERATED EVIDENCE

I have pointed out that most research syntheses focus on main effect questions but then also test for moderators by grouping studies according to differences in the way the research was carried out. In essence, then, these moderator analyses are testing for interaction effects, that is, they ask whether the main effect relationship is different depending on the level or categories of a third variable, in this case a characteristic of the study. This leads us to consider an important distinction between the types of evidence contained in research syntheses.

There are two different sources of evidence about relationships contained in research syntheses. The first type is called *study-generated evidence*. Study-generated evidence is present when a single study contains results that directly test the relation being considered. Research syntheses also contain evidence that does not come from individual studies, but rather from the variations in procedures across studies. This type of evidence, called *synthesis-generated evidence*, is present when the results of studies using different procedures to test the same hypothesis are compared to one another.

There is one critical distinction between study-generated and synthesis-generated evidence: *Only study-generated evidence based on experimental research allows the synthesist to make statements concerning causality.* An example will clarify the point. With regard to choice and motivation studies, suppose we were interested in whether the number of options a participant is given to choose among influences the effect of choice on motivation. Suppose also that 16 studies were found that directly assessed the impact of number of options by randomly assigning participants to experimental conditions, one in which participants chose between only two alternatives and another in which more than two alternatives were available. The accumulated results of these studies could then be interpreted as supporting or not supporting the idea that the number of choice options *causes* increases or decreases in motivation. Now, assume instead that we uncovered eight studies that compared only a two-option choice condition to a no-choice control group and eight other studies that compared a multiple-option (more than two) choice condition to a no-choice control group. If this synthesis-generated evidence revealed larger effects of choice on motivation when more options were given, then we could infer an association but not a causal relation between the number of options and motivation.

Why is this the case? Causal direction is not the problem with synthesis-generated evidence. It would be foolish to argue that the amount of motivation exhibited by participants caused the experimenters' decision about the number of options. However, still problematic is another ingredient of causality—the absence of potential third variables causing the relationship. A multitude of third variables are potentially confounded with the original experimenters' decisions about how many choice options to give participants. For instance, the participants in multiple-option studies may have been more likely to be adults while two-option studies were more likely to be conducted with children.

Synthesis-generated evidence cannot legitimately rule out as possible true causes any other variables confounded with the study characteristic of interest. This is because the synthesists did not randomly assign the number of choice options to experiments. It is the ability to employ random assignment of participants that allows primary researchers to assume that third variables are represented equally in the experimental conditions. So, a synthesis encompassing studies that all compared varying choice-option conditions to a no-choice control group can make causal statements about the effect of choice per se but not about the effect of the number of options on the effect of choice. Here, only an association can be claimed.

Summary

It is important for synthesists to keep the distinction between study-generated and synthesis-generated evidence in mind. *Only evidence coming from experimental manipulations within a single study can support assertions concerning causality.* However, the lesser strength of synthesis-generated evidence with regard to causal inferences does not mean this evidence should be ignored. The use of synthesis-generated evidence allows you to test relations which may have never been examined by primary researchers. For example, it may be the case that no previous primary study has examined whether the relation between homework and achievement is different for assignments of different length, or whether different types of interventions differ in their effects on subsequent physical activity. By searching across studies for variations in assignment length or intervention type and then relating this to the effect of homework on achievement or interventions on physical activity, synthesists can produce the first evidence about these potentially critical moderating variables. Even though this evidence is equivocal, it is a major contribution of research synthesis and a source of potential hypotheses for future primary research.

ARGUING FOR THE
VALUE OF THE SYNTHESIS

Research syntheses should be placed in a theoretical, historical, and/or practical context. Why are attitudes toward rape important? Do theories predict how and why particular individual differences will relate to rape attitudes? Are there conflicting predictions associated with different theories? Why do older adults need physical activity? Where did the idea for activity interventions come from? Are intervention components grounded in theory or in practical experience? Are there debates surrounding the utility of exercise programs?

Contextualizing the problem of a research synthesis does more than explain why a topic is important. Providing a context for the problem also provides the rationale for the search for moderators of the principal findings. It is an important aid in identifying variables that you might examine for their influence on outcomes. For example, self-determination theory proposes that having a choice will improve intrinsic motivation to engage in a task but providing rewards will undermine future task motivation. This suggests that studies of choice that also provided rewards might produce different results from studies with no rewards.

Also, many social interventions, such as assigning homework, have claims associated with them that suggest they will influence more than one outcome variable. For example, homework proponents provide a list of claimed positive effects that include academic and nonacademic outcomes. Likewise, homework opponents provide their own list of possible negative effects. It is important that research synthesists present a list as complete as possible of the positive and negative effects of the intervention. These effects might be offered by theorists, researchers, proponents, and opponents.

Again, both quantitative and qualitative research can be used to place the research problem in a meaningful context. Narrative or qualitative descriptions of relevant events can be used to discover the salient features of the problem at hand. These can be the source of important queries for research synthesists to ask of the quantitative evidence. Quantitative surveys also can answer specific questions across a broader array of problem instantiations. In addition to establishing the importance of the problem, surveys can answer questions such as, "How available are physical activity intervention programs?" and "What are the characteristics of participants in these intervention programs?"

If a Synthesis Already
Exists, Why Is a New One Needed?

Sometimes, the value of a synthesis is easy to establish: A lot of past research has been conducted and it is yet to be accumulated, summarized, and integrated. However, if a topic has a long history of research, it is not surprising to find that previous attempts at integration already exist. Obviously, these efforts need to be scrutinized carefully before the new synthesis is undertaken. Past syntheses can help establish the necessity for a new one. This assessment process is much like that used in primary research before undertaking a new study.

There are several things you can look for in past syntheses that will help your new effort. First, previous syntheses can be used, along with the other background documents you find, to identify the positions of other scholars in the field. In particular, the past syntheses can be used to determine whether conflicting conclusions exist about what the evidence says and, perhaps, what has caused the conflict.

Second, an examination of past syntheses can assess the earlier efforts' completeness and validity. For example, the synthesis on activity interventions found two narrative reviews of past research on older adults but no meta-analyses. The only meta-analysis included adults of all ages. Thus, we could argue that the benefits of meta-analysis accompanied our new effort.

Past syntheses also can be an important aid in identifying interacting variables that the new synthesists might wish to examine. Rather than restart the compilation of potential moderating variables, previous synthesists (along with primary researchers, both quantitative and qualitative) will undoubtedly offer many suggestions based on their own intellect and reading of the literature. If more than one synthesis of an area has been conducted, the new effort will be able to incorporate all the suggestions.

Finally, past syntheses allow you to begin the compilation of a relevant bibliography. Most syntheses will have fairly lengthy bibliographies. If more than one exists, their citations will overlap somewhat, but not perfectly. Along with other techniques described in the next chapter, the research cited in past syntheses provides an excellent place for you to start the literature search.

The Effects of Context on Synthesis Outcomes

Differences in how a problem is placed in its theoretical or practical context affects the outcomes of syntheses by leading to differences in the way study operations are treated *after* the relevant literature has been identified. Synthesists can vary in the attention they pay to theoretical and practical distinctions in the literature. Thus, two research syntheses conducted using identical conceptual definitions and the same set of studies can still reach decidedly different conclusions if one synthesis examined information about theoretical and practical distinctions in studies to uncover moderating relationships that the other synthesis did not test. For example, one synthesis might discover that the effect of homework on achievement was associated with the grade level of students, whereas another synthesis never addressed the question. Thus, to evaluate whether (a) the importance of the problem has been established and (b) a list of important potential moderators of findings has been identified, the next question to ask about your research syntheses is,

Is the problem placed in a meaningful theoretical, historical, and/or practical context?

EXERCISES

1. Identify two research syntheses that claim to relate to the same or similar hypotheses. Find the conceptual definitions used in each. Describe how the definitions differ, if they do. Which synthesis employs the broader conceptual definition?

2. List the operational characteristics of studies described as the inclusion and exclusion criteria in each of the two syntheses. How do they differ?

3. List the studies deemed relevant in each synthesis. Are there studies that are included in one synthesis and not the other? If so, why did this happen?

4. What type of relationship is posited as existing between the variables of interest in the two syntheses? What types of research designs are covered in the syntheses? Do the posited relationships and covered design correspond? Why?

5. What rationales are given for the two research syntheses? Do they differ?

3

Step 2

Searching the Literature

What procedures should be used to find relevant research?

Primary Function Served in the Synthesis

1. To identify places to find relevant research (e.g., reference databases, journals)
2. To identify terms used to search for relevant research in reference databases

Procedural Variation That Might Produce Differences in Conclusions

1. Variation in searched sources might lead to systematic differences in the retrieved research

Questions to Ask When Evaluating the Literature Search in a Research Synthesis

1. Were complementary searching strategies used to find relevant studies?
2. Were proper and exhaustive terms used in searches and queries of reference databases and research registries?

This chapter describes

- Objectives of a literature search
- Methods for locating studies relevant to a synthesis topic
- Direct, quality-controlled, and secondary channels for obtaining research reports and
  - How research enters different channels
  - How searchers access different channels
  - What biases may be present in the kinds of information contained in different channels
- Problems encountered in retrieving studies

In primary social science research, participants are recruited into studies through subject pools, newspaper advertisements, schools, doctors' offices, and so on. In research synthesis, the studies of interest are found by conducting a search for reports describing past relevant research. Regardless of whether social scientists are collecting new data or synthesizing results of previous studies, the major decision they make when finding relevant sources of data involves defining the *target population* that will be the referent of the research (Fowler, 2002). In primary research, the target population includes those individuals or groups that the researcher hopes to represent in the study. In research synthesis, the target population includes all the studies that test the hypothesis or address the problem.

The *sample frame* of an investigation in the case of primary research includes those individuals or groups the researcher pragmatically could obtain. In the case of research synthesis, it includes obtainable study reports. In most instances, researchers will not be able to access all of a target population's elements. To do so would be too costly because some people (or documents) are hard to find or refuse to cooperate.

POPULATION DISTINCTIONS IN SOCIAL SCIENCE RESEARCH

Both primary research and research synthesis involve specifying target populations and sampling frames. In addition, both types of investigation require the researcher to consider how the target population and sampling frame may differ from one another. The trustworthiness of any claims about the target population will be compromised if the elements in the sampling frame differ in systematic ways from the target population. Because it is easier to alter the target of an investigation than it is to locate hard-to-find people or studies, both primary researchers and research synthesists may find they need to respecify their target population when an inquiry nears completion.

The most general target population for social science research could be characterized roughly as "all human beings," either as individuals or in groups. Most topics, of course, delineate the elements to be less ambitious, such as "all students" in a study of the effects of homework or "all adults over 50 years of age" in a study of the effects of activity interventions.

Sampling frames in social science research typically are much more restricted than targets. So, participants in an exercise intervention might all be drawn from a similar geographic area. Most social scientists are aware of the gap between the diversity of participants they hope the results of their research refer to and those people actually available to them. For this reason, they discuss limits on generalizability in their discussion of the study's results.

As I noted in Chapter 1, research syntheses involve two targets. First, *synthesists hope their work will cover all previous research on the problem.* Synthesists can exert some control over reaching this goal by how they conduct their literature search, that is, through their choices of information sources. How this is done is the focus of this chapter. Just as different sampling methods in primary research can lead to differences in who is sampled (e.g., phone surveys reach different people than mail surveys), different literature-searching techniques lead to different samples of studies. Likewise, just as it is more difficult to find and sample some people than others, it is also more difficult to find some studies than others.

In addition to wanting to cover all previous research, *synthesists also want the results of their work to pertain to the target population of people (or other units) that are relevant to the topic.* Our synthesis of homework research hoped that students at grade levels kindergarten through 12, not just high school students, for example, would be represented in past studies. Our ability to meet this goal was constrained by the types of students sampled by primary researchers. If first and second graders were not included in previous homework studies, they will not be represented in a synthesis of homework research. Thus, research synthesis involves a process of sampling samples. The primary research includes samples of individuals or groups, and the synthesist retrieves primary research. This process is something akin to cluster sampling, with the clusters distinguishing people according to the research projects in which they participated.

Also different from primary research, synthesists typically are not trying to draw representative samples of studies from the literature. Generally, they attempt to retrieve an entire population of studies. This formidable goal is rarely achieved, but it is certainly more feasible in a synthesis than in primary research.

METHODS FOR LOCATING STUDIES

How do you go about finding studies relevant to a topic? There are numerous techniques scientists use to share information with one another. These techniques have undergone enormous changes in the past 20 years. In fact, it is safe to say that the ways scientists transmit their work to one another has changed more in the last two decades than it did in the preceding three centuries, dating back to the late 17th century, when scholarly journals first appeared. The change is primarily due to the use of computers and the Internet to facilitate human communication.

The Fate of Studies From Initiation to Publication

A description of the many mechanisms that searchers can use to find studies will be most instructive if we begin with an account of the alternative possible fates of studies once they have been proposed. My colleagues and I (Cooper, DeNeve, & Charlton, 1997) conducted a survey of 33 researchers who had several years earlier proposed 159 studies to their university's institutional review board. The survey asked the researchers how far along each of the studies had gotten in the process from initiation to publication. Figure 3.1 summarizes their responses. Of the 159 studies, 4 were never begun, 4 were begun but data collection was never completed, and 30 were completed but the data were never analyzed. From the point of view of research synthesists, these 38 studies are of little interest because a hypothesis was never tested. However, once a study's data have been analyzed (as happened for about 76% of the proposed studies), then the result is of interest because it represents a test of the study's hypotheses. Not only does the study now include information on the truth or falsity of the hypothesis, but what happens to the study next may be influenced by what the data revealed. For example, Figure 3.1 indicates that about 13% of studies with analyzed data produced no written report, and several reasons were given for why this was the case. Some of these reasons seem related to the outcome itself, especially the reason that the results were not interesting and/or not statistically significant. Next, we see in Figure 3.1 that only about half of the written summaries of research were prepared for a journal article, book chapter, or book. And finally, of these, somewhere between 75% and 84% eventually found their way into print.

As we examine the different retrieval techniques used by people searching for studies, it will be important to keep in mind that *the difficulty in finding research, and the value of different searching techniques, will be a function of how far along the study went—or currently is, for recently completed work—in the process from data analysis to publication,* as outlined in Figure 3.1. For example, to anticipate the discussion that follows, it is clear that studies that had data analyzed but never were written up will only be retrievable by directly contacting the researchers. Studies that appear in journals will be easy to find, but may overrepresent significant and/or novel findings.

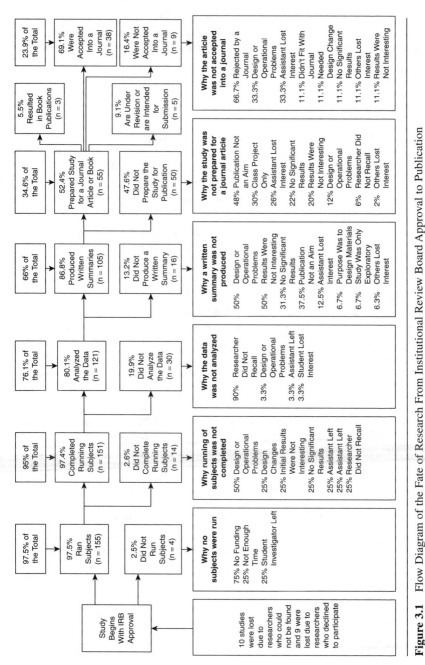

Figure 3.1 Flow Diagram of the Fate of Research From Institutional Review Board Approval to Publication

SOURCE: From "Finding the missing science: The fate of studies submitted for review by a human subjects committee," by H. Cooper, K. DeNeve, & K. Charlton, 1997, *Psychological Methods, 2,* p. 448–449. Copyright 2001 by the American Psychological Association.

Some Ways Searching Channels Differ

The section that follows will present descriptions of the major techniques you can use to find research. I will attempt to evaluate the kind of information found using each technique by comparing search results that used it exclusively to that of the target population "all relevant research," or, put differently, "all relevant studies for which data were analyzed." Regrettably, there are only limited empirical data on differences in scientific information obtained using different search techniques, so many of my comparisons will involve some speculation on my part. The problem is complicated further by the fact that the effect of a technique's characteristics on its outcomes probably varies from topic to topic.

Also, the proliferation of ways to share information makes it increasingly difficult to find just a few descriptors that help us think about how the search techniques differ and relate to one another. Mechanisms for communication have arisen in a haphazard fashion, so no descriptive dimension perfectly captures all their important features. Still, there are several features that are useful in describing the different search techniques. One important feature that distinguishes scientific communication techniques relates to *how research gets into the channel*. Channels can have relatively open or restricted rules for entry. Open entry permits the primary researcher (the person who wants to put something in the channel) to enter the channel directly and place their work into its collection of information. Restricted entry requires primary researchers to meet the requirements of a third party—some person or entity between themselves and the person searching for information—before their work can be included. The most important of these requirements is the use of *peer review* to ensure that research meets certain standards of relevance, quality, and importance. In fact, all channels have some restrictions on entries, but the type and stringency differ from channel to channel. It is these restrictions that most directly affect how the research in the channel differs from all relevant research.

A second important feature of search techniques concerns *how searchers obtain information from the channel*. Channels have more or less open or restricted requirements regarding how to access their content. A channel is more restricted if it requires the searcher (the person seeking information from the channel) to identify very specifically what or whose documents they want. A channel is more open if the searchers can be more broad or general in their request for information. These access requirements also can influence the type of research a searcher will find in a channel.

The importance of these distinctions will become clear as I describe how they relate to specific search techniques. For purposes of exposition, I have grouped the techniques under the headings "Direct-to-Researcher Channels," "Quality-Controlled Channels," and "Secondary Channels."

DIRECT-TO-RESEARCHER CHANNELS

Direct-to-researcher techniques for obtaining study reports are characterized by the fact that synthesists are attempting to locate investigators who may or may not have relevant studies rather than to locate the reports themselves. There are no formal restrictions on the kinds of requests that can be made through such direct contact or who can exchange it. The information exchanged can be very general (e.g., anything to do with interventions to increase activity) or very specific (e.g., studies of the effects of interventions on older adults' frequency of aerobic exercise), and the types of information about studies can be anything from unanalyzed data to published reports. In all but one case, there is no third party that mediates the exchange of information between the searcher and researcher. The principal forms of direct-to-researcher communication involve *personal contacts, mass solicitations, traditional invisible colleges,* and *electronic invisible colleges.* The distinctions between these forms of communication are described in the following paragraphs and summarized in Table 3.1.

Personal Contact

The first information available to synthesists is, of course, their own research. Before anyone else sees research results, the primary investigators see it themselves. So, we began our search for studies about the effects of homework on achievement by including our own studies that were relevant to the issue.

Although this source may seem almost too obvious to mention, it is a critical one. It is important for research synthesists to keep the role of their own work in proper perspective. Primary research that synthesists personally have conducted has a strong impact on how they interpret the research literature as a whole (Cooper, 1986). Typically, as researchers, we expect that all research should come to the same conclusions as our studies. However, comparing any single researcher's own studies to all the research that has been done on a topic reveals it can differ markedly on a number of important dimensions, many of which might influence results. Each researcher is likely to repeat some of the same operations across studies, using only a few measurement devices and/or instructions to participants. For example, studies of homework that one researcher conducts might exclusively use students' class grades as the measure of achievement. Other researchers might use textbook unit tests or standardized tests but not class grades. Also, participants in one researcher's studies might be drawn from the same institutions (e.g., a researcher always

Table 3.1   Direct-to-Researcher Channels for Locating Studies

Channel	Restrictions on How Research Gets In	Restrictions on How Searcher Gets In	Restrictions on Types of Information
Personal contact	Researcher must be known to searcher	Searcher must know how to contact researcher	Studies may be relatively homogeneous in methods and results
Mass solicitation	Researcher must hold status known to searcher (e.g., member of a relevant organization)	Searcher must have address for contact	Studies may be homogeneous in methods and results, if solicitation is based on membership in organization with particular bias
Traditional invisible college	Research must be "approved" by prominent researchers	Searcher must know who are prominent researchers and contact them	Studies may be homogeneous in methods; results may be overly consistent with perspective of prominent researchers
Electronic invisible college	Researcher must subscribe to computer listserv or bulletin board	Searcher must subscribe to same listserv or bulletin board or make request to someone who is a subscriber	Studies may be homogeneous in methods and results if listserv or bulletin board is based on membership in organization with particular bias

uses students in a nearby school district) and geographical area. This makes participants homogeneous on some dimensions (say, socioeconomic status) and different from participants in other researchers' studies. Even research assistants will be more homogeneous within the same laboratory in potentially relevant ways (e.g., training) than a random sample of all research assistants working on studies related to the topic.

Other one-on-one contacts—that is, people you contact directly or who contact you to share their work because they know the things you are interested in—take you outside your own laboratory, but perhaps not far outside. Students and their professors share ideas and pass on to one another papers and articles they find that are of mutual interest. Colleagues who have collaborated in the past or have met and exchanged ideas previously also will let one another know when new studies become available. A colleague down the hall might run across an article on homework in a journal or conference program and, knowing of my interest in the topic, might pass it on to me. Occasionally, readers of a researcher's past work will point out literature they think is relevant to the topic but was not cited in the report. This sometimes happens when the research report appears in print, but also as part of the manuscript review process. It would not be uncommon for a reviewer of a homework manuscript I submitted for journal publication to suggest some additional relevant articles that were not referenced in my work. These would be added to our list of relevant research as we begin our homework synthesis.

Limitations of information obtained by personal contact. Personal contact is generally a restricted communication channel. A searcher must know of, and individually contact, the primary researchers to obtain relevant information. Or the primary researchers must know the searcher is interested in what they do in order to initiate the exchange of information. So, much like a researcher's own work, information found through personal contacts, be they friends or colleagues, generally will reflect the methodological and theoretical biases of the searcher's informal social system. It most likely will be more homogeneous in findings than "all relevant research." That is not to say that personal contacts will never reveal to searchers findings that are inconsistent with their expectations but rather that this is somewhat less likely to happen than it is to reveal research that confirms expectations (and looks like the kind of research the colleagues do). Therefore, *personal contacts with friends and colleagues must never be the sole source of studies in a research synthesis.* Research synthesists who rely solely on these techniques to collect relevant work are acting like surveyors who decide to sample only their friends. That said, Figure 3.1 also suggests that these personal contacts may be the only way to obtain studies that analyzed data but never resulted in a written research report.

Mass Solicitations

Sending a common solicitation to a group of researchers can produce less biased samples of information. These contacts require you, first, to identify groups whose individual members might have access to relevant research reports.

Then, you obtain lists of group members and contact the members individually—typically by e-mail—even if you do not know them personally. For our homework search, we contacted the dean, associate dean, or chair of 77 colleges, schools, or departments of education at institutions of higher education and requested they transmit to their faculty our request that they share with us any research they had conducted, or knew of, that related to the practice of assigning homework.

Limitations of information obtained through mass solicitation. Mass solicitations can reveal a more heterogeneous sample of studies than personal contact, depending on the technique used to generate the mailing list. For example, it is hard to see how our strategy of contacting deans, associate deans, and department chairs would lead to a terribly biased sample of studies (although we did not know exactly which deans actually forwarded our e-mail, and this might have been related to what types of information they thought we would be "happiest" to receive). With regard to Figure 3.1, I suspect that information on studies that have only resulted in data analysis are less likely to be retrieved through mass mailing than personal contact because the searcher is less likely to be known to the solicitation recipient.

Traditional Invisible Colleges

Another channel of direct communication, a bit less restrictive than personal contacts, is the *invisible college*. According to Crane (1969), invisible colleges are formed because "scientists working on similar problems are usually aware of each other and in some cases attempt to systematize their contacts by exchanging reprints with one another" (p. 335). Through a sociometric analysis, Crane found that most members of invisible colleges were not directly linked to one another but were linked to a small group of highly influential members. In terms of group communication, traditional invisible colleges are structured like wheels—influential researchers are at the hub and less established researchers are on the rim, with lines of communication running mostly between a hub and spoke and less often among peripheral members.

The structural characteristics of the traditional invisible college are dependent on the fact that in the past the informal transmission of information between scientists occurred one-on-one, primarily through the mail and by telephone. These two mediums required that only two people at a time could exchange information (though multiple two-way communications might occur in parallel through, say, mass mailings). Also, the two communicators had to know and choose to talk to one another. Thus, influential researchers acted as hubs, both restricting the input (entry) and directing the output of (access to) information to a group of researchers known to them.

Today, traditional invisible colleges still exist but they have lessened in importance because of the ease and speed with which researchers can communicate with one another. For our homework search, we sent similar e-mails to 21 scholars who our reference database search (discussed in the following section) revealed had been the first author on two or more articles on homework and academic achievement between 1987 and the end of 2003. Among these 21 researchers, there were about a half dozen we already knew were active homework researchers. So, you might say that our decision to identify homework researchers by finding those who had multiple publications in recent years was a strategy to find people likely to be the hubs of homework wheels. Prominent researchers who publish frequently in an area are likely to get contacted more often than researchers just starting out.

Limitations of information obtained through traditional invisible colleges. The influence of prominent researchers over the information communicated through traditional invisible colleges holds the key to assessing the biases in the information transmitted through this channel. Synthesists gathering research solely by contacting prominent researchers will probably find studies that are more uniformly supportive of the beliefs held by these central researchers than are studies gathered from all sources. This is because new or marginal researchers who produce a result in conflict with that of the hub of an invisible college should be less likely to try to enter their work into this channel. If they do, they are less likely to see their work widely disseminated throughout the network. Disconfirming findings may lead a researcher already active in an invisible college to leave the network. Also, because the participants in a traditional invisible college use one another as a reference group, it is likely that the kinds of operations and measurements used in their research will be more homogeneous than those used by all researchers who might be interested in a given topic.

Electronic Invisible Colleges:
Listservs, Distribution Lists, and Bulletin Boards

While traditional invisible colleges still exist today, there exists also a newer type of "invisible" college. With the advent of the Internet, the need has diminished for communication hubs that hold together groups of scientists interested in the same topic. The Internet allows searchers to send the same information request simultaneously to a group whose members may be largely unknown to one another.

Electronic invisible colleges operate through the use of computerized list management programs, called *listservs*. These programs maintain mailing lists and automatically send e-mail messages to members. So, for our homework synthesis, we identified a group called the National Association of Test Directors, composed of the directors of research or evaluation in over 100 school districts. We contacted the manager of the listserv and asked this person to send our request for studies to members. If you are a member of a listserv that is relevant to your topic, you may be able to make this request directly of the other members.

Sometimes groups of researchers may not be associated with a formal listserv but rather communicate through informal *distribution lists* that are maintained by individuals. In other instances, researchers may be members of an *electronic bulletin board* or *discussion group*, on which members hold electronic discussions by submitting topics and receiving comments from other subscribers. Any of these can be used to make requests for research reports.

How do literature searchers know what listservs and bulletin boards are out there? The best way of finding listservs and discussion groups or bulletin boards is to do a web search including the terms "discussion group," "electronic bulletin board," or "listserv" and descriptors of the topic of interest. Mailing lists also can be found by visiting Internet sites of research organizations.[1]

Limitations of information obtained through electronic invisible colleges. A large majority of subscribers to a listserv, distribution list, or discussion group who receive messages asking for help in identifying studies relevant to a particular topic probably could not help and will not respond, but if even a few do know of studies, this can be very helpful. Especially, these channels can help you locate new research—perhaps in report form but not yet submitted for publication or in the publication queue but not yet published—or old research that never made its way into another communication channel.

Invisible colleges, listservs, distribution lists, bulletin boards, and discussion groups, unless they are associated with stable organizations, can be temporary, informal entities that often deal with special problems. They can vanish when the problem is solved or the focus of the discipline shifts. They can become out of date by including researchers whose interests have moved on from the topic. They can exclude new researchers who have recently entered the field and do not yet know of their existence. That is why *it is good practice to use both listserv and distribution lists along with the more direct personal contacts* described previously.

The listservs and electronic distribution lists can be less restrictive than a traditional invisible college because while an individual may act as the list coordinator (the hub), many lists are not moderated by individuals at all. Instead, the computer often acts as the hub of the communication wheel. It disseminates the communications that come to it without imposing any restrictions on content. In moderated mailing lists, the list of members can

---

[1] Another strategy would be to start a distribution list related to the topic of interest. This strategy would take longer to pay off but might reap great rewards when it did so.

be held privately and admittance and/or content may be screened, so these can function more like traditional invisible colleges.

Anyone can join many listservs and distribution lists, once they know that the list exists, by sending a simple command to its host computer. Other listservs require more formal membership. So, I could not join the National Association of Test Directors listserv because I am not a test director (we had to contact the list coordinator and ask that person to send it for us). Generally, however, literature searchers who use these channels to gather research should obtain a more heterogeneous set of studies than would be the case using a traditional invisible college or personal contacts.

Still, the listserv or distribution list will not produce studies as diverse in method and outcome as "all relevant research." Subscribers may still share certain biases. For example, I might try to gather research investigating homework by contacting the listserv of the American Psychological Association's Division of Educational Psychology. Subscribers to this list might overrepresent researchers who do large-scale surveys or experiments and underrepresent researchers who do ethnographic studies. And of course, in order to use these listservs, you must know they exist, suggesting that less established researchers are less likely to know of and contribute to them.

In sum, then, all the direct channels discussed so far share an important characteristic: There are no restrictions on what two colleagues can send to one another. Therefore, samples of studies found through personal contacts, mass solicitations, invisible colleges, listservs, and the like are more likely to contain studies that have not undergone scrutiny by others than will the corpus of all relevant research. Because of the reasons suggested in Figure 3.1, many of these studies may never appear in more restricted communication channels. In addition, many of the direct channels for scientific communication are likely to retrieve studies that are more homogeneous in methods and results than all conducted studies that are relevant to the topic.

QUALITY-CONTROLLED CHANNELS

Quality-controlled channels of communication require research to meet certain criteria related to the way the research was conducted before the reports can gain entry. Whether or not the criteria are met typically is judged by other researchers who are knowledgeable about the research area, so in this way this channel resembles the traditional invisible college. It is different from the invisible college, however, in that in most instances a report submitted for inclusion in a quality-controlled channel will likely be judged by more than one person. The two major quality-controlled channels are *conference presentations* and *scholarly journals*. Their characteristics are summarized in Table 3.2.

Table 3.2   Quality-Controlled Channels for Locating Studies

Channel	Restrictions on How Research Gets In	Restrictions on How Searcher Gets In	Restrictions on Types of Research Getting In
Professional conference paper presentations	Research must pass weak peer review	Searcher must be aware of conference	Statistically significant and interesting results more likely to appear
Peer-reviewed journals	Research must pass strict peer review	Searcher must subscribe to or be aware of the journal	Statistically significant and interesting results more likely to appear; journals likely to be homogeneous in methods

Conference Presentations

There are a multitude of social science professional societies, structured both by professional concerns and topic areas, and many of them hold yearly or biannual meetings. By attending these meetings or examining the papers given at them, you can discover what others in your field are doing and what research has recently been completed.

As an example of a search for conference presentations, in preparing this chapter I visited the website of the American Educational Research Association (AERA) and followed its link to the 2008 convention program. Along the way, I had to identify myself as a member or guest, and I had different privileges depending on what my status was. Appropriately, none of these privileges related to my access to the program proper; however, different organizations may have different rules and may restrict access to programs.

Next, I entered the search term "homework" and received the titles of 20 presentations, along with information about the session at which the paper was scheduled to be presented and the sponsoring division of the organization. A separate link for each presentation then took me to a page with the title, authors, their professional affiliations, and a brief abstract of the paper. As is typical of websites for convention programs, there was no link to a complete paper or to specific contact information for the authors. Still, with their name and affiliation, I could easily search for contact information on the Internet and send each author a request for a copy of the paper (and for other related papers they may have).

I could do similar searches separately for each AERA meeting program back to 2004. I also could conduct similar searches for papers presented at other related meetings (e.g., the Society for Research in Child Development) as well as regional educational research associations. Or if I wanted to do a more general search of conference proceedings, I could use the databases *PapersFirst* or *Proceedings* (available through my institutional library). These databases contain papers presented at conferences worldwide.

Limitations of information obtained through conference proceedings. In comparison to personal contacts, the research found through conference proceedings is less likely to reveal a restricted sample of results or operations and more likely to have undergone peer review. However, the selection criteria for meeting presentations are usually not as strict as those required for journal publication; in general, a larger percentage of presentations submitted to conferences are accepted than are manuscripts submitted to journals that use peer review. Also, the proposals that researchers submit for evaluation by a conference committee are often not very detailed. Finally, some researchers are invited to give papers by the people who put together the meeting agenda. These invited addresses generally are not reviewed for quality (they are assumed to be high quality based on the past work of the invitee).

A search for presentations complements a search of published studies because presentations given at meetings are likely to present data that never will be submitted for journal publication or have not yet made their way through the publication process. Researchers may never follow up a presentation by preparing a manuscript or they may present a paper before a publishable manuscript has been written, reviewed, or accepted. Journals also often have long lag times between when a manuscript is submitted and when it is published. McPadden and Rothstein (2006) found that about three quarters of the best papers presented at Academy of Management conferences eventually were published and the average time to publication was about 2 years after submission. Nearly half of the published papers included more or different data than were described in the conference proceedings. These new data included the addition of more outcome variables, an important component of a thorough research synthesis. A less selective sample of all papers presented at annual conferences of the Society for Industrial and Organizational Psychology revealed that only about half were eventually published and 60% of these contained data that were different from those reported in the conference paper.

Scholarly Journals

Synthesists can learn of research done in a topic area by examining the journals they subscribe to personally or believe are relevant and have access to through colleagues or their library. Journal publication is still the core of the formal scientific communication system. Journals are the traditional link between primary researchers and their audience.

Limitations of information obtained through journals. There would be some serious biases in a literature search that used personal journal reading as the sole or major source of research. The number of journals in which relevant research might appear is generally far greater than those that a single scientist examines routinely. As early as 1971, Garvey and Griffith noted that scholars had lost the ability to keep abreast of all information relevant to their specialties through personal readings and journal subscriptions. Thus, scientists tend to restrict the journals they read routinely to ones that operate within networks of journals (Xhignesse & Osgood, 1967). *Journal networks* comprise a small number of journals that tend most often to cite research published in other network journals.

Given that personal journal reading is likely to include journals in the same network, it would not be surprising to find some commonalities shared by network members. As with personal contacts and traditional invisible colleges, we would expect greater homogeneity in both research findings and operations within a given journal network than in all the research available on a topic area.

The appeal of using personal journal subscriptions as a source of information lies in their ease of accessibility. The content of these journals also will be credible to the reference group the synthesists hope will read their work. So, *personal journal readings should be used to find research for a synthesis, but this should not be the sole source of studies.*

Electronic journals. The journals a researcher routinely consults for work related to their interests can come to them on printed pages or electronically. Electronic journals, or *ejournals*, disseminate and archive full-text reports of scholarly work using computer storage media (see Peek & Pomerantz, 1998, for a history of electronic journals). Many journals appear in both paper and electronic form. Other journals are strictly paper or strictly electronic.

There are two characteristics of electronic journals that distinguish them from paper journals. First, many more electronic journals than printed journals do not use peer review procedures to screen the work they publish. It is critical for you to know which journals you have accessed do and do not evaluate submitted articles so you can use this information to assess both the potential methodological rigor of the studies and the likelihood of bias against null findings (see the following section). Second, relative to paper journals, electronic journals can have much shorter times between when a paper is accepted and when it is published. Due to the storage capacity and favorable economics of computer technology, an article accepted for publication in an electronic journal can become available to readers faster than articles accepted for printed journals. Of course, this distinction is disappearing as printed journals are using electronic editing procedures that are cutting down the time for both reviewing and editing accepted material.

A search for electronic journals that might be of interest to you can begin with the Internet. For example, a list of electronic journals can be found on the website http://library.georgetown.edu/newjour/. Or, more specifically, the American Educational Research Association's Special Interest Group on Communication of Research maintains a list of open-access electronic journals at http://aera-cr.asu.edu/ejournals/. Using the search terms "electronic journals" and a descriptor of almost any discipline in the social sciences in an Internet search engine will uncover scores of Internet-based journals for you to peruse.

Peer Review and Publication Bias

Most scientific journals (and conference programs) use peer review to decide whether or not to publish a particular research report. Upon submission, the journal editor sends the report to reviewers, who judge its suitability for publication. The primary criteria reviewers use will be the methodological quality of the research and the presence of safeguards against inferential errors. However, journal reviewers will also consider the appropriateness of the manuscript's content to the substantive focus of the journal they are reviewing for and whether the article makes an important contribution to the particular research literature. Largely, these last two criteria are irrelevant to the objectives of a research synthesist. As a synthesist, you want articles related to your topic even if they are somewhat inconsistent with the foci of the journals you read. Also, a report of a study that is not terribly significant in its contribution, perhaps because it reports a direct replication of earlier findings, might not meet a journal's criterion for importance but it still can be very important for inclusion in a synthesis.

Also of great concern is that *research published in many journals is more likely to present statistically significant findings—that is, findings that reject the null hypothesis with a probability of $p < .05$ (or some other significance criterion)—than all research on the topic.* This *bias against null findings* is present in the decisions made by both reviewers and primary researchers. To demonstrate, Atkinson, Furlong, and Wampold (1982) conducted a study in which they asked consulting editors for two APA journals in counseling psychology to review manuscripts. The manuscripts were identical in all respects except whether the hypothesized relation was statistically significant. They found that significant results were more than twice as likely to be recommended for publication compared to nonsignificant results. Further, they reported that the manuscripts with statistically significant results were rated to have better research designs than the ones with nonsignificant results, even though the methods were the same.

Primary researchers also are susceptible to bias against null findings. Greenwald (1975) found that researchers said they were inclined to submit significant results for publication about 60% of the time. On the other hand, researchers said they would submit the study for publication only 6% of the time if the results failed to reject the null hypothesis. Examining actual decisions by researchers, Figure 3.1 reveals a similar bias. Researchers' decisions not to submit statistically nonsignificant results are probably based on their beliefs that nonsignificant findings are less interesting than statistically significant ones. Also, they probably believe that journals are less likely to publish null results.

The bias against null findings in journal publication (and conference presentations) ensures that the size of correlations or differences between the mean scores of groups reported in published works will be larger than the differences you would be likely to find in all relevant research. Begg and Berlin (1988) gave a detailed account of the statistical characteristics of prejudice against the null hypothesis. Lipsey and Wilson (1993) empirically demonstrated the bias against null findings. They examined 92 meta-analyses that presented separate estimates of a treatment's effect found in published and unpublished research reports. The published estimates were about one-third greater than the unpublished ones.

Bias against null findings is not the only source of bias that influences the results of published research. For example, researchers whose findings conflict with the prevailing beliefs of the day are less likely to submit their results for publication, even if they are statistically significant, than researchers whose work confirms commonly held beliefs (Nunnally, 1960). Likewise, journal reviewers appear to look less favorably on studies that conflict with conventional wisdom than studies that support it. Bradley (1981) reported that 76% of university professors answering a mail questionnaire said they had encountered some pressure to conform to the subjective preferences of the reviewers of their work. These phenomena have been labeled collectively *confirmatory bias*.

The existence of *bias against null findings and confirmatory bias means that quality-controlled journal articles (and conference presentations) should not be used as the sole source of information for a research synthesis* unless you can convincingly argue that these biases do not exist in the specific topic area. For the homework research synthesis, my personal journal library included five journals that we examined for relevant studies: the *American Educational Research Journal*, the *Educational Psychologist*, the *Elementary School Journal*, the *Journal of Educational Psychology*, and the *Journal of Experimental Education*.

SECONDARY CHANNELS

Secondary channels provide information about primary research by gathering references from other sources, such as journals, government agencies, and even from researchers directly, and then creating databases for searchers to use. They are constructed by third parties for the explicit purpose of providing literature searchers with lists of studies relating to a topic. The major secondary channels, summarized in Table 3.3, are *research report reference lists, bibliographies, research registers,* and *reference databases,* including *citation indexes.*

Research Report Reference Lists

Using the reference lists at the end of research reports to locate other reports that might be relevant to a search is sometimes called the *ancestry approach,* or, more informally, footnote chasing. It involves examining the research reports you have already acquired to see if they contain references to studies as yet unknown to you. Then, you judge the list entries themselves for their relevance to the problem. If a reference may be relevant, you retrieve its abstract or full report. The reference lists of these reports then can be scrutinized for further leads. In this way, you work your way back through a literature until either the important concepts disappear or the studies become so old you judge their results to be obsolete.

There is another way to chase references made possible through the use of a secondary source called the Web of Science. When you are viewing the full record of an article in the Web of Science, there is a link on the page, labeled "View Related Records." Clicking on the link will display all articles that refer to at least one of the same earlier writings. Fortunately, the articles with shared references are listed high to low by the number of references they share with the article. The assumption here is that articles sharing more references are more likely to be related to one another. For example, when I used Web of Science to retrieve the full record for an article on the association between homework and achievement that my lab had published (Cooper, Jackson, Nye, & Lindsay, 2001), the record told me that the article contained 18 references.

Table 3.3   Secondary Channels for Locating Studies

Channel	Restrictions on How Research Gets In	Restrictions on How Searcher Gets In	Restrictions on Types of Information
Research report reference lists	Research must be known to article's authors	Searcher must subscribe to or be aware of the journal	Studies in the same journal network are more likely to be cited, producing homogeneity in methods and results
Research bibliographies	Compiler must be aware of research	Searcher must be aware of bibliography	Few restrictions, but possible bias toward particular methodologies
Prospective registers	Researcher must know about the register or be obligated to have research listed in it	Searcher must be aware of register	Prospective registers likely overrepresent large-scale and/or funded research
Internet	Researcher must make work available on the Internet	Searcher must choose search terms	Few, if any, restrictions; search terms will limit documents retrieved
Reference databases	Research must be in covered source	Searcher must choose search terms	Depending on database, may favor published research; recent research is missing; search terms will limit documents retrieved
Citation indexes	Research must be published	Searcher must know article that is cited by other articles	Mostly published research; recent research missing; search terms will limit documents retrieved

When I clicked on the "View Related Records" link, the new page told me that there were 5,180 articles that shared at least one reference in common with our article. The first two shared six references, the next five shared five references, and so on. I could then click on the link to each of these articles to find its full record.

Limitations of information obtained through the ancestry approach. Reference lists in primary research reports are rarely exhaustive compendia of the relevant research. In fact, authors are often advised to keep these to a minimum and cite only the most directly related material. They are meant to provide context for interpreting the new primary research. Further, primary report reference lists will tend to cite other work available through the same outlet or the small group of outlets that form an exchange network, like a journal network. Also, studies referred to in other study reports seem to be more likely to have statistically significant results (Dickerson, 2005). Therefore, you should expect more homogeneity in research methods and results found through primary report reference lists than would be present in all relevant studies.

Another form of reference list is provided by previous research synthesists. Obviously, these can be especially helpful sources of relevant studies and will likely not contain the number and networking restrictions associated with references in primary research reports. However, even though these will be more comprehensive, you should not assume previous syntheses are based on all relevant research. To determine this, you would need to (a) read and evaluate the literature search strategies used by the synthesists and (b) determine whether their inclusion and exclusion criteria match your own. They also may be dated, thus missing the most recent research.

In sum, searching reference lists, either through the ancestry approach or through related records, will overrepresent published research because it is generally easier to find than unpublished work. Also, the most recently completed research will not appear on these lists because of the lag between when a final manuscript is submitted and when it is published. However, while reference lists in reports should not be used as a sole means for finding studies, they are generally productive sources of relevant research. Although we did not keep track of the precise numbers, we found many homework research articles by examining report reference lists.

Research Bibliographies

Research bibliographies can be either evaluative or nonevaluative listings of books, journal articles, and other research reports that are relevant to a particular topic area. Bibliographies are sometimes maintained by individual scientists, groups of scientists within a particular research area, or formal organizations. For example, while I am not aware of individuals or organizations that maintain bibliographies on homework, I do know that the Harvard Family Research Project maintains a database called the *Out-of-School Time Program Research and Evaluation Database*. This database contains profiles about research and evaluations conducted on both large and small out-of-school programs and initiatives. Each profile contains an overview of the program or initiative as well as detailed information about each report produced about that program.

Limitations of information obtained through bibliographies. The use of bibliographies prepared by others can be a tremendous time saver. The problem, however, is that most bibliographies are likely to be of much greater breadth than the searcher's interest. Also, it is likely that most bibliographies will need updating for recent research. Even with these precautions, comprehensive bibliographies generated by interested parties can be a great help to you. The compiler has spent many hours obtaining information, and the biases involved in generating the bibliographies may counteract biases that exist in the other techniques you use to find research.

Prospective Research Registers

Prospective research registers are unique in that they attempt to include not only completed research but also research that is in the planning stage or is still underway (see Berlin & Ghersi, 2005). Today, such registers are more commonly available in the medical than in the social sciences. Still, there are ways to find lists of social science research projects that are currently underway or have recently been completed. For example, the websites of many private foundations or government agencies that sponsor research can be visited to seek a list of current or recent research grants. For a topic such as homework, I might visit the websites of the W. T. Grant Foundation, the Spencer Foundation, the U.S. Department of Education's Institute for Education Science, and the U.S. National Institutes of Health.

As with bibliographies, a difficulty in finding pertinent research registers is in knowing where to start. Librarians and knowledgeable colleagues can be a big help here.

Limitations of information obtained through prospective research registers. From the searcher's point of view, identifying a prospective research register with relevant studies can provide access to ongoing and unpublished research that is not filtered through personal allegiances. In the case of funded research, you know the results will be available regardless of the study's outcome. This can be a great complement to other search channels.

That said, prospective research registers are likely to overrepresent large-scale and funded research projects. My example of foundations and government projects makes this clear. Also, the comprehensiveness of the register is of greatest importance to the literature searcher. Therefore, it is critical that searchers determine (a) how long a register has been in existence and (b) how the research included in the register got to be there.

The Internet

The capability of the Internet to assist in the transfer of information has revolutionized modern society; scientific communication has been no less affected than other areas of human interaction. The critical task for research synthesists using the Internet is to develop a strategy for finding websites with information that addresses their problem. *Search engines*, programs that search for and then index websites, are used for this purpose. Three widely used search engines can be found at www.google.com, www.search.yahoo.com, and www.ask.com. Studies of content overlap suggest that more than 80% of the pages in the major search engine's database exist only in that database and first page results overlap only .6% across the three search engines (http://searchengineland.com/070601-094554.php). So, *it is good practice to use more than one search engine to be certain you are conducting a thorough search of the Internet.* A good comparison of the features of the three most popular search engines (with some instruction on how best to use them) is provided by the University of California at Berkeley Libraries and can be found at http://www.lib.berkeley.edu/TeachingLib/Guides/Internet/SearchEngines.html.

The searcher provides a search term, phrase, or set of terms and phrases to the search engine. All the search engines in some way permit the use of *Boolean syntax operators* to expand or restrict the search. Boolean operators allow the searcher to use set theory to help define the items that will be retrieved by a search. However, how websites are represented and the precise commands used to do the Boolean syntax search will differ somewhat for each search engine. All three search engines mentioned in the previous paragraph provide online assistance to help you learn how to use them.

The result of a search will be a list of websites that fit the keyword description, most often because the website contains the keyword or words somewhere on the web page. The order in which the websites appear on the results page will be a function of the degree of match between search terms and the website content as well as how frequently the website is viewed.

As an Internet search example, while preparing this chapter I began a search for homework research by asking the three search engines to list for me all websites that included the term "homework." Bad idea: Google found about 51,200,000 websites, Yahoo gave me 151,000,000, and Ask.com gave me 29,560,000. Of course, many of these websites include homework assignments posted by teachers on the Internet, tips on how to do homework, newspaper articles about homework, and so on. The numbers were no less daunting when I added the term "research" to the search and required that both be present for the website to be retrieved. Even requiring that the two terms appear adjacent to one another led to 70,000 sites in Google, 255,000 in Yahoo, and 14,500 in Ask.com.

As these results suggest, using the Internet to find scientific research on a specific topic can be overwhelming and time consuming. It would be foolish to go to each of these websites to see if it reported research relevant to the research synthesis (and not found through other channels). The Internet contains much more than research information. To overcome this problem, a searcher can use one of the more specialized search engines. For example, Google has a specialized search engine called Google Scholar (http:// scholar.google.com/intl/en/scholar/about.html). This search engine is restricted to scholarly documents available on the Internet and permits the specification of searches that can take many of the irrelevant documents out of the search results. So, searching "homework" in Google Scholar retrieved 274,000 documents. But when I used the Advanced Search feature to specify that both the terms "homework" and "effects" had to appear in the title of a document indexed only in the social sciences, arts, or humanities, I found 222 websites. When I used "homework" and "research," 93 documents were found.

An Internet search using the terms "research engines" and "social science" will lead to other sites that list search engines more specific to your purposes and potentially related to your topic. The search engines listed in these sites primarily provide computer access to research registers and to the reference databases that I will describe shortly.

The strategies for searching the Internet I have described are only some examples of numerous approaches. I am being deliberately general here because these resources change quickly. With practice, you will become more familiar with the resources available to you and how to construct searches that produce relevant material.

Limitations of information obtained through the Internet. Internet websites can be constructed by anyone who has (or knows someone who has) the required expertise. Thus, there is little restriction on what information can be made available on websites. And of course, this can be both a good and a bad thing because the amount of information can be exhaustive but overwhelming and with no quality check on content.

Reference Databases

Finally, the sources of information likely to prove most fruitful to research synthesists are called reference databases. These are indexing services maintained by both private and public organizations associated with social science disciplines. Our search for homework studies used four reference databases. We searched the *Education Resource Information Center (ERIC*, http://www.eric.ed.gov/), *PsycINFO* (http://www.apa.org/psycinfo/), *Sociological Abstracts*, and *Dissertation Abstracts* electronic databases for documents cataloged between January 1, 1987, and December 31, 2003. Because these databases and their interfaces are constantly being updated, I recommend that you visit their web pages or your library's resource pages to get the most current information about them and many other databases. One good general source of information on databases is the *Gale Directory of Databases* (Hall & Romaniuk, 2008).

Limitations of information contained in reference databases. Even though reference databases are superb sources of studies, they still have limitations. First, there can be a time lag between when a study is completed and when it will appear in the reference database, though technology has reduced this lag dramatically. Still, the study must be written up and submitted, accepted into its primary outlet, appear in print or online, and then cataloged into the reference database. So, the most recently completed research—the type you would find by contacting researchers or contained in prospective registers (and perhaps on the Internet)—will not appear in reference databases. Second, each reference database contains some restrictions on what is allowed to enter the system based on topical or disciplinary boundaries. Therefore, if you are interested in an interdisciplinary topic you will need to access more than one reference database. For example, studies about homework certainly interest education researchers but might also appear in psychology or sociology journals. Third, some reference databases contain only published research, others both published and unpublished research, and others just unpublished research (e.g., dissertation abstracts). So, if you want to minimize publication bias, it is important to find out the coverage of the databases you plan to use and try to include databases that assemble unpublished as well as published documents.

Citation indexes. A citation index is a unique kind of reference database that identifies and groups together all published articles that have referenced (cited) the same earlier publication. In this way, the earlier publication becomes the indexing term for the more recent articles. In contrast to using research report reference lists to look for the ancestors of a report, the citation index uses a *descendancy approach*, looking for the descendants of an article. Three citation indexes produced by the Institute for Scientific Information are available through most research libraries and can be entered through the Web of Science. It provides access to the *Science Citation Index Expanded* (which includes published articles in science journals from 1900 to the present), the *Social Sciences Citation Index* (beginning in 1956), and the *Arts & Humanities Citation Index* (beginning in 1975). As noted, the Web of Science also provides cited reference searching and thus allows users to move forward and backward through the literature.

An example will make the citation search strategy clear. At the beginning of the search for homework research, we were aware of an important and well-known published document (our earlier research synthesis) that had a high likelihood of being cited in many subsequent investigations on homework. With this knowledge, we entered the citation indexes by looking up this reference (Cooper, 1989). The *Science Citation Index Expanded* and the *Social Sciences Citation Index* databases were searched from 1987 to 2004 to identify studies that had cited this book. The index gave a listing of each article that had cited the book by the article's author, source, and date of publication. We then could look at these articles to see if they contained results we could use in our new synthesis. We could have used the same strategy again using several different important articles.

Past research is not the only way to track down descendents. The search for studies concerning individual differences in rape attitudes also used the *Social Sciences Citation Index* to great effect even though we could not identify seminal research articles. Here, five frequently used measures of attitudes toward rape were identified and the articles in which the measures were originally described were used to access the citation index. We found 545 citations of the five scales and examined their abstracts to determine if the studies were relevant to the study of individual differences.

Limitations of information contained in citation indexes. Citation indexes limit entry to references in published research, both journals and books. Therefore we can expect a bias against the null hypotheses in citations in the same way we expect this in the references we find in research reports. However, their coverage is quite exhaustive within these categories. Also, citation indexes will miss more recent publications because of the time it takes to index documents.

Database vendors. All major research libraries have numerous reference databases available. Reference librarians can help you identify the databases most appropriate for your search and can provide the introductory instructions needed to access them. Once you have identified the databases of relevance to your search, the database interface will contain step-by-step, menu-driven instructions that make them easy to use. However, the same database can be provided to your library by more than one vendor and the results of your search using the same database may be slightly different depending on which vendor you choose. This likely happens because of differences in the frequency with which the databases are updated.

CONDUCTING SEARCHES OF REFERENCE DATABASES

Research libraries employ trained specialists who can conduct your search or help you through the process. It is good practice to discuss your search with a trained research librarian before you begin; they are likely to have suggestions about places to look that you have not thought of. Also, there are many publications that can help you start thinking about a search, including *Library Use: Handbook for Psychology* (Reed & Baxter, 2003) and *The Oxford Guide to Library Research* (Mann, 2005). Reed and Baxter (2009) provide a more indepth treatment of reference database searching strategies in the context of research synthesis.

Typically, you begin your reference database search by deciding which databases to access. So, I started a search for homework research by deciding to search *PsycINFO, ERIC, Sociological Abstracts,* and *Dissertation Abstracts.* Before entering any of these databases, I checked to see if more than one vendor offered them. I found that my university offered *PsycINFO* through two vendors. One vendor permitted me to search both *PsycINFO* and *ERIC* at the same time. Therefore, using this vendor would save me the effort of removing duplicate documents from separate searches of each database. I also found little difference in the number of documents retrieved using the term "homework" in the *ERIC* data using the two different vendors. (I chose *ERIC* to run this test because I anticipated that it is the database that would reveal the most relevant documents.) So, I chose the vendor that permitted me to search jointly *ERIC* and *PsycINFO.*

Next, I chose the terms I used to search for documents. A searcher can browse through thesauri that accompany the different databases to identify terms that might not have initially come to mind. You can also use examples of documents you hope to retrieve and see what terms are used to index these documents or that appear in their title or abstract. This gives you some concrete idea about the material desired. If a search does not include these documents, something has gone awry. Regardless of how terms to use in a search are identified, when you evaluate the search procedures used in a research synthesis, you should ask the question,

> *Were proper and exhaustive terms used in searches and queries of reference databases and research registries?*

I began my search simply with the term "homework" because I first wanted to explore whether related terms exist. My search engine told me that the *ERIC Thesaurus* relates the term "homework" to the terms "assignments" and "home study." I can then use an "explode" function to expand these terms and examine yet more terms. These terms seemed too far afield ("instruction" comes up as a term related to "assignments" and "distance education" related to "home study"), so I decided to use just "homework" without much concern that too many relevant documents will be missed. The thesaurus for *PsycINFO* told me that the term "homework" was added in 1988. It also told me that the definition of homework used in the database was "assignment given to students or clients to be completed outside regular classroom period or therapeutic setting." Here, then, I encountered an instance in which the same term is used in two very different contexts, one academic and one therapeutic. This alerted me to the possible need to restrict my search in some way to exclude therapeutic homework in a clinical situation. The PsycINFO thesaurus offered three related terms: "note taking," "psychotherapeutic techniques," and "study habits." I decided that none of these would likely add many relevant studies if "homework" is already in the search.[2]

Next, I set my search parameters. I decided to use the search terms "homework" and "achievement." I wanted both terms to appear (so I used the AND Boolean operator, not the OR operator). The addition of achievement to the search should exclude all or most of the research in which homework is part of a therapeutic regimen. My search engine then gave me a series of other decisions to make regarding whether I wanted to restrict my search to, for example, only journal articles, only articles intended for specific audiences, and only studies using particular research methodologies. Consistent with my problem definition, I decided to leave the search unrestricted except for two parameters. First, I wanted documents that pertained to elementary and secondary homework only, not early childhood or postsecondary education. Second, I only wanted documents that appeared since 1987, the last time we synthesized the research on homework.

---

[2] In some databases, you may run into a distinction between *natural language* key words or search terms and *controlled vocabulary*. Natural language consists of the words researchers and searchers use to describe research. Controlled vocabulary consists of terms added to document records by the database constructors to describe documents. Today, the distinction will not much change what you do, but you may be happy that the controlled vocabulary has been added to the record because it tends to diminish the scatter of a literature.

Finally, I decided that I only wanted to see documents that use the two terms "homework" and "achievement" in the abstract. I could restrict documents to ones that use homework in the title but that seems too restrictive; I am aware that there are some studies that use homework as one of many predictors of achievement and therefore it is likely to be mentioned in the abstracts of these articles but not in the title. Including all documents that mention homework anywhere in the text seemed too inclusive. In making these decisions, I was making trade-offs between the precision and recall of my search. The more precise my search, the more likely it is that I will miss some relevant studies. The higher the recall of my search, the more likely it is that I will retrieve many document records that are irrelevant to my search.

On the day I conducted this search, I found 431 documents that met the inclusion criteria. I could then repeat my search with the other databases, keeping my search parameters as similar as possible.

Let me also illustrate a search of a citation index. From the Web of Science home page provided by my library, I clicked on a tab labeled "Cited Reference Search." First, I provided the last name and first name initial of the author (I use Cooper H), the cited work (my book titled *Homework*; if this had been a journal article, I would enter the journal title), and the year of the publication I was interested in (in this case, 1989). This is a very restricted search, as it is looking for citations to only a single publication. Had I entered only "Cooper H" and left the cited work and year blank, I would retrieve citations to all documents authored by scholars who share this last name and first initial. Next, the page allowed me to restrict my search to certain years (I chose 1989 to the present, since it would be impossible for the book to have been cited by a publication that appeared before the book was published) or to any of the three citation databases. I chose to search all three. The search found references to the book in 89 documents. I could then restrict the search further by several types of citing documents and by language.

As my example reveals, another limitation on the exhaustiveness of searches based solely on reference databases derives not from what they contain but from how they are accessed by searchers. *Even if a database were to have exhaustive coverage of the journals that are relevant to your topic, you will not necessarily be able to describe your topic in a manner that ensures you uncover every relevant article in it.* The search may not "recall" all the wanted information. Like searching the Internet, searchers must enter the database by specifying search terms associated with particular research topics. Searchers who are unaware or omit terms that apply to documents relevant to their interests are likely to miss articles. All searchers make trade-offs between (a) the likelihood of missing relevant documents and (b) including lots of irrelevant documents.

DETERMINING THE
ADEQUACY OF LITERATURE SEARCHES

The question of which and how many sources of information to use in a search has no general answer. The appropriate sources will be a function partly of the topic under consideration and partly of the resources available to you. As a rule, however, *searchers must always use multiple channels with different entry and access restrictions so that they minimize any systematic differences between studies that are and are not found by the search.* If a searcher has uncovered different studies through channels that do not share similar entry and access restrictions, then the overall conclusions of the synthesis should be replicable by someone else using different, but also complementary, sources for primary research. This rule embodies the scientific principle of making results replicable. So, an important question to ask about the adequacy of the search strategy used in a research synthesis is,

Were complementary searching strategies used to find relevant studies?

Reference databases and research registers, if they are available, should form the backbone of any comprehensive literature search. These sources probably contain the information most closely approximating all research. Typically, they cast the widest net. Their restrictions are known and can be compensated for by the use of other complementary search strategies.

Earlier in this chapter, I mentioned that concentrating on only quality-controlled sources would produce a set of studies that overrepresented statistically significant results. However, because these sources involve peer review, it could be argued that this research has undergone the most rigorous methodological appraisal by established researchers and probably is of the highest quality. As we shall see in Chapter 5, publication does not ensure that only studies of high quality will be included in the synthesis. Faulty studies often make their way into print. Also, well-conducted studies may never be submitted for publication.

A focus on only published research might be legitimate in two circumstances. First, published research often contains several dozen, or in some cases hundreds, of relevant studies. In such an instance, it is likely that while the published research may overestimate the certainty with which a null hypothesis can be rejected and the size of the relationship, it probably will not incorrectly identify the direction of a relationship. The suggested magnitude of the relation can be adjusted for the possibility of bias against null results (I will return to this in Chapter 7). Also, enough instances of a hypothesis test will be covered to allow a legitimate examination of which study characteristics covary with study outcomes.

Second, there are many hypotheses that have multiple tests in the literature that were not the primary focus of the research. For instance, many psychological and educational studies include the participants' sex as a variable in the data analysis and report hypothesis tests of sex differences, although these are only an ancillary interest of the primary researchers. The bias toward significant results in publications probably does not extend much beyond the primary hypothesis. Therefore, a hypothesis that appears in many articles as a secondary interest of the researchers will be affected by bias against null results to a lesser degree than the researcher's primary focus.

Generally speaking, however, focusing on only published studies is not advisable. The possibility of bias against the null hypothesis is too great. In addition, *you should not restrict your search to published outlets even if you ultimately decide to include only published work in your synthesis.* To make a well-informed choice about what to put in and leave out, and even to help you decide what the important issues are in a field, you need to have the most thorough grasp of the literature.

Finally, the information contained in channels involving personal contact with researchers is not likely to reflect information gleaned from all potential sources. However, research found by contacting researchers directly likely will complement that gained through other channels because it is likely to be more recent.

PROBLEMS IN
DOCUMENT RETRIEVAL

Depending on the databases you use and the nature of your topic (especially the age of the research you want to retrieve), once you have your search results, you will be able to retrieve relevant articles through three different media: print, microfiche, and online. Digitization of documents has made retrieval much easier, and as more documents are stored and accessed online, you will find retrieval is just a few key strokes away.

However, some deficiencies in document retrieval procedures will frustrate you regardless of how thorough and careful you try to be. Some potentially relevant studies do not become public and defy the grasp of even the most conscientious searchers. Other documents you will become aware of but you will be unable to obtain.

Every research synthesist will find that some documents of potential relevance (based on their title or abstract) cannot be obtained from their personal journals or institutional library's print or microfiche collections and will not be available electronically. To what lengths should you go to retrieve these documents? The use of interlibrary loans is a viable route. Interlibrary loans can be used to obtain dissertations and master's theses, or dissertations can be purchased from Proquest UMI (originally, University Microfilms International). Also, contacting the primary researchers directly is another possibility, although personal contact often results in only a low rate of response. Whether or not a primary researcher can be located and induced to send a document is influenced in part by the age of the requested material, whether it is digitized, and the status of the requester.

In general, when deciding how much effort should be expended trying to retrieve documents that are difficult to obtain, you should consider (a) the likelihood that the needed document actually contains relevant information, (b) the percentage of the total known documents that are difficult to find and how their results might differ from the results of studies you have, (c) the cost involved in undertaking extraordinary retrieval procedures (e.g., interlibrary loan is cheap, buying dissertations is expensive), and (d) any time constraints operating on you.

THE EFFECTS OF LITERATURE
SEARCHING ON SYNTHESIS OUTCOMES

At the beginning of this chapter, I mentioned that literature searches have two different targets—previous research and individuals or groups relevant to the topic area. Therefore, it is necessary for you to address the adequacy of your accessed studies with respect to each of the targets. You must ask (a) how the retrieved studies might differ from all studies and (b) how the individuals or groups contained in retrieved studies might differ from all individuals or groups of interest.

Much of this chapter has dealt with how to answer the first of these questions. Every study does not have an equal chance of being retrieved. It is likely that studies easily obtained through your retrieval channels are different from studies that never become available. Therefore, you must pay careful attention to what the results of inaccessible studies might be and how this might differ from what is found in studies that have been retrieved (again, I return to this topic in Chapter 7).

The synthesist's second population of interest, referring to individuals or other basic units of analysis, injects a note of optimism into the discussion. There is good reason to believe research syntheses will pertain more directly to a target population than will the separate primary research efforts in the topic area. The overall literature can contain studies conducted at different times, on units with different characteristics, and in different locations. A literature can also contain research conducted under different testing conditions with different methods. For certain problem areas containing numerous replications, the diversity of samples accessible to a synthesist should more closely approximate the target population of the primary researcher.

Of course, we must bear in mind that the biases against null results and contradictory findings may affect the available samples of people as well as studies. *To the extent that more retrievable studies are associated with particular subpopulations of elements, retrieval biases will be associated with not only the outcomes of studies but also with the characteristics of study samples.*

The most important way to ensure that the sample of studies in your syntheses is representative of all research on your topic is to conduct a broad and exhaustive search of the literature. While the law of diminishing returns applies here, a complete literature search has to include at least

- a search of reference databases,
- a perusal of relevant journals,
- the examination of references in past primary research and research syntheses, and
- personal contacts with active and prominent researchers.

The more exhaustive a search, the more confident you can be that other synthesists using similar, but perhaps not identical, sources of information will reach the same conclusions. Table 3.4 presents an example of a log that can be used to keep track of the techniques you used to search the literature.

Also, in your analysis of your synthesis' results, you should present indices of potential retrieval bias, if they are available. For instance, many research syntheses examine whether any difference exists in the results of studies that are published versus those that are unpublished. Others examine the distribution of results to see if they suggest that some results are missing. Techniques for conducting these analyses are discussed in Chapter 7.

Table 3.4 A Log for Keeping Track of a Search of the Literature

Direct-to-Researcher Search Techniques	Used?	Who Was Contacted?	Date Sent	Date Reply Received	Nature of Reply
Personal contact	__ Yes Date___ __ No Reason:	Researcher Names _____ _____ _____ _____	||||	||||	||||
Mass solicitation	__ Yes Date___ __ No Reason:	Organization Names _____ _____ _____ _____	||||	||||	||||
Traditional Invisible College "Hubs"	__ Yes __ No If no, reason:	Researcher Names _____ _____ _____ _____	||||	||||	||||

(Continued)

Table 3.4 (Continued)

		Organization Names		Number of Documents Examined	Number of Relevant Documents Found
Electronic invisible college; listservs, bulletin boards, discussion groups	__ Yes Date___ __ No Reason:	_____ _____ _____ _____			
Quality-Controlled Search Techniques	Used?	Organization Names or Journal Titles	Years Searched	Number of Documents Examined	Number of Relevant Documents Found
Professional conference paper presentations	__ Yes Date___ __ No Reason:	Organization Names _____ _____ _____	__-__ __-__ __-__	____ ____ ____	____ ____ ____
Peer-reviewed journals	__ Yes Date___ __ No Reason:	Journal Titles _____ _____ _____	__-__ __-__ __-__	____ ____ ____	____ ____ ____

Secondary Searching Techniques	Used?		Years Covered	Number of Documents Examined	Number of Relevant Documents Found
Research report reference lists	__ Yes Date ____ __ No Reason:	# of Reports Examined ____	__—__	____	____
Research bibliographies	__ Yes Date ____ __ No Reason:	Source (Name) of Bibliography _____ _____ _____ _____	_—_ _—_ _—_ _—_	____ ____ ____ ____	____ ____ ____ ____
Prospective registers	__ Yes Date ____ __ No Reason:	Register Names _____ _____ _____ _____	_—_ _—_ _—_ _—_	____ ____ ____ ____	____ ____ ____ ____

(Continued)

Table 3.4 (Continued)

Secondary Search Techniques	Used?		Years Searched	Search Terms	Other Restrictions
Internet	___ Yes Date___ ___ No Reason:	Search Engines _____ _____ _____		_____ AND/OR _____ AND/OR _____ AND/OR ___	_____ _____ _____
Reference databases	___ Yes Date___ ___ No Reason:	Database Names _____ _____ _____	_ _ _ _ _ _	_____ AND/OR _____ AND/OR _____ AND/OR ___	_____ _____ _____
Citation indexes	___ Yes Date___ ___ No Reason:	Index Names _____ _____ _____	_ _ _ _	_____ AND/OR _____ AND/OR _____ AND/OR ___	_____ _____

EXERCISES

1. Using the topic area you identified in Chapter 2, conduct a search of a reference database. Perform a parallel search of the Internet. How are the outcomes different? Which was more useful and cost-effective?

2. For a topic of your choice, choose the channels you would use to search the literature and the order in which you would access them. For each step in the search, describe its benefits, limitations, and cost-effectiveness, given your topic.

4

Step 3

Gathering Information From Studies

What procedures should be used to extract information from each study report?

Primary Functions Served in the Synthesis

1. To create a coding frame for obtaining information from studies

2. To train coders

3. To assess the accuracy of extracted information

Procedural Variation That Might Produce Differences in Conclusions

1. Variations in the information gathered from each study might lead to differences in what is tested as an influence on cumulative results

2. Variations in coder training might lead to differences in entries on coding sheets

3. Variation in rules for deciding what study results are viewed as independent might lead to differences in the amount and specificity of data used to draw cumulative conclusions

Questions to Ask When Evaluating the Information Gathered From Each Study to Be Included in a Research Synthesis

1. Were procedures used to ensure the unbiased retrieval of information from study reports?

This chapter describes

- How to construct a coding guide that will gather the important information about studies to be included in a research synthesis
- How to train coders so the information about studies will be gathered reliably
- Issues in judging whether separate outcomes from the same study should be considered independent outcomes
- What to do when information about a study is missing

So far, you have formulated the problem you want to explore in your research synthesis. You know the crucial issues that have come to the attention of theorists, researchers, and previous synthesists. And your literature search is underway. The next step in your synthesis is to begin the construction of your *coding guide*. The coding guide is the device you (and those who are assisting you) will use to gather information about each study. Most of this information will come from the study report itself but some may come from other sources as well.

DEVELOPING A CODING GUIDE

If the number of studies involved in your synthesis is small, it may not be necessary before you begin to examine the literature to have a precise and complete idea about what information to collect about the studies. The relevant reports, if only a dozen or so exist, can be retrieved, read, and reread until you have a good notion of what aspects of the studies would be interesting to code or how often the important characteristics suggested by others actually appear in the studies. For example, you might be interested in whether the effect of homework is moderated by the socioeconomic status (SES) of students but you find that very few studies report the SES of the students taking part.

Of course, *if you read the entire literature first and then decide what information to code about each study, your choices of codes are post hoc and should not be solely dictated by what your reading suggested will be significant predictors of results.* If you do this, the probability levels associated with the predictors are not accurate estimates (they are too low). Still, small sets of studies allow you to follow up on ideas that emerge only after all the studies have been read. Then, you can return to previously read studies to code the new information you did not realize was important during the first reading.

If you expect to uncover a large number of studies, reading then rereading reports may be prohibitively time-consuming. In this case, it is necessary to consider carefully what data will be retrieved from each research report before the formal coding begins.

When an area of research is large and complex, the construction of a coding guide can be no small task. The first draft of a coding guide should never be the last. First, you need to list all the characteristics of studies you want to gather. Then, you need to consider what possible values studies might take on each variable. For example, in a research synthesis of interventions to increase physical activity among older adults, you would certainly want to gather information on the age of participants. You might decide that your definition of "older adults" includes people over the age of 55, but participants still might be much older than 55 and this might influence the effects of the intervention. So, you might want your coding guide to help you gather information on the range in age among participants. Therefore, the coding guide should contain a question about the age of the youngest participant in the study, one about the oldest participant, and the mean and/or median age of participants.

After you have this preliminary set of coding questions and response categories, you need to show this first draft to knowledgeable colleagues for their input. They are certain to suggest additional codings and response categories, and point out instances in which your questions and responses are ambiguous and thus difficult to understand. After taking their advice, you should code a few randomly selected studies using the coding guide. This will add further precision to questions and response categories.

An important rule in constructing a coding guide for research synthesis is that *when many studies are involved, any information that might possibly be considered relevant should be retrieved from the studies*. Once data coding has begun, it is exceedingly difficult to retrieve new information from studies that have already been coded. Some of the information you gather on the coding sheets may never be examined in your completed synthesis. Sometimes, too few studies will report information about the variable of interest. In other cases, studies will not vary enough across values of a characteristic (for example, most homework studies were done in public schools, very few in private schools) to allow valid inferences. Still, it is much less of a problem to gather more information with your coding guide that you will eventually find useful than it is to have to return to reports to get information that was neglected the first time through.

INFORMATION TO INCLUDE ON A CODING GUIDE

While the content of every research synthesis coding guide will be unique to the question asked, there are certain broad types of information that every synthesist will want to gather from primary research reports. Here, I will classify these types of information into eight categories:

1. The report

2. The predictor or independent variable

   a. If the report describes an experimental manipulation, information about the manipulated conditions, that is, the intervention (if the study is applied in nature, such as homework or exercise programs) or the independent variable (if the study is testing basic theoretical predictions, such as the effects of task choice)
   b. If the report describes nonmanipulated predictor variables, information about how these were collected and their psychometric characteristics (for example, the scales used to measure participants' individual differences)

3. The setting in which the study took place

4. Participant and sample characteristics

5. The dependent or outcome variables and how they were measured (such as achievement, amount of physical activity, motivation, or rape myth acceptance)

6. The type of research design

7. Statistical outcomes and effect sizes

8. Coder and coding process characteristics

In this chapter, I will focus on six of the eight types of information about a study. I will return to discuss how to code research designs in Chapter 5 and statistical outcomes in Chapter 6, when each of these topics is covered in more detail.

A general coding guide will never capture all the important aspects of all studies. The questions that should guide your construction of the material to be retrieved from studies should include

- Theoretical and applied concerns

  o Do theories suggest what study characteristics might be important and how the studies might differ on these characteristics?
  o Are there issues in practical application that suggest that the way studies are conducted could relate to the impact of the intervention or policy?

- Methodological issues
  - How might methods vary in ways that could relate to study outcomes?
  - Are there disputes in the literature that relate to how studies are conducted?

Finally, completed coding sheets are often characterized by numerous entries left unfilled (I will return to this later) and notes in margins. Coders sometimes will feel as though they are slamming round pegs into square holes. Perfection is never achieved. Therefore, *it is good practice to leave coders space to make notes about on-the-spot decisions they made.* In general, the rules for constructing a coding guide are similar to those used in creating a coding frame for a primary research effort (Bourque & Clark, 1992), and a more detailed description of the process in research synthesis can be found in Wilson (2009) and Orwin and Vevea (2009).

Characteristics of the report. Table 4.1 provides an example of a coding guide for report characteristics. Note that an "R" is placed before each question number in the first column. This was done to distinguish questions about the report from questions about other features of the study, which will be given other letters, such as "I" for intervention characteristics and "O" for outcome characteristics. Doing this is really a matter of personal taste. You could also just number the questions successively. Also, note that all possible responses to each question are listed below the question and each response is given a number that will be entered by the coder into the spaces provided in the second column. Some responses are simply "other." This code will be used if the coder finds a report characteristic that does not correspond to any response listed above it. When the "other" response is used, the coder is asked to provide a brief written description of the characteristic. Some of the questions also provide a "can't tell" response. Coders will use a question mark in the response space for "can't tell." This makes it easy to distinguish missing information from other coded values. I have repeated the "can't tell" response in most of the questions, but to save space, coders could be instructed simply to use this convention throughout the coding sheet. Finally, the question column of the coding sheet can ask coders to give the page number on which the information was found in the report (see Question R3). Later, if coders have concerns about how they coded particular pieces of information or if two coders disagree about a code, having its location reported on the coding sheet will ease the process of finding the information for later checking. To save space, I have only shown this once in the tables, but it can appear for just about every question. If coders are working from their own copies of reports, you can also ask them to circle or highlight the place in the report where information was found and put the question number from the coding guide on the report as well. Then, it is easy to see where each code came from.

Table 4.1   Example Coding Sheet for the Report Identification Section of a Coding Guide

Report Characteristics	
R1. What is the report ID number?	__ __ __ 1 2 3
R2. What was the first author's last name? (First six letters; enter ? [a question mark] if you can't tell.)	__ __ __ __ __ __ 4 5 6 7 8 9
R3. What was the year of appearance of the report or publication? (Enter ? if you can't tell.) Page found _____	__ __ __ __

R4. What type of report was this?
  1 = Journal article
  2 = Book or book chapter
  3 = Dissertation
  4 = MA thesis
  5 = Private report
  6 = Government report (state, federal, or district)
  7 = Conference paper
  8 = Other (specify) _____
  ? = Can't tell
	__

R5. Was this a peer-reviewed document?
  0 = Not peer reviewed
  1 = Peer reviewed
  ? = Can't tell
	__

R6. What type of organization produced this report?
  1 = University
  2 = Government entity (specify) _____
  3 = Contract research firm (specify)_____
  4 = Other (specify) _____
  ? = Can't tell
	__

R7. Was this research funded?
  0 = No
  1 = Yes
  ? = Can't tell
 	
R7a. If yes, who was the funder?
  1. Federal government (specify) _____
  2. Private foundation (specify) _____
  3. Other (specify) _____
	__
	
	__

In the second column, where the coder will enter the responses, the number of spaces for each response corresponds to the number of columns needed to represent all possible values of that variable in a data file, one column for a variable with up to 10 possible numerical values (0 to 9), two columns for up to 100 possible values, and so on. Also, you might place under each response space the column of the data file in which the variable can be found. This marker might make it easier to transfer the data from the coding sheet into a data file and to do so with less error. To save space here, I have only demonstrated this for the first two questions in Table 4.1. In practice, these numbers would continue successively throughout the coding guide. Sometimes this marker will be unnecessary because a computer program will transfer the data to a data file automatically.

You will want to start by giving each report a unique identification number (Question R1). Later, you will also give unique numbers to each study in a report (if there is more than one study in it), to each unique sample within a study for which separate data are reported, and to each outcome reported within each sample.

Next, you will want to include on your coding sheet enough information about the first author of the study so that if you later want to group studies by their author (perhaps to test whether different authors get different results), you will be able to do so. In Table 4.1, the first six letters of the first author's name are used for this purpose (Question R2). Note that this is one of only two responses in the coding guide example that do not use numbers (the other asks for the postal code of the state in which the study was conducted). The choice of six letters is arbitrary; you can use as many as you feel you will need to identify each author uniquely.

Third, you will want to know the year in which the report appeared. This might be used later to examine temporal trends in findings, or simply to help uniquely identify the study (along with the first author's name) in summary tables.

Fourth, you will want to describe the type of report and whether the report had undergone some form of peer review before it appeared. This information will later be used to test for the possibility of publication bias. Note here that the response categories are *mutually exclusive* (every report should fall into only one category) and *exhaustive* (every report will have a category).

Finally, you might be interested in what type of organization produced the report and whether or not the report was done with some type of funding support. This information can be critical if you discover that the funders of some studies might have had a monetary or other interest in whether studies had a particular outcome, for example, if a chain of gymnasiums supports a study on the value of exercise for older adults. If so, you might want to see if such studies produce different results from unfunded studies. It will be more or less important that you gather this information depending on your research problem.

Experimental conditions, if any. You will need to describe carefully the details of any experimental conditions—that is, the intervention or independent variable—if these were part of the study. This portion of the coding guide describes the relevant operations that define the experimental conditions and the categories that capture the variations in how the conditions might have been operationalized. What was experienced by people in the experimental condition? What was the intensity and duration of the intervention? As important as it is to describe what happened in the experimental condition, it is equally important to describe how the control or comparison group was treated. Was there an alternate intervention? If so, what was it? If not, what did participants in the comparison conditions do, or how were controls obtained? Differences among studies on any of these variables would be prime candidates for causes of differences in study outcomes.

Table 4.2 provides some examples of the types of information that might be gathered on a coding sheet for studies comparing students who did homework with students who did not do homework. First, note that the homework intervention coding sheet gives each intervention described within the report a unique study number. This allows for the possibility that there might be more than one study of homework described in a single report, or that there might be more than one homework intervention within the same study (for example, some students did an hour of homework, other students did a half hour, and still others did no homework at all).

The next question asks whether this homework intervention meets each of three characteristics that define homework. If any of these three are answered "no," it might lead to the study being excluded from the analysis. The next five questions ask about other characteristics of assignments that the synthesists might want to test as moderators of the effects of the homework intervention. There might be more of these. Note that Question I3 (i.e., what was the subject matter of the homework assignment?) uses letters to distinguish seven different coded responses and each is given a "yes" or "no" answer. The reason for this is that a homework assignment might cover any one of the six subject matters or any combination of two or more. There are dozens of such combinations. So, it would be tedious for you and coders if you listed them all out, especially since you know that most of the combinations would never be coded. By coding the subject matters using just these seven codes (which still give you precise information about each study), you can then examine how frequently each combination occurs and have the computer create new variables based on the codes. For example, you might find that most studies cover only one subject matter but a few cover both reading and language arts. So, you could instruct the computer to create a new variable that has eight values, one for each instance in which only one subject matter gets a 1 and

Table 4.2   Example Coding Sheet for Homework Interventions (Selected Questions)

Information About the Homework Intervention *Complete these questions separately for each homework intervention described in the study report.*	
I1. What is this study's ID number?	___
I2. Which of the following characteristics were part of the homework intervention? (Place a 1 in each column that applies, 0 if not, ? if not reported.) a. Focuses on academic work b. Assigned by classroom teachers (or researcher via teacher) c. Meant to be done during nonschool hours or during study time at school	 ___ ___ ___
I3. What was the subject matter of assignments? (Place a 1 in each column that applies, 0 otherwise) a. Reading b. Other language arts c. Math d. Science e. Social studies f. Foreign language g. Other (specify) _____	 ___ ___ ___ ___ ___ ___ ___
I4. How many homework assignments were assigned per week? (Enter ? if not reported.)	___
I5. What was the expected amount of time needed to complete each assignment, in minutes? (Enter ? if not reported.)	___
I6. Were assignments graded? 0 = No 1 = Yes ? = Can't tell	 ___ ___ ___
I7. Was the homework used in determining class grades? 0 = No 1 = Yes ? = Can't tell	 ___ ___ ___

I8. Was evidence reported that the homework intervention was or was not implemented in a manner similar to the way it was defined? (An example of when you would answer "not implemented as specified" to this question would be if the report says the homework was meant to be assigned three times a week but was only assigned once a week.)

0 = Not implemented as specified
What information?
_____

1 = Implemented as specified
What information?
_____

? = Nothing reported about the fidelity of implementation

———

I9. Was there evidence that the group receiving homework might also have experienced a changed expectancy, novelty, and/or disruption effect that was not also experienced by the control group?
0 = No change in expectancy, etc.
1 = Yes, change in expectancy, etc.
? = Nothing reported about change in expectancy, etc.

———

I10. How was the comparison group treated?
0 = No homework and no other compensating activity
1 = Other compensating activity (specify)
_____

? = Not reported

———

I11. Were the homework and comparison group drawn from the same local pool? (Students drawn from the same school building and attending the same grade are considered to be from the same local pool.)
0 = No
1 = Yes
? = Not reported

———

I11a. If yes to I11, did the students, parents, and/or teachers in either the homework or comparison group know who was in which condition?
0 = No
1 = Yes
? = Not reported

———

the others get a 0, a seventh in which both reading and language arts get a 1, and an eighth for all other combinations.

Question (I8) relates to the *fidelity* with which the homework intervention was carried out. If the way homework was actually carried out in studies was different from the intended treatment, this might raise questions about whether the study was a fair test of homework's effects. For this question, the coding sheet also provides a note that is meant to help the coder remember a coding convention that was established to clarify how to code a study. In this case, the meaning of "implemented in a similar manner" might be ambiguous, so the note clarifies its meaning. Using these notes (one appears for Question I11 as well) will help ensure that different coders use the guide in the same manner, thus reducing differences between them (and also within a particular coder's responses from study to study). The next question (I9) asks whether there was evidence that the homework intervention was *confounded* with other differences in the way the experimental and control group were treated. If such confounds exist, this would compromise the study's ability to draw causal inferences about the effects of homework. Answers to both of these questions might lead to the study being excluded from the synthesis, or the information might be used to group studies to see if these characteristics were associated with study outcomes.

Question I10 and I11 relate to the control participants. Question I10 asks about how the control was treated, and Question I11 tries to get at whether the participants in each condition knew there were other participants in the study who were being treated differently. If so, this might have influenced how they behaved. Each of these questions (I10–I11) relates to the construct validity of the treatment manipulation.

Setting of the study. This information most often includes the geographic location of the study (e.g., country, state, or part of the country; urban, suburban, or rural community). If the studies might have been conducted within an institutional setting, for example, schools or hospitals or gymnasiums, this information could be gathered as well. Further, some studies will always be conducted within institutional contexts (for example, homework studies always occur within school), so differences in institutions might be of interest (for example, was it a public or private school, did the school have a religious affiliation, etc.). Table 4.3 presents some example questions related to setting that might appear on a homework coding sheet.

Participants and samples. Another type of information typically collected from research reports concerns the characteristics of the participants included in the primary research. This can include the age, race and/or ethnic group, and social class of participants, as well as any restrictions placed by the primary

Table 4.3 Example Coding Sheet for Study Setting Characteristics in a Homework Synthesis

Setting Characteristics	
S1. Were the participants: (Place a 1 in each column that applies, 0 if not, ? if not reported.) a. In the United States b. In a country other than the United States (specify country)	 —— ——
S2. What state was the study conducted in? (Use postal codes.)	——
S3. What type of community was the study conducted in? 1 = Urban 2 = Suburban 3 = Rural ? = Can't tell	——
S4. What type of school was the study conducted in? 1 = Public school 2 = Private school 3 = Private school with a religious affiliation (specify religious group) _____ ? = Can't tell	——
S5. What classroom types were represented among the settings? (Place a 1 in each column that applies, 0 if not, ? if not reported.) a. Regular education b. Special education c. Other (specify) _____ d. No classroom types given	 —— —— —— ——

researchers regarding who could participate in the study. Table 4.4 provides some examples of participant and sample characteristics that might be important in a study of the effects of homework. Also, note that yet another unique sample ID number must be provided here because some studies might present information on separate samples within the study. For example, a study might break out its samples and results based on whether students were gifted or average. To capture this distinction, each sample would get a different sample number and Question S2 would be answered differently for each sample.

Table 4.4   Example Coding Sheet for Participant and Sample Characteristics in a Homework Synthesis

Participant and Sample Characteristics *Complete these questions separately for each sample within a homework intervention for which there is a separate outcome.*

P1. What is this sample's ID number?	___
P2. Which of the following labels were applied to students in this sample? (Place a 1 in each column that applies, 0 if not, ? if not reported.) a. Gifted b. Average c. "At risk" d. Underachieving/below grade level e. Possessing a learning deficit f. Other (specify) _____	 ___ ___ ___ ___ ___ ___
P3. What was the socioeconomic status (SES) of students in the sample? (Place a 1 in each column that applies, 0 if not, ? if not reported.) a. Low SES b. Low-middle SES c. Middle SES d. Middle-upper SES e. Upper SES f. Only labeled as "mixed"	 ___ ___ ___ ___ ___ ___
P5. What were the grade levels of the students in the sample? (Place a 1 in each column that applies, 0 if not. Use options n through q only if no specific grade information was reported.) a. K b. 1 c. 2 d. 3 e. 4 f. 5 g. 6 h. 7 i. 8 j. 9 k. 10	 ___ ___ ___ ___ ___ ___ ___ ___ ___ ___ ___

Participant and Sample Characteristics *Complete these questions separately for each sample within a homework intervention for which there is a separate outcome.*	
l. 11 m. 12 n. Labeled as "elementary school" o. Labeled as "middle school" p. Labeled as "junior high school" q. Labeled as "high school" r. No grade level information given	— — — — — — —
P6. What sexes were represented in the sample? (Place a 1 in each column that applies, 0 if not.) a. Males b. Females c. No sex information given	 — — —
P6a. If reported, what was the percentage of females in the sample? (Use ? if not reported.)	—

Predictor and outcome characteristics. For studies that do not involve experimental manipulations but rather associate measured variables, one as the predictor of another (e.g., individual differences predicting rape attitudes), or for the outcomes of studies with experimental manipulations (e.g., measures of exercise by older adults after an intervention, or motivation after a choice manipulation), you will want to retrieve information concerning the types of outcomes and whether or not they were standardized measures, and evidence about the outcomes' validity or reliability, if this information is available.

Table 4.5 provides some questions that might be asked about the outcomes of a homework study. Note that the first question requires, yet again, that a unique number be given to each outcome. So, we now have a four-tiered system that, when the ID numbers are strung together, uniquely identifies each outcome within each sample, each sample within each study, and each study within each report. In some studies, outcomes will be reported for, say, more than one grade level or more than one measure of achievement. When such a study is uncovered, the coder would fill out separate sheets for each two-group combination. For example, a study with both a standardized test and class grade measure of achievement reported separately for students in fifth and sixth grade would have four outcome coding sheets associated with it, two each for fifth and sixth graders.

Table 4.5 Example Coding Sheet for Outcomes in a Homework Synthesis

Outcome Measure *Complete these questions separately for each relevant outcome within each sample.*	
O1. What is this outcome's ID number?	——
O2. What subject matter did this outcome measure? (Place a 1 in each column that applies, 0 otherwise) a. Reading b. Other language arts c. Math d. Science e. Social studies f. Foreign language g. Other (specify) _____ h. Not a subject matter test	 —— —— —— —— —— —— ——
O3. What type of outcome measure is this? 1 = Standardized achievement test (specify) _____ 2 = Another test measuring achievement (e.g., teacher- developed, textbook chapters) 3 = Class grades after homework 4 = Multiple types of student achievement measures 5 = Student study habits and skills ? = Can't tell	 ——
O4. Was evidence presented regarding whether the validity/reliability of this outcome measure reached an acceptable criterion? (Note: Place a 1 in each column if acceptable, 0 if not, 9 if not reported. A statement indicating that internal consistency was "acceptable" is sufficient, even if the specific value was not reported. A citation to an external source is sufficient.) a. Internal consistency b. Test-retest correlation c. Other (specify) _____	 —— —— ——
O5. In days, when was the outcome measure administered relative to the end of the homework intervention? (Enter 0 if outcome measure was given on the last day of the homework study. Enter ? if unable to determine.)	 ——

Note as well that it is not just different measures of the same construct that can create multiple measures associated with the same sample (within the same study within the same report). It is also possible for researchers to collect the same measure two or more times. That is one reason why Question O5 is included on the outcome coding sheet. Also, researchers might collect data on more than one construct. For example, the homework synthesis might not have focused exclusively on achievement but might also have collected outcomes related to study skills and/or attitudes toward school. If this were the case, the outcomes coding sheets would be expanded to include questions and responses related to measures of these constructs.

The fourth question (O4) on the outcome coding sheet relates to the validity and reliability of the measure. These questions can be phrased in lots of different ways, depending on the level of detail you wish to gather. The example requests information that is not very specific, asking the coders only whether the measure reached an "acceptable" level of reliability.

Coder and coding characteristics. The coding guide should contain a section for the coders to enter their names or ID number and the date on which they coded the study (see Table 4.6). You might also ask coders to state the amount of time it took to code the study, for accounting purposes. In some instances, this information might be formally incorporated into your data files. This section can also provide coders with space to make any narrative comments about the coding process they want to share with you.

Low- and High-Inference Codes

Most of the information requested in the example coding guides might be thought of as *low-inference codes.* That is, they require the coder only to locate the needed information in the research report and transfer it to the coding sheet. In some circumstances, coders might be asked to make some *high-inference codes* about the studies. It might have occurred to you that there were some inferences that coders were asked to make on the homework coding sheets. For example, I noted previously that coders using the example guide for outcomes (Table 4.4) would be asked to code whether the estimates attained for the internal consistency, test-retest reliability, and other validity/reliability estimates for measures were "adequate" (Question O4). If left to their own devices, the judgment of "adequacy" would indeed be an inference, one that might vary from coder to coder. However, if you gave coders a threshold that defined "adequate," the need for inference would have been removed from these questions. So, the question might have been rephrased to say, "Was an estimate of internal consistency present? If yes, was it above .8?" Or the coders might have been

Table 4.6   Example Coding Sheet for Coder and Coding Information

Coder and Coding Characteristics	
C1. What is your coder ID number?	___
C2. On what date did you complete coding this study?	__/__/__
C3. In minutes, how long did it take you to code this study?	___ ___ ___
Notes (provide below any notes about the study or concerns you had regarding your codes):	

asked to gather the exact values of the internal consistency estimates. The exact values then could be used to test whether this measure of the validity/reliability of the measures was related to study outcomes.

Other high-inference codes involve attempting to infer how an intervention or experimental manipulation might have been interpreted by the individuals presented with it. A synthesis by Carlson and Miller (1987) provides a good example. They summarized the literature on why negative mood states seem to enhance the likelihood that people will lend a helping hand. In order to test different interpretations of this research, they needed to estimate how sad, guilty, angry, or frustrated different experimental procedures might have made participants feel. To do this, a group of judges were asked to read excerpts from the methods sections of relevant articles. The judges then used a 1 to 9 scale to rate, for example, the "extent to which subjects feel specifically downcast, sad, or depressed as a result of the negative-mood induction" (p. 96). These judgments were then added to the coding sheets for each study.

These high-inference codes create a special set of problems for research synthesists. First, careful attention must be paid to the reliability of high-inference judgments. Also, judges are being asked to play the role of a research participant, and the validity of role-playing methodologies has been the source of much controversy (Greenberg & Folger, 1988). However, Miller, Lee, and Carlson (1991) empirically demonstrated that high-inference codes can lead to valid judgments and can add a new dimension to synthesists' ability to interpret literatures and resolve controversies. This technique deserves a try if you feel you can validly extract high-inference information from articles and persuasively explain your rationale for doing so (i.e., how it will increase the value of your synthesis).

SELECTING AND TRAINING CODERS

The coding of studies for a research synthesis is not a one-person job. Even if a single person eventually does gather information from all the studies, the research synthesists must demonstrate that this person did a good job of data extraction. There is simply too much room for bias (conscious or unconscious), for idiosyncratic interpretation of coding questions and responses, and for simple mechanical error for the unverified codes of a single person to be considered part of a scientific synthesis of research. For example, Rosenthal (1978) looked at 21 studies that examined the frequency and distribution of recording errors. These studies uncovered error rates ranging from 0% to 4.2% of all the data recorded; 64% of the errors in recording were in a direction that tended to confirm the study's initial hypothesis.

Recording errors are not the only source of unreliability in study coding. Sometimes, codes cannot be reliably applied because the reports of studies are not clear. Other times, ambiguous definitions provided by the research synthesists lead to disagreement about the proper code for a study characteristic. Finally, as I noted earlier, the predispositions of coders can lead them to favor one interpretation of an ambiguous code over another.

Stock and colleagues (Stock, Okun, Haring, Miller, & Kinney, 1982) empirically examined the number of unreliable codings made in a research synthesis. They had three coders (one statistician, and two post-Ph.D. education researchers) record data from 30 documents into 27 different coding categories. Stock and colleagues found that some variables, such as the means and standard deviations of the ages of participants, were coded with perfect or near-perfect agreement. Only one judgment, concerning the type of sampling procedure used by the researchers, did not reach an average coder agreement of 80%.

Demonstrating that the coding definitions are clear enough to generate consistent data across coders and that the coders have extracted information from the reports accurately—that is, gave responses to the coding questions little different from those that would have been given by any other coder—will involve training at least two coders. Doing so is especially important if the number of studies to be coded is large or if persons with limited research training are called on to do the coding. It is rare today to find a research synthesis in which a single coder gathered information from all studies. And these are looked on skeptically. Most syntheses involve at least two coders gathering information from at least a portion of the studies. Some syntheses involve teams of three or more coders. In any case, *it is good practice to treat the coding of studies as if it were a standard exercise in data gathering.*

Some synthesists will have every study coded independently by more than one coder, called *double coding*. The codings for every study are then compared, and discrepancies are resolved in a meeting of the coders or by a third party. This procedure can greatly reduce potential bias, make evident different interpretations of questions and responses, and catch mechanical errors.

While all synthesists must demonstrate the reliability of their codings, how far they can go to ensure reliability will be a function of the number of studies to be coded, the length and complexity of the coding guide, and the resources available to accomplish the task. Clearly, syntheses involving larger numbers of studies with complex coding sheets will require more coding time. Unless lots of time is available, more studies to code will make it more difficult to have every study coded twice. In some cases, if there is complex information to be coded, synthesists can decide to double code some of the information on the coding sheet but not other information. The synthesists must determine how to get the most trustworthy codes possible given their limited resources.

Double coding is not the only way you can enhance the reliability of codes. First, you can pick coders who have the background and interest needed to do a good job. People with lots of experience reading and conducting research make better coders than novices. Training can overcome some limitations of inexperience, but not all.

Second, coding sheets can be accompanied by code books that define and explain distinctions in each study characteristic. In the examples given in Tables 4.1 through 4.6, some of these definitions appear directly on the coding sheet. A code book with other definitions and conventions for coding particular questions could accompany the coding sheets.

Third, prior to actual coding, discussions and practice examples should be worked through with coders. *It is important to pilot test your coding guide using the individuals who will actually do the coding.* Use a few research reports, preferably chosen to represent what you know are diverse types of research contained in the literature, and talk through how the coding would proceed. The coders will raise concerns you had not thought of and this will lead to greater clarity in questions, responses, and conventions to use when reports are unclear.

Fourth, the coders should gather information for the same few studies independently and share their responses in a group. You should discuss mistakes with them. Even greater clarity in the coding guide will result. At this stage and during subsequent coding, some synthesists will attempt to keep the coders unaware of certain aspects of the studies. Some will remove information about the study's authors and affiliation from the report so that coders will not be influenced by any knowledge they may have about the researchers. Some synthesists have the different sections of the report coded by different coders so that, for example, the results of a study do not influence the ratings it might get on the quality of the study design. These procedures are more important to follow when (a) coding decisions might involve high-inference judgments, (b) the research area is distinguished by polarized opinions and findings, and/or (c) the coders are themselves very knowledgeable about the area and might have their own opinions about what the results of studies "should" be.

Estimating reliability. Once these steps have been completed, you are ready to assess reliability. This should happen before coders are given lots of studies to code and again periodically during coding. It is usually important to obtain numerical estimates of coder reliability. There are many ways to quantify coder reliability and none appears to be without problems (see Orwin & Vevea, 2009, for a general review of evaluating coding decisions). Two methods appear most often in research syntheses. *Most simply, research synthesists will report the agreement rate between pairs of coders.* The agreement rate is the number of agreed-on codes divided by the total number of codes. Typically, this will be broken out by each coding question. If the number of codes is large, the synthesists may just provide the range of agreement percentages and then discuss any that might seem problematically low. For example, in the synthesis of studies relating choice to intrinsic motivation, we found that out of a total of 8,895 codes, there were 256 disagreements, or coders disagreed 2.88% of the time. The question that gave coders the most trouble involved the description of the control group, with disagreements occurring 9.4% of the time for this variable.

Also useful is Cohen's kappa, a measure of reliability that adjusts for the chance rate of agreement. Kappa is defined as the improvement over chance reached by the coders. Often kappa is presented along with the percent agreement.

As mentioned previously, some synthesists will have each study examined by two coders, will compare codes, and then will have discrepancies resolved through discussion or by consulting a third coder. This procedure leads to very high reliability and often is not accompanied by a quantitative estimate of reliability. In order to get an effective reliability for double coding, you would have to form two teams of two coders and an arbiter and compare the results of the two teams' deliberations. You can see that this process in unlikely to result in many differences between the teams.

Other synthesists have individual coders mark the codes they are least confident about and discuss these codes in group meetings. This procedure also leads to highly trustworthy codes. Regardless of what techniques are used, the question to ask when evaluating the methods of data collection used to carry out research syntheses is,

> Were procedures used to ensure the unbiased and reliable (a) application of criteria to determine the substantive relevance of studies and (b) retrieval of information from study reports?

Transferring Information to the Data File

In the foregoing paragraphs, I describe techniques for ensuring that information about each study was correctly recorded into coding sheets. I suggest that the best way to do this is to have each study coded by more than one researcher and then compare their codes to one another. Even if the coders agree on the coding sheets, *it is good practice to have two people transfer the results from the coding sheets into separate data files—the files that will be used by the computer when the data are analyzed.* Then, these files can be compared to one another to determine if any errors have been made when data were transferred from the coding sheets to the computer file. If only one coder is used, this person can be asked to do the data entry twice. Although this task may seem simple, errors in data transcription are to be expected (Rosenthal, 1978), especially when the task data are complex. Of course, if a computer program is used that transfers codings directly into a data set ready for the computer, this type of check is unnecessary.

PROBLEMS IN GATHERING
DATA FROM STUDY REPORTS

In Chapter 3, I discussed some deficiencies in study retrieval that will frustrate synthesists regardless of how thorough and careful they try to be. Among these, some potentially relevant studies do not become public and defy the grasp of even the most conscientious search procedures. Other studies you will learn about but will not be able to obtain.

Perhaps the most frustrating occurrence in collecting the evidence is when synthesists obtain primary research reports but the reports do not contain the needed information. Reports could be missing information on study characteristics, preventing the determination of whether study outcomes were related to how the study was conducted, or even whether the study was relevant at all. Or information could be missing on statistical outcomes, preventing synthesists from estimating the magnitude of the difference between two groups or the relationship between two variables.

Imprecise Research Reports

Incomplete reporting will be of most concern to research synthesists who intend to perform meta-analyses. What should the meta-analyst do about missing data? Several conventions can be suggested to handle the most common problems.

Incomplete reporting of statistical outcomes. Research reports sometimes lack important information about the results of statistical procedures carried out by the primary researchers. Statistical data are often omitted when the researcher was testing to reject the null hypothesis and it is not rejected. Instead of giving the exact results of the statistical test, the researchers simply say it did not reach statistical significance. In these cases, the researchers are also less likely to provide the correlation or means and standard deviation associated with the finding. Sometimes they do not even tell which direction the correlation or comparison of group means was in.

You have limited options when you know a relationship or comparison has been tested but the primary researchers do not provide the associated means and standard deviations, inference test value, *p*-level, or effect size. One option is to contact the researchers and request the information. As I noted in Chapter 3, the success of this tactic will depend partly on whether the researchers can be located and the status of the requester. The likelihood of compliance with the request will also depend on how easy it is for the researchers to retrieve the information. There is less chance a request will be fulfilled if the study is old, if the desired analyses are different from those originally conducted, or if a lot of data are asked for.

The chance of getting a response from researchers will increase if you can make the request as easy to fulfill as possible. This might include providing the researchers with a table in which they simply need to plug in the values you need. Never ask for more information or more detailed information than you need. The more information you ask for, the more authors may worry that you think they did something wrong and suspect that you are interested in more than just including their study in a meta-analysis. (Of course, it is also important to follow up with authors if you think you have uncovered an erroneous result.)

Another approach to finding missing data is to examine other documents that describe the study being reported. For example, if you have found a journal article that reports some but not all the results you need, but the accompanying Author Note says the study was conducted as a doctoral dissertation, it might be that the dissertation itself contains the information. Often, dissertations have appendices that include thorough descriptions of results. Or some research reports prepared by government agencies and contract research firms are written with audiences in mind who will not be interested in the details. These organizations also might have available more technical reports with lots more information in them.

If you cannot retrieve the needed data, another option is to treat the outcome as having uncovered an exact null result. That is, for any statistical analysis involving the missing data, a correlation of 0 is assumed, or the means being compared are assumed to be exactly equal. It is reasonable to expect that this convention has a conservative impact on the results of the meta-analysis. In general, when this convention is used, the cumulative average relationship strength will be closer to zero than if the exact results of nonsignificant relationships were known. However, adding zeros to your data set for missing values will change the characteristics of your distribution of findings. For these reasons, it is rare for meta-analysts to use this procedure anymore.

A fourth option is simply to leave the comparison out of your meta-analysis. This strategy will likely lead to a higher average cumulative relationship than if the missing value were known. All else being equal, nonsignificant findings will be associated with the smaller relationship estimates in a distribution of sampled estimates. However, most meta-analysts choose this fourth option, especially if the number of missing values is small relative to the number of known values. Also, if meta-analysts can classify missing value outcomes according to the direction of their findings, that is, if they know which group had the higher mean or whether the correlation was positive or negative, these outcomes can be included in vote count procedures (discussed in Chapter 6). Using vote counts, it is possible to estimate the strength of a relationship (see Bushman & Wang, 1996). Also discussed in Chapter 7 are ways to test meta-analytic results to see whether the conclusions would be different using different methods to handle missing data. When statisticians analyze the same data using different statistical assumptions, it is called *sensitivity analysis* (see Chapter 7).

Incomplete reporting of other study characteristics. Research reports also can be missing information concerning the details of study characteristics other than their outcomes. For example, reports might be missing information on the composition of samples (say, in a homework study the students' economic background), the setting (e.g., whether the school was in an urban, suburban, or rural community), or treatment characteristics (e.g., the number of homework assignments each week and their length). Meta-analysts want this information so they can examine whether treatment effects or relationship magnitudes are associated with the conditions under which the study was conducted.

You have several options when study information of this sort is missing. First, you can ask yourself whether the information might be available in sources other than the research report. For example, the homework coding guide contains a question about whether the school was in an urban, suburban, or rural community and what the students' economic status was. If you know the school district in which this study took place, this information might be available on the district or state website. If information on the psychometric characteristics of measures is not reported, these might be found in reports on the instruments themselves.

Most simply, you can leave the study with missing information out of the analysis, although it may be included in other analyses for which the needed information is available. For example, homework studies missing information on the students' economic background (a frequent occurrence) simply cannot be used in the analyses testing whether this characteristic influences the effect of homework, but they can be used in analyses looking at grade level, a characteristic rarely missing from reports.

Alternatively, it is sometimes appropriate to assume that a missing value suggests what the value is. This will happen because the researchers have assumed the information is taken for granted. For example, homework researchers are likely in nearly all instances to mention if a study was conducted in an all-boys or all-girls school. So, when the sex composition of classes is not mentioned, it is probably safe to assume that both boys and girls were present, and perhaps in roughly equal numbers. You might have coders use "?" for this code but then have the computer consider this code to mean "both boys and girls." If you do this, you should mention the convention in your methods section. Also, if possible, you might run this analysis twice, once with the recoded studies included and once without.

The amount of concern a meta-analyst should have over missing study characteristics will depend partly on why the data are missing. Some data will be missing at random. That is, there will be no systematic reason why some reports include information on the characteristic while others do not. If this is the case, then the outcome of an analysis examining the relationship between study outcomes and study characteristics will be unaffected by the missing data except, of course, for a loss of statistical power.

If the reason data are missing relates systematically to study outcomes, or to the values of the missing data themselves, then the problem is more serious. In this case, the missing data might be affecting the results of the analysis. For example, suppose health researchers are more likely to report that the participants in their study were all females or all males if the result indicates a significant effect of an activity intervention. Nonsignificant effects are more often associated with mixed-sex samples, but this is unknown to the meta-analyst because researchers who find nonsignificant results are less inclined to report the sample's composition. In such a case, the meta-analyst would have a hard time discovering the relationship between the sex composition of the intervention study and the magnitude of the intervention's effect (e.g., exercise is more or less effective when groups are composed of the same sex).

Pigott (2009) suggests several other strategies for dealing with missing study characteristics. First, missing values can be filled in with the mean of all known values on the characteristic of interest. This strategy does not affect the outcome of the cumulative analysis, except to raise its power. It is most appropriate when the meta-analyst is examining several study characteristics together in one analysis. In such a case, a single missing value may delete the entire study and this may not be desirable. Second, the missing value can be predicted using regression analysis. In essence, this strategy uses known values of the missing variable found in other studies to predict the most likely value for the missing data point. Pigott also describes several more complicated ways to estimate missing data.

In most instances, I would advise meta-analysts to stick with the simpler techniques for handling missing data. As techniques become more complex, more assumptions are needed to justify them. Also, when more complicated techniques are used, it becomes more important to conduct sensitivity analysis. It is always good to compare results using filled-in missing values with results obtained when missing values are simply omitted from the analysis.

IDENTIFYING INDEPENDENT COMPARISONS

Another important decision that must be made when data are being gathered involves how to identify independent estimates of relationship strength or group differences. Sometimes a single study may contain multiple tests of the same comparison or relation. This can happen for several reasons. First, more than one measure of the same construct might be used by the researchers and each measure is analyzed separately. For example, a researcher of choice effects might measure intrinsic motivation using both participants' self-reports and observations of their activities during a free-play period. Second, measures of different constructs might be taken, such as several different personality variables all related to attitudes toward rape. Third, the same measure might be taken at two or more different times. And finally, people in the same study might be broken out into different samples and their data analyzed separately. This would occur, for instance, if a rape-attitude researcher gave the same measures to all participants but then separately examined results for males and females. In all these cases, the separate estimates in the same study are not completely independent—they share methodological and situational influences. In the case of the same measure taken at different times, the study results even share influences contributed by having been collected on the same people with the same measures.

The problem of nonindependence of study results can be taken even further. Sometimes a single research report can describe more than one study. So, the two studies likely were conducted in the same context (e.g., the same laboratory), perhaps with the same research assistants, and with participants drawn from the same participant pool. Also, multiple research reports in the same synthesis often describe studies conducted by the same principal investigators. The synthesists might conclude that studies conducted by the same researchers at the same site, even if they appear in separate reports over a number of years, still contain certain constancies that imply the results are not completely independent. The same primary researcher with the same predispositions may have used the same laboratory rooms while drawing participants from the same population.

Synthesists must decide when statistical results will be considered independent tests of the problem under investigation. Several alternatives can be suggested regarding the proper *unit of analysis* in research syntheses.

Research Teams as Units

The most conservative way to identify independent results uses the laboratory or researcher as the smallest unit of analysis. Advocates of this approach would argue that the information value of repeated studies by the same research team is not as great as an equal number of studies reported from separate teams. This approach requires the synthesists to gather all studies done by the same research team and to come to some overall conclusion concerning the results for that particular group of researchers. Therefore, one drawback is that this approach requires the synthesists to conduct syntheses within syntheses, since decisions about how to cumulate results first must be made within research teams and then again between teams.

The research-team-as-unit approach is rarely used in practice. It is generally considered too conservative and too wasteful of information that can be obtained by examining the variations in results from study to study, even within the same laboratory. Also, it is possible to ascertain whether research teams are associated with systematic differences in study outcomes by using the researchers as a study characteristic in the search for outcome moderators.

Studies as Units

Using the study as the unit of analysis requires the synthesists to make an overall decision about the results reported in an individual study. If a single study contains information on more than one test of the same group comparison or relation, the synthesists can calculate the average of these results and have that represent the study. Alternatively, the median result can be used. Or if there is a preferred type of measurement, for example, a particular rape-attitude scale with good measurement characteristics, this result can represent the study.

Using the study as the unit of analysis ensures that each study contributes equally to the overall synthesis result. For example, a study estimating the relationship between rape attitudes and need for power using two different attitude scales and reporting separately for men and women would report four nonindependent correlations. By cumulating these correlations (using one of the techniques suggested previously) so that a single correlation represents this study ensures equal consideration will be given to another study with one sex group and one attitude measure.

Samples as Units

Using independent samples as units permits a single study to contribute more than one result if the tests are carried out on separate samples of people. For example, synthesists could consider statistical tests on males and females within the same study of rape attitudes as independent but not consider as independent tests that used alternate measures of the same attitude construct given to the same people.

Using samples as independent units assumes that the largest portion of the variance shared by results in the same study comes from data collected on the same participants. This shared variance is removed (by combining results from different measures within samples) but other sources of dependency (e.g., researchers, settings) that exist at the study level are ignored.

When meta-analysts calculate an average comparison or relationship across units, *it is good practice to weight each independent unit—be it a sample within a study or the entire study—by its sample size.* Then, weightings are functionally equivalent whether independent samples within studies or entire studies are used as units of analysis. For example, a study with 100 participants would be weighted by 100 if the study is used as the unit, or its two samples would each be weighted by 50 if the sample is used as the unit (more will be said about this procedure in Chapter 6).

Comparisons or Estimates as Units

The least conservative approach to identifying independent units of analysis is to use each individual group comparison or estimate of relationship strength as if it were independent. That is, each separate comparison or estimate calculated by primary researchers is regarded as an independent estimate by the research synthesist. This technique's strength is that it does not lose any of the within-study information regarding potential moderators of the studies' outcomes. Its weakness is that it is likely to violate the assumption made in the meta-analytic statistical procedures that the estimates are independent. Also, the results of studies will not be weighted equally in any overall conclusion about results. Instead, studies will contribute to the overall finding in relation to the number of statistical tests contained in them, regardless of their sample size. In the example concerning rape attitudes and need for power, the study with four related comparisons (for two sexes on two measures) will have four times the influence on the overall results as a second study with one comparison (but an equal total sample size). This is generally not a good weighting criterion.

Shifting Unit of Analysis

A compromise approach to identifying comparisons is to employ a *shifting unit of analysis.* Here, each outcome is initially coded as if it were an independent event. Thus, the single study that contained four estimates of the relationship between attitudes toward rape and need for power would have four outcome coding sheets filled out for its four results. Two of these outcome coding sheets would be linked to two different sample coding sheets associated with this study. Then, when an overall cumulative result for the synthesis is calculated—that is, when the question, "What is the overall relationship between attitude about rape and need for power?" is answered—the outcome results would first be combined so that each study (requiring that all four results be combined) or each sample (combining two outcomes for each sample) contributed equally to the overall finding. Of course, each result should still be weighted by its sample size. These combinations would then be added into the analysis across all studies.

However, the shifting unit approach allows that when examining potential moderators of the overall outcome, a study's or sample's results would be aggregated only *within* the separate categories of the moderator variable. An example should make this clearer. Suppose you have chosen to use studies as the basic unit of analysis. If a rape-attitude and need-for-power study presented correlations for males and females separately, this study would contribute only one correlation to the overall analysis—the average of the male and female correlations—but two correlations to the analysis of the impact of sex on the size of the correlation—one for the female group and one for the male group. To take the process one step further, assume this study reported different correlations between rape attitudes and need for power within each sex for two different attitude measures, that is, four correlations in all. Then, the two correlations for different attitude scales would be averaged for each sex when the analysis examining the moderating influence of sex was conducted. Likewise, the two sex-related correlations would be averaged for each scale when the type of attitude measure was examined as a moderator.

In effect, the shifting-unit technique ensures that for analyses of influences on study estimates of relationship strength, a single study can contribute one data point to each of the categories distinguished by the moderating variable. This strategy is a good compromise that allows studies to retain their maximum information value while keeping to a minimum any violation of the assumption of independence of statistical tests. However, the approach is not without problems. First, creating and recreating average effect sizes for analysis of each different moderator can be time consuming and difficult in some statistical packages. Also, when the meta-analysts wish to study multiple influences on study outcomes in a single analysis, rather than one influence at a time, the unit of analysis can quickly decompose into individual comparisons.

The synthesis of studies examining correlates of rape attitudes included 65 research reports containing 72 studies with data on 103 independent samples. Primary researchers calculated a total of 479 correlations. Clearly, using the individual correlations as if they were independent results would grossly exaggerate their cumulative information value. For the overall analysis, then, the 103 independent samples were used as the unit and all correlations were averaged within samples. However, an analysis of differences in average correlations for different rape attitude scales was based on 108 correlations, because five primary researchers had given two scales to the same sample of participants.

Statistical Adjustment

Gleser and Olkin (2009) discuss statistical solutions to the problem of non-independent tests. They propose several procedures that statistically adjust for interdependence among multiple outcomes within studies and for different numbers of outcomes across studies. The key to successfully using these techniques lies in the synthesists having credible estimates of the interdependence of the statistical tests. For instance, assume a study of correlates of rape attitudes includes both a measure of myth acceptance and victim blame. In order to use the statistical techniques, the synthesists must estimate the correlation between the two scales for the sample in this study. Data of this sort often are not provided by primary researchers. When not given, it might be estimated from other studies or the analysis could be run with low and high estimates to generate a range of values.

THE EFFECTS OF DATA
GATHERING ON SYNTHESIS OUTCOMES

Variation in the procedures used by research synthesists to gather information from studies can lead to systematic differences in how studies are represented in the research synthesis data set. This in turn can lead to differences in what the synthesists conclude about the literature. Variation can happen in at least three ways.

First, if the synthesists only cursorily detail study operations, their conclusions may overlook important distinctions in results. A conclusion that the synthesis results indicate no important influences on study outcomes can occur either because no such influences truly exist or because the synthesists missed representing important influences in their data set. A lack of overlap in the study details considered relevant by different synthesists studying the same problem will create variation in their conclusions. However, the notion that a synthesis leads to more trustworthy results if it includes more tests of potential influences on the overall synthesis result must be tempered by the fact that the more influences tested, the more likely it is that chance alone will lead to significant findings. So, *best practice suggests that you be judicious in your choices of what influences to test.* Still, as noted before, the coding guide should be constructed to be exhaustive; not everything coded will be tested.

Second, synthesists can come to different conclusions about a research literature because they code studies with different accuracy. If two syntheses vary in how carefully variables are defined and coders are trained, they likely will also vary in the number of errors in their data sets, and possibly in their conclusions, because of these errors. Clearly, all else being equal, the synthesis with the more rigorous coding procedures is the one with more credibility.

And finally, the conclusions of syntheses can vary because the synthesists have used different rules for judging study results as independent tests of the problem. Here, some synthesists may place greater importance on ensuring independence while others consider it more valuable to extract as much information as possible from their data.

EXERCISES

For studies on a topic of interest to you,

1. draw up a preliminary coding guide,

2. find several reports that describe research that is relevant to the topic, and

3. apply the coding guide to several studies, some of which you have not read before.

What did you learn about your problem definition and the research methods used in attempts to study it?

5

Step 4

Evaluating the Quality of Studies

What research should be included or excluded from the synthesis based on (a) the suitability of the methods for studying the synthesis question and/or (b) problems in research implementation?

Primary Function in Research Synthesis

To identify and apply criteria that separate studies conducted in ways that correspond with the research question from studies that do not

Procedural Variation That Might Produce Differences in Conclusions

Variation in criteria for decisions about study inclusion might lead to systematic differences in which studies remain in the synthesis

Questions to Ask When Evaluating the Correspondence Between the Methods and Implementation of Individual Studies and the Desired Inferences of the Synthesis

1. If studies were excluded from the synthesis because of design and implementation considerations, were these considerations (a) explicitly and operationally defined and (b) consistently applied to all studies?

2. Were studies categorized so that important distinctions could be made among them regarding their research design and implementation?

This chapter describes

- Problems with judging the methodological adequacy of primary research
- Different approaches to describing the design and implementation of studies
- How to identify studies that report results so extreme that their exclusion from a synthesis may be warranted

The data evaluation stage of a scientific investigation involves making judgments about whether individual data points are trustworthy enough to be included as part of the findings. The researcher asks, "Is this data point a legitimate test of the hypothesis under consideration? Or did something happen while it was collected that compromised its ability to speak to the hypothesis?" Data evaluation first requires you to establish criteria for judging the adequacy of the procedures used to gather the data for testing the relationship of interest. Next, you must examine each data point to determine if any irrelevancies or errors might have affected it. Then, you must determine whether these influences are substantial enough to dictate that the data point either should be dropped from your study or interpreted with caution.

The evaluation of individual data points must be carried out whether the data are the scores of individual participants in primary research or the outcomes of studies in a research synthesis. Both primary researchers and research synthesists examine their data looking for "contaminants" or other indicators that suggest the outcome for the individual participants (in primary research) or individual studies (in research synthesis) may not be trustworthy. Also, they look to see if data points are statistical outliers. This occurs when the value of a data point is so extreme relative to other scores in the data set that it is unlikely to be a member of the same population of values.

The techniques for identifying data that might be contaminated by irrelevancies are different for the two types of research. In primary research, an individual participant's responses are sometimes discarded because the researcher has evidence that the participant did not attend to the appropriate stimuli or that the response instructions were misunderstood. If deception or some other form of misdirection was used in the research, a participant's data may be discarded because the participant did not believe the cover story or deduced the hidden hypothesis.

In research synthesis, there is one important criterion, beyond the conceptual relevance of the study, for questioning the trustworthiness of data: the degree to which the study's design and implementation permit you to draw the inferences that guide your work. If a study's methods are not fully commensurate with your intended inferences, you can make either a discrete decision—whether or not to include the study at all—or a continuous one—whether to weight the study's findings less than other studies. A large part of this chapter will be devoted to criteria for judging this match between the design and implementation of studies and the inferences that can be drawn from them.

You may have noticed that I have couched my discussion of judging study research methods in terms of the correspondence between what inferences the methods can support and what inferences the synthesists want to make. You may have wondered, "Why not simply talk about study quality? Aren't some studies high quality and others low quality?" The answer is that there are certainly some criteria that can be offered as indicators that one study is of "higher quality," or "better," than another. I would suggest that the trustworthiness of measurements may be such a universal criterion, though what makes a measure trustworthy may differ greatly depending on the question it is meant to answer. So, studies with more valid measures can be viewed as of higher quality regardless of whether the variable being measured is achievement, amount of physical activity, or attitude toward rape.

However, other criteria are more context dependent; they depend on the type of relationship that is under consideration. For example, a study of the effects of interventions to get older adults to exercise more often that randomly assigns participants to intervention and control conditions would be a "better" study (all else being equal) of the intervention's *causal* effects than one that allowed participants to choose whether or not to engage in the intervention. Likewise, a study that begins with older adults who chose to participate in the intervention but then matched participants so that the comparison and intervention groups were roughly equivalent on important third variables is "better" for drawing causal inferences than one that used no equating procedure. On the other hand, random assignment of participants is irrelevant to a study of individual differences in rape attitudes. While we might desire to know whether these individual differences "cause" differences in rape attitudes, no one has yet devised a method for randomly assigning people to different sexes, ages, or personalities. So, correlational studies that are of minimal value for uncovering causal relationships may be of high value for studying naturally occurring associations. The "quality" of the study depends on the question it is being used to answer.

While it is true that using the term "quality" to discuss differences between studies' methods may be good shorthand, it is not good practice if it creates the impression that one set of quality criteria can be applied to all studies regardless of the nature of the inferences called for by the problem under consideration. So, I will use the term "quality" for expository purposes, but you should keep in mind that I am using it in the sense that *high quality means high correspondence between methods and desired inferences.*

PROBLEMS IN JUDGING RESEARCH QUALITY

Predispositions of the Judge

Most social scientists agree that the correspondence between methods and inferences should be the primary criterion, if not the only criterion besides substantive relevance, for decisions about how to treat a study in a research synthesis. However, the predispositions of researchers about what the outcome of studies *should* be can have a strong impact on how studies are evaluated. So, it is important to examine the sources and effects of synthesists' prior beliefs about a research area.

Almost every primary researcher and research synthesist begins an inquiry with expectations about its outcome. In primary research, methodologists have constructed elaborate controls to eliminate or minimize the role of artifacts in producing results. Most notable among these are controls for *experimenter expectancy effects*, that is, techniques to ensure that the experimenter does not treat participants in different conditions in such a manner as to increase the likelihood that the hypothesis under consideration is confirmed.

In research syntheses, protections against expectancy effects are fewer and less foolproof. As the research is being collected, coded, and evaluated, synthesists are most often aware of the outcomes of the studies they are considering. This leads to the possibility that the evaluation of a research project's methodology will be influenced by the evaluator's predisposition toward its outcomes. The impact of predispositions on syntheses was so great in the past that it is worth again quoting Glass (1976) on the old process:

> A common method for integrating several studies with inconsistent findings is to carp on the design or analysis deficiencies of all but a few studies—those remaining frequently being one's own work or that of one's students or friends—and then advance the one or two "acceptable" studies as the truth of the matter. (p. 4)

Mahoney (1977) performed an experiment that directly tested the impact of predispositions on the evaluation of research. He sampled guest editors for the *Journal of Applied Behavior Analysis* and asked them to rate several aspects of a controlled manuscript. Mahoney found that the methods, discussion, and contribution of the manuscript were evaluated more favorably if the study confirmed the raters' predisposition about the results. In a related study, Lord, Ross, and Lepper (1979) found that readers rated studies that supported their attitudes as more methodologically sound than studies with counterattitudinal results. More strikingly, the undergraduates who participated in the Lord and colleagues study showed *polarization* in attitudes despite the fact that they all read the same research abstracts. That is, even though all participants read one study that supported their prior belief and one that refuted it, after reading the two studies, participants saw more support for their initial positions.

Thus, it appears that predispositions favoring a result can influence synthesists' judgments about whether a piece of research is a good test of the hypothesis under consideration. If a study disconfirms the synthesists' predispositions, they may be more likely to find some aspect of the study that renders it irrelevant or methodologically unsound. On the other hand, studies that confirm predispositions may be included although their relevance is questionable or their methods are a bad match for the hypothesis.

One way to minimize the impact of predispositions on the evaluation of research would be to have information gathered from studies by coders who are unaware of the studies' outcomes. This can be done by having separate coders unfamiliar with the topic area code different parts of the research article. For example, one coder might code the method section of a report while another coder codes the results section. However, Schram (1989) evaluated this "differential photocopying" procedure. She found it created new problems and did not lead to much higher interrater reliability.

The potential for coding study methods in a way that "favors" studies with results consistent with the coder's predispositions provides another reason why *it is good practice to (a) make the criteria for coding decisions explicit before coding begins and (b) have each study coded by at least two researchers working independently* (see Chapter 4). The first of these procedures serves to minimize the chance that coders will unconsciously shift their evaluative criteria to favor studies that favor their expectations about results. The second increases the chance that if one coder's codes do reflect their predispositions, this can be caught and fixed before the studies' information is entered into the database.

Judges' Disagreement
About What Constitutes Research Quality

Another problem with making quality judgments is that even "disinterested" judges of research can disagree on what is and is not a high-quality study. For example, numerous demonstrations have examined the reliability of evaluations made about manuscripts submitted to journals in the fields of psychology (Fiske & Fogg, 1990; Scarr & Weber, 1978), education (Marsh & Ball, 1989), and medicine (Justice, Berlin, Fletcher, & Fletcher, 1994). These studies typically calculate some measure of agreement between the recommendations made by manuscript readers concerning whether or not a manuscript should be accepted for publication. Typically, the level of agreement is surprisingly low.

In an interesting demonstration, Peters and Ceci (1982) resubmitted 12 published articles to the journals in which they initially appeared. The manuscripts were identical to the originals except that the names of the submitters were changed and their affiliations were changed from "high-status" to "low-status" institutions. Only 3 of the 12 articles were detected as being resubmissions. Of the 9 articles that completed the rereview process, 8 were not accepted for publication.

In many respects, the judgments of manuscript evaluators are more complex than those of research synthesists. The manuscript evaluator must consider several dimensions that do not interest the research synthesist, including the clarity of writing and the interests of the journal's readership. Also, a journal editor will sometimes deliberately choose evaluators who represent different perspectives. However, the editor still hopes that the evaluators will agree on the disposition of the manuscript. And, of course, if perfectly objective criteria were available (and were employed), the evaluators would come to concurring decisions.

Some of the differences between judgments by manuscript evaluators and research synthesists were controlled in a study conducted by Gottfredson (1978). He removed much of the variability in judges' ratings that might be due to differing initial biases by asking authors to nominate experts competent to evaluate their work. Gottfredson was able to obtain at least two expert evaluations for each of 121 articles. The experts evaluated the quality of the articles on a three-question scale that left the meaning of the term "quality" ambiguous. An interjudge agreement coefficient of $r = .41$ was obtained. On a 36-item evaluation scale, which tapped many explicit facets of research quality, an interjudge agreement coefficient of $r = .46$ was obtained. These levels of agreement are probably lower than we would hope.

Why do overall judgments of quality differ? In addition to differences in the judges' predispositions, it is possible to locate two other sources of variance in quality judgments: (a) the relative importance judges assign to different research design characteristics and (b) judgments about how well a particular study met a criterion. To demonstrate the first source of variance, I conducted a study in which six experts in school desegregation research were asked to rank the importance of six design characteristics for establishing the "utility or information value" of a school desegregation study (Cooper, 1986). The six characteristics were (a) the experimental manipulation (or in this case, the definition of desegregation), (b) the adequacy of the control group, (c) the validity of the outcome measure, (d) the representativeness of the sample, (e) the representativeness of the environmental conditions surrounding the study, and (f) the appropriateness of the statistical analyses. The intercorrelations of the rankings among pairs of experts varied from $r = .77$ to $r = -.29$, with the average correlation being $r = .47$. Thus, it was clear that judges differed in how important they thought different evaluative criteria were, even before applying them to particular studies.

In sum, the studies of judges' assessments of methodological quality indicate evaluator agreement is less than we would like. *One way to improve the reliability of quality judgments would be to add more judges to the evaluation of any given study.* So, for example, a rating of a study (or the decision to include or exclude a study from a research synthesis) based on five judges' average ratings will correspond better with the average rating of five other judges (drawn from the same population of judges) than will the ratings of two judges with any other two judges. However, it is rare that such large pools of judges can be used to make quality judgments about studies in a research synthesis. Two or three is often the practical limit.

Differences Among Quality Scales

I mentioned earlier that two sources of variance in judges' ratings were (a) the relative importance they assign to different research design characteristics and (b) how well they think a particular study met a particular criterion. A technique many research synthesists have used in an attempt to address the first of these concerns involves using *quality scales*. Here, the synthesists use a predeveloped scheme that tells judges what evaluative dimensions are important. Also, the scales typically use a prearranged weighting scheme so that the same weight is placed on a dimension of quality when it is applied to each study. The synthesists hope that by asking coders to apply the same set of explicit criteria, it will lead different coders to more transparent and consistent ratings. The goal of quality scales is to take some of the subjectivity out of the rating process.

While certainly an improvement over allowing each judge to determine his or her own quality criteria, quality scales have met their goals with limited success. In medical research, Peter Jüni and his colleagues (1999) demonstrated that quality scales may create consistency among those using the same scale but it does not mean that *different scales* will come to the same judgments. Jüni and colleagues applied 25 different scales (constructed by other researchers) to the same set of studies and then conducted 25 meta-analyses, one using each scale. They found that the conclusions of the meta-analyses differed dramatically depending on the scale that was used. For six of the scales, the high-quality studies suggested no difference between a new and old treatment, whereas the low-quality studies suggested a significant positive effect for the new treatment. The pattern was reversed for seven other quality scales. The remaining 12 quality scales resulted in conclusions that showed no difference between the results of high- and low-quality studies. Thus, even though the quality scales may improve somewhat the reliability of judges using the same scale, the validity of the conclusions they lead us to is still suspect.

Jeff Valentine and I (Valentine & Cooper, 2008) suggested several reasons why the quality scales seem to lead to such poor agreement. First, just as individual judges can disagree about what characteristics of research are important for quality judgments, quality scales do not necessarily agree about this either.

For example, in the Jüni and colleagues study, some of the scales focused almost exclusively on the studies' ability to permit causal inferences; other scales addressed multiple characteristics, such as the representativeness of the sample and statistical power.

Second, most quality scales still leave room for judges' subjective assessments to enter the evaluation process. The scales use terms such as "adequate," "appropriate," and "sufficient" to describe design features (e.g., "Was the internal consistency of measures adequate?"), without providing operational definitions for these adjectives. What may be adequate for one judge may be inadequate for another. This means that even though the important characteristics are identified, the reliability of codes for any single dimension will still be less than perfect. It also suggests that while identifying the characteristics makes judgments more transparent, it is still not perfectly clear what the criteria are for applying each of the evaluative labels.

Third, similar to individual researchers, most scales apply different schemes to weight the importance of different methodological characteristics. Typically, quality scales assign a certain portion of the scale's points to each of the characteristics. So, even when scales use the same characteristics, there can be variation among scales about the importance that should be assigned to each characteristic. For example, Jüni and colleagues found that some scales assigned 16 times more weight than other scales to the same design feature. Part of this difference was explainable by the fact that the scales used different numbers of design features and part to the fact that the scale developers might have valued the same design feature differently.

Reliance on a single score to express quality. Typically, the scores from the various items on a quality scale are summed to a single score. These were the scores that Jüni and colleagues (1999) used to categorize studies into high- and low-quality groupings when they did their 25 meta-analyses. Valentine and Cooper (2008) questioned whether it makes sense to reduce the evaluation of a study to a single dichotomous judgment (Is this study good or bad?) or even to a single continuous judgment (What is this study's quality score?). The single-score approach results in one number that is summed across very different aspects of study design and implementation, many of which are not necessarily related to one another. For example, there is no necessary relationship between the process used to assign participants to experimental conditions and the quality of outcome measures used in a study. So, one study of homework might randomly assign participants to conditions but use a self-report of grades as the measure of achievement. A second study might use matching of students who did and did not do homework on their own but use grades taken from student records. In such a case, the first study has a stronger design for making causal inferences but the second study has a more valid outcome measure. When a scale combines these two elements of study design into a single score, it may obscure these important differences between them; these two studies might get identical or similar scores. If the two studies produce different results, how should we interpret this difference?

A Priori Exclusion of Research Versus A Posteriori Examination of Research Differences

The role of predispositions and the disagreement about what characteristics of research design define "quality" demonstrate how subjectivity intrudes on our attempts to be scientifically objective. The point is important because research synthesists often debate whether or not *a priori* judgments of research quality should be used to exclude studies from their work. This debate was first captured in an exchange of views between Hans Eysenck (1978) and Gene Glass and Mary Smith (1978) concerning Smith and Glass's (1977) early meta-analysis of research on psychotherapy. Smith and Glass (1977) synthesized over 300 studies examining the effectiveness of psychotherapy with no *a priori* exclusion of studies due to methodology. Eysenck felt this strategy represented an abandonment of scholarship and critical judgment:

> A mass of reports—good, bad, and indifferent—are fed into the computer in the hope that people will cease caring about the quality of the material on which the conclusions are based. . . . "Garbage in—garbage out" is a well-known axiom of computer specialists; it applies here with equal force. (p. 517)

Eysenck concluded that "only better designed experiments than those in the literature can bring us a better understanding of the points raised" (p. 517).

Glass and Smith (1978) made several points in rebuttal. First, they argued that the poor design characteristics of different studies can "cancel" one another out, if the results of different studies are consistent. Second, as noted earlier, the *a priori* quality judgments required to exclude studies are likely to vary from judge to judge and be influenced by personal biases. Finally, Glass and Smith claimed they did not advocate the abandonment of quality standards. Instead, they regarded the impact of design quality on study results as "an empirical *a posteriori* question, not an *a priori* matter of opinion" (Glass, McGaw, & Smith, 1981, p. 222). They suggested that synthesists thoroughly code the design aspects, good and bad, of each study and then demonstrate if, in fact, the outcomes of studies are related to how the studies were conducted.

I suspect that the best approach to the debate about when, if ever, to exclude studies from a research synthesis is best resolved by a combination of approaches.

Generally, the decision to include or exclude studies on an *a priori* basis requires you to make an overall judgment of study quality that is often subjective and others may find unconvincing. But there could be instances in which, for example, so many high-quality studies exist that low-quality studies can be dismissed without concern. Thus, it is important that you ask this question about how a research synthesis was conducted:

> If studies were excluded from the synthesis because of design and implementation considerations, were these considerations (a) explicitly and operationally defined and (b) consistently applied to all studies?

Generally, however, *it is good practice to carefully enumerate study characteristics and to compare the results of studies using different methods to determine if studies' methods and results covary with one another.* If it is empirically demonstrated that "good" studies (that is, studies that permit inferences most correspondent with the inferences you wish to make) produce results different from "bad" studies, the results of the good studies ought to be believed. In this case, no harm is done to the validity of your inferences by looking at the "bad" studies and perhaps something is learned about how to conduct future research. When no difference in results is found, it seems sensible to retain (some or all of) the "bad" studies because they contain other variations in methods (such as different samples and locations) that, by their inclusion, may help you answer many other questions surrounding the problem area. In most cases, letting the data speak—that is, including nearly all studies and examining empirically the differences in results associated with methods—substitutes a discovery process for the predispositions of the synthesist. I will return to this issue again after I suggest a scheme for coding the methodological characteristics of studies.

APPROACHES TO CATEGORIZING RESEARCH METHODS

The decision to examine empirically the impact of methodology on research results does not relieve you of all evaluation responsibilities. You must still decide what methodological characteristics of studies need to be coded. As I pointed out previously, these decisions will depend on the nature of the question under scrutiny and the types of associated research. If a problem has been addressed mainly through experimental manipulations in laboratory settings, as has been, for example, the effects of choice on intrinsic motivation, a different set of methodological characteristics of studies will be important than if correlational designs are at issue, as in studies of the relationship between individual differences and attitudes about rape. Two broad approaches to coding research methods can be identified, though they are rarely used in their pure form. The first approach requires the synthesist to make judgments about the *threats to validity* that exist in a study. The second approach requires the detailing of the objective design characteristics of a study, as described by the primary researchers.

Threats-to-Validity Approach

When Campbell and Stanley (1963) introduced the notion of "threats to validity," they literally transformed the social sciences. They suggested that a set of extraneous influences associated with each research design could be identified that "might produce effects confounded with the experimental stimulus" (p. 5). Different research designs had different validity threats associated with them. Designs could be compared according to their inferential capabilities. More importantly, less-than-optimal designs could be triangulated so that strong inferences could result from multiple studies when the single "perfect" study could not be performed.

Campbell and Stanley's (1963) notion held the promise of increased sensitivity and objectivity in discussions of research quality. However, it was not long before some problems in the application of their scheme became apparent. The problems related to creating an exhaustive list of threats to validity and identifying what the implication of each threat might be.

Initially, Campbell and Stanley (1963) proposed two broad classes of validity threats. Threats to *internal validity* related to the causal correspondence between the experimental treatment and the experimental effect. To the extent that this correspondence was compromised by deficiencies in research design, the ability to interpret a study's results as evidence of a causal relationship would be called into question. Campbell and Stanley listed eight threats to internal validity. Threats to *external validity* related to the generalizability of research results. Evaluating external validity required assessing the representativeness of a study's participants, settings, treatments, and measurements. While the external validity of a study could never be assessed definitively, Campbell and Stanley suggested four classes of threats to representativeness.

Bracht and Glass (1968) offered an expanded list of threats to external validity. They felt that "external validity was not treated as comprehensively as internal validity in the Campbell-Stanley chapter" (p. 437). To rectify this omission, Bracht and Glass identified two broad classes of external validity: *population validity*, referring to generalization to persons not included in a study, and *ecological validity*, referring to settings not sampled. Two specific threats to population validity were described, along with 10 threats to ecological validity.

Campbell (1969) added a ninth threat to internal validity, called "instability," defined as "unreliability of measures, fluctuations in sampling persons or components, autonomous instability of repeated or equivalent measures" (p. 411).

Next, Cook and Campbell (1979) offered a list of 33 specific threats to validity grouped into four broad classifications. The notions of *construct validity* and *statistical conclusion validity* were added to internal and external validity. Construct validity referred to "the possibility that the operations which are meant to represent a particular cause or effect construct can be construed in terms of more than one construct" (p. 59). Statistical conclusion validity referred to the power and appropriateness of the data analysis technique. And finally, Shadish, Cook, and Campbell (2002) updated the list of threats categorized into the four broad classifications.

From this brief history, the problems in using a strict threats-to-validity approach to assess the quality of empirical studies should be clear. First, different researchers may use different lists of threats. For instance, should the threat of "instability" offered by Campbell (1969) constitute one threat, as originally proposed, or several threats (e.g., low statistical power, unreliability of measures), as redefined by Shadish and colleagues (2002)? Or should ecological validity constitute one threat or up to 10 different threats? A second problem is the relative weighting of threats—is the threat involving historical confounds (other societal events that happened concurrent with the experimental manipulation) weighted equally with the threat involving restricted generalizability across constructs? Expert methodologists may even disagree on how a particular threat should be classified. For instance, Bracht and Glass (1968) listed "experimenter expectancy effects" as a threat to external validity while Shadish et al. (2002) listed it as a threat to the construct validity of causes.

All these problems aside, the threats-to-validity approach to the evaluation of research still represents an improvement in rigor, and is certainly preferable to the *a priori* single judgment of quality it replaces. Each successive list of threats represents an increase in precision and a deepening understanding of the relationship between research design and inferences. Also, the list of validity threats gives the synthesist an explicit set of criteria to apply or modify. In that sense, synthesists who use the threats-to-validity approach make their rules of judgment open to criticism and debate. This is a crucial step in making the research evaluation process more objective.

Methods-Description Approach

In the second approach to evaluating study design and implementation, the synthesist codes the objective characteristics of each study's methods as they are described by the primary researchers. For example, experimental designs—how comparisons between groups treated differently are constructed—relate mainly to eliminating threats to internal validity. Campbell and Stanley (1963) described 3 preexperimental designs, 3 true experimental designs, and 10 quasi-experimental designs, and the list of design variations has been expanded several times since (see Shadish et al., 2002). So, in this approach, rather than evaluate the internal validity of a study's design—an abstract assessment that could lead to disagreement—the coder simply retrieves the design type by matching the design used in the study to a design on a list of possibilities. This is a low-inference code that should be fairly consistent across coders; when inconsistencies appear, it should be fairly easy to resolve disagreements. In most areas of research, considerably fewer than all the available designs will be needed to describe exhaustively how comparisons were constructed in the relevant research.

One problem with the methods-description approach to evaluating studies is shared with the threats-to-validity approach (and was evident in the use of quality scales)—different synthesists may choose to list different methodological characteristics. So, while the methods-description approach may lead to more reliable coding, it does not solve the problem of what characteristics to code in the first place.

Another problem with the methods-description approach is that the list of methodological characteristics that might need to be coded can become extremely long. Remember, there are four classes of threats to validity—internal, external, construct, and statistical validity—and each may require the coding of numerous design and implementation characteristics to capture every aspect of methodology that might influence whether the threat is a concern in a given study. And it may not be advisable to test every one of these characteristics as a moderator of study results because the number of tests would be so large, some will be significant by chance alone (i.e., the Type I error rate will be inflated). So, there may be a trade-off between the threats-to-validity and methods-description approaches involving parsimony versus reliability.

A judgment about the threat to validity called *low statistical power* (related to statistical conclusion validity) provides a good example. A coder making an overall judgment about whether a study has a good chance to reject a false null hypothesis must do so by combining several explicit study characteristics: size of the sample, whether a between- or within-subjects design was used, the inherent power of the statistical test (e.g., parametric versus nonparametric), the number of other sources of variance extracted in the analysis, and even the expected size of the relationship under study. Using the threats-to-validity approach, two coders of the same study might disagree on whether or not a study has low statistical power because they weighted these factors differently or perhaps failed to consider the same factors. However, they might agree perfectly on their codings of these separate components. This speaks in favor of using the methods-description approach. But using the methods-description approach still leaves room for subjectivity; when is sample size too small for adequate statistical power? And, if the number of codes required (I listed five for just one of dozens of threats to validity) becomes too large, relating them all to study outcomes jeopardizes the validity of the results of the research synthesis; with so many tests, a few will be significant by chance. If chance is playing a role in generating significant findings, the pattern of results will be difficult to interpret. This speaks in favor of using the threats-to-validity approach.

A Mixed-Criteria Approach: The Study DIAD

The pros and cons of the two approaches makes one wonder if there is a way to combine them that maximizes the strengths and minimizes the weaknesses of each. In such a strategy, you might code many of the potentially relevant aspects of research methodology and perhaps build a scheme for explicitly combining them into judgments about the different validity threats, not unlike my previous example regarding statistical power. Some threats to validity might have to be coded directly. For instance, the threats to internal validity involving aspects of the control group—diffusion of treatments, compensatory rivalry, or resentful demoralization of participants receiving the less desirable treatment—are probably best coded directly as threats to validity, though deciding whether they are present or absent still relies heavily on the description of the study presented by the primary researcher. While this mixed-criteria approach does not remove all problems from evaluating studies (I will describe several in the following paragraphs), it would be a step toward the use of explicit and objective quality criteria that also takes into account the utility of the resulting descriptions of studies.

Jeff Valentine and I (Valentine & Cooper, 2008) attempted to create an instrument for use in research synthesis that evaluated studies using this mixed-criteria approach. The result was called the Study Design and Implementation

Assessment Device, or the Study DIAD. The Study DIAD provides a framework for synthesists to build an evaluative scale unique to their topic area and allows them to choose from several different levels of abstractness for describing the correspondence between a study's methods and desired inferences. However, it requires the user (a) to be detailed and explicit about the chosen criteria, (b) to define these criteria prior to beginning the evaluation of studies, and (c) to apply the criteria consistently across all studies. The Study DIAD is based on the assumption that the user wants to draw causal inferences about the effectiveness of an intervention; for example, do interventions meant to promote physical activity among older adults cause participants to exercise more? However, it is divided into sections corresponding to the four classes of validity, so it can be used for other types of research as well. A full exposition of the Study DIAD is available elsewhere (see Valentine & Cooper, 2008), but a brief introduction should give you an idea of how it combines the threats-to-validity and methods-description approaches, how it works, and whether using it might be appropriate for your synthesis.

At the most abstract level, the Study DIAD provides the user with answers to four global questions relating to the construct, internal, external, and statistical conclusion validity of a study. These questions are

1. Fit Between Concepts and Operations: Were the participants in the study treated and the outcomes measured in a way that is consistent with the definition of the intervention and its proposed effects?

2. Clarity of Causal Inference: Did the research design permit an unambiguous conclusion about the intervention's effectiveness?

3. Generality of Findings: Was the intervention tested on participants, settings, outcomes, and occasions representative of its intended beneficiaries?

4. Precision of Outcome Estimation: Could accurate estimates of the intervention's impact be derived from the study report?

The term "intervention" is used in the Study DIAD to stand for any treatment or experimental manipulation. So, all four of these questions would be relevant to our examples involving research on the effectiveness of homework, programs to increase physical activity among older adults, and the effects of choice on intrinsic motivation; they all seek to uncover causal relationships. However, because the studies of choice and intrinsic motivation were conducted in laboratories (with great experimental control), they should all have good internal validity, so the "Clarity of Causal Inference" question likely could be omitted from the Study DIAD for this synthesis. Our fourth example, individual differences in attitudes toward rape, is not concerned with causal relationships, so Question 2 also would

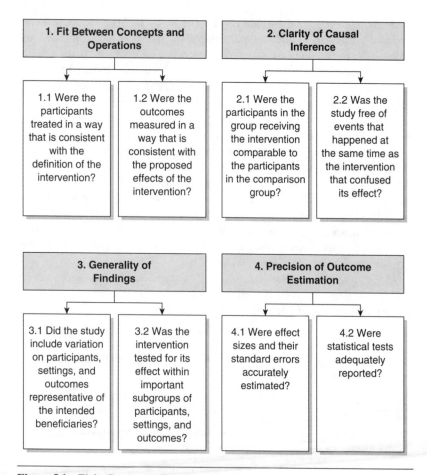

Figure 5.1   Eight Composite Questions About Study Quality Taken From the Study DIAD

SOURCE: Valentine and Cooper (2008, p. 140). Copyright 2008 by the American Psychological Association. Reprinted with permission.

be irrelevant to assessing the correspondence between study methods and inferences in that research synthesis. The other three global questions on the Study DIAD are relevant to all the examples.

At a slightly more specific level, the Study DIAD decomposes the four global questions into eight composite questions. These are presented in Figure 5.1. Here, the four global questions are each divided into two more specific questions. It might have occurred to you that the four global and eight composite questions could be used to form a quality scale by themselves. In other words, judges might simply be asked to answer each of these questions for each study (or to give the study a score on a continuous measure). This would be an example of a pure threats-to-validity approach to quality assessment and would exhibit the strengths and weaknesses associated with such an approach.

But the Study DIAD goes a step further by attempting to operationally define the methodological characteristics of studies that go into answering each of the eight composite and four global questions. Accomplishing this task requires that the instrument (a) identify the particular design and implementation features that must be considered when answering each of the eight composite questions and (b) providing a way (an algorithm) to "sum up" the chosen positive and negative methodological features to get to the answers to the eight (and then the four) questions. To do this, the Study DIAD requires coders to answer about 30 questions regarding a study's design and implementation. These are presented in Table 5.1 with the question number associated with each indicating which global and composite question that particular methodological feature is related to.

Looking over the questions in Table 5.1, you might wonder how we decided which aspects of design and implementation should be represented in the Study DIAD. Here, we faced the same problem encountered by everyone who attempts to develop a quality scale. To make these decisions, first, we considered the content of other scales and many methods textbooks and articles. Second, we shared early drafts of the Study DIAD with 14 highly regarded research methodologists. Then, we sought input on the instrument at a public meeting attended by over 150 people. We also accepted comments on a draft of the instrument sent to us through the What Works Clearinghouse's website. In all, over 60 comments were received. So, the consensus surrounding the 30-odd questions about study design and implementation on the Study DIAD probably is higher than most sets of such questions used in most quality scales.

That said, you next might also recognize that the questions in Table 5.1 still involve some degree of judgment on the part of the coder; the 30 questions still include terms like "adequate" and "fully." So, the Study DIAD goes yet a step further by requiring the users, before the instrument is applied, to more precisely define the terms listed in Table 5.1 that otherwise would be open to varying interpretations. The mechanism for doing this is presented in Table 5.2, which contains a document that needs to be completed by the research synthesists before the Study DIAD can be applied. The first column contains the request for the definitions of terms. Note that these definitions are specific to the research area under consideration. Some are highly related to the specific content area, such as the important characteristics of the intervention (Question 1

Table 5.1   Questions About Study Design and Implementation From the Study DIAD

1.1   Were the participants treated in a way that is consistent with the definition of the intervention?

    1.1.1   To what extent does the intervention reflect commonly held or theoretically derived characteristics about what it should contain?

    1.1.2   Was the intervention described at a level of detail that would allow its replication by other implementers?

    1.1.3   Was there evidence that the group receiving the intervention might also have experienced a changed expectancy, novelty, and/or disruption effect not also experienced by the comparison group (or vice versa)?

    1.1.4   Was there evidence that the intervention was implemented in a manner similar to the way it was defined?

1.2   Were the outcomes measured in a way that is consistent with the proposed effects of the intervention?

    1.2.1   Do items on the outcome measure appear to represent the content of interest to this synthesis (i.e., have face validity)?

    1.2.2   Were the scores on the outcome measure acceptably reliable?

    1.2.3   Was the outcome measure properly aligned to the intervention condition?

2.1   Were the participants in the group receiving the intervention comparable to the participants in the comparison group?

    2.1.1   Was random assignment used to place participants into conditions? (If no, answer the next questions.)

        2.1.1a   For quasi-experiments: Were adequate equating procedures used to recreate the selection model?

    2.1.2   Was there differential attrition between intervention and comparison groups after equating occurred?

    2.1.3   Was there severe overall attrition after equating occurred?

2.2   Was the study free of events that happened at the same time as the intervention that confused its effect?

    2.2.1   Was there evidence of a local history event?

    2.2.2   Were the intervention and comparison groups drawn from the same local pool? (If yes, answer the next question.)

        2.2.2a   If yes, were intervention conditions known to study participants, providers, data collectors, and/or other authorities?

    2.2.3   Did the description of the study give any other indication of the strong plausibility of other intervention contaminants?

3.1   Did the study include variation on participants, settings, and outcomes representative of the intended beneficiaries?

    3.1.1   Did the sample contain participants with the necessary characteristics to be considered part of the target population?

3.1.2 To what extent did the sample capture variation among participants on important characteristics of the target population?

3.1.3 To what extent did the study include variation on important characteristics of the target setting?

3.1.4 To what extent were important classes of outcome measures included in the study?

3.1.5 Did the study measure the outcome at a time appropriate for capturing the intervention's effect?

3.1.6 Was the study conducted during a time frame appropriate for extrapolating to current conditions?

3.2 Was the intervention tested for its effect within important subgroups of participants, settings, and outcomes?

3.2.1 To what extent was the intervention tested for effectiveness within important subgroups of participants?

3.2.2 To what extent was the intervention tested for effectiveness within important subgroups of settings?

3.2.3 Was the intervention tested for its effectiveness across important classes of outcomes?

4.1 Were effect sizes and their standard errors accurately estimated?

4.1.1 Was the assumption of independence met, or could dependence (including dependence arising from clustering) be accounted for in estimates of effect sizes and their standard errors?

4.1.2. Did the statistical properties of the data (e.g., distributional and variance assumptions, if any, presence of outliers) allow for valid estimates of the effect sizes?

4.1.3 Were the sample sizes adequate to provide sufficiently precise estimates of effect sizes?

4.1.4 Were the outcome measures sufficiently reliable to allow adequately precise estimates of the effect sizes?

4.2 Were statistical tests adequately reported?

4.2.1 To what extent were sample sizes reported (or estimable) from statistical information presented?

4.2.2 To what extent could directions of effects be identified for important measured outcomes?

4.2.3a To what extent could effect sizes be estimated for important measured outcomes?

4.2.3b Could estimates of effect sizes be computed using a standard formula (or algebraic equivalent)?

in Table 5.2). Others might be a bit more general but still might vary as functions of the topic. For example, the criteria for the minimum acceptable attrition (that is, loss of participants from the study; Questions 12 and 13) probably have some general boundaries but also might be different for studies on the effectiveness of homework and studies on the effectiveness of an intervention for increasing physical activity among older adults.

Table 5.2 also shows in the second column the composite question that each answer applies to. In the third column, the table shows you how the questions might be answered by synthesists who were going to apply the Study DIAD to studies about the effectiveness of homework. So, for example, the coders applying the Study DIAD to each study are not asked to make a decision about what a minimally acceptable internal consistency is for outcome measures; in the example, this is the measure of achievement (Question 4 in Table 5.2). Instead, the coders are told that the principal investigators have chosen .60 to be the minimal acceptable level of this type of reliability. In this way, all of the judgments in the eight composite questions are given operational definitions.

In the final steps for using the Study DIAD, a set of algorithms are applied to the answers to the design and implementation questions (Table 5.1) so that they are combined to answer the eight composite questions in Figure 5.1. Table 5.3 presents one of these eight algorithms. Algorithms also exist for combining the eight composite questions into the four global questions. As an example, Table 5.4 shows the results of applying the Study DIAD to a study by McGrath (1992) on the effects of homework on academic achievement.

For any study, the Study DIAD results in three sets of answers to questions about its methods, or its "quality" for testing the hypothesis of interest: (a) about 30 design and implementation questions, (b) 8 composite questions, and (c) 4 global questions. Really, any of these characterizations of the study can be used to "judge" the study or to see if features of a study's methods are related to the study's outcome. In fact, if you wanted to exclude studies *a priori* based on Study DIAD results, you could set a minimum profile that the study had to meet or exceed in order to be included in the synthesis. For example, the McGrath study might be excluded because it got only a "Maybe yes" on Global Question 2 about internal validity.

The Study DIAD is a complex and time-intensive instrument to apply, one that takes careful thought and sufficient training to be used properly. But this complexity is a reflection of the fact that coming to careful and transparent decisions about research quality is not a simple task. If we acknowledge this fact in our work, then the Study DIAD has many characteristics to its credit. First, the 30-odd characteristics of a study's design and implementation that form the core of the instrument (presented in Table 5.1) were arrived at using

(Text continued on page 141)

Table 5.2 Contextual Questions That Need Answers From the Users in Order to Apply the Study DIAD

Contextual Question	Study DIAD Composite Question	Example of Answer to Questions for Evaluating Research on the Effects of Homework on Academic Achievement
1. What commonly shared and/or theoretically derived characteristics of the intervention should be present in its definition and implementation?	Fit Between Concepts— Intervention	• Focuses on academic work • Assigned by classroom teacher (or researcher via teacher) • Meant to be done during nonschool hours or during study time at school
a. Which of these characteristics are necessary to define interventions that "fully," "largely," and "somewhat" reflect commonly shared and/or theoretically derived characteristics?		• For "fully," all three must be present • There will be no "largely" or "somewhat" studies

b. What variations in the intervention are important to examine as potential moderators of effect size?		• Frequency of assignments
		• Expected amount of time spent on each assignment
		• Subject matter(s) covered
		• Degree of individualization
		• Compulsory vs. voluntary nature of assignments
		• Purpose
		  o Practice (reinforcement, rehearsal)
		  o Preparation (introduce a new skill)
		  o Integration (combine two new skills)
		  o Extension (apply to a new content area)
		  o Enrichment
		• Amount of time to complete
		• Individual or group assignment

(Continued)

Table 5.2 (Continued)

Contextual Question	Study DIAD Composite Question	Example of Answer to Questions for Evaluating Research on the Effects of Homework on Academic Achievement
2. What important characteristics of the intervention would we need to know in order to reliably replicate it with different participants, in other settings, at other times?	External Validity	• Frequency of assignments • Expected amount of time spent on each assignment • Actual amount of time spent on each assignment • Subject matter(s) covered • Grade level(s) of students • Degree of individualization • Compulsory vs. voluntary nature of assignments • Individual or group assignment

3. What are the important classes of outcomes?	Fit Between Concepts— Outcomes	• Achievement tests
		  o Standardized
		  o Other test
		• Class grades
		• Study habits and skills
		• Student attitudes toward
		  o School
		  o Subject matter
		• Student self-beliefs
		• Parent attitudes toward school

a. What classes of outcomes are needed to conclude that a reasonable range of operations and/or methods have been included and tested?		• Any two classes of outcomes is a reasonable range
4. Does the principal investigator have a minimum level of score reliability for outcomes to be considered in the review? If so, what are	Fit Between Concepts— Outcomes	• Yes, internal consistency estimate > .60

Contextual Question	Study DIAD Composite Question	Example of Answer to Questions for Evaluating Research on the Effects of Homework on Academic Achievement
the specific minimum reliability coefficients for internal consistency, temporal stability, and/or interrater reliability (as appropriate)?		
5. Considering the context of this study, during what interval of time should it have been conducted to be relevant to current conditions?	External Validity— Sampling	• 1982–2007
6. Considering the context of this study, what are the characteristics of the intended beneficiaries of the intervention?	External Validity— Sampling	• K–12 students • Students in the United States, Canada, United Kingdom, Australia
7. What are the important characteristics of participants that might be related to the intervention's effect and must be equated if a study does not use random assignment?	Causal Inference— Selection	• Pretest of outcome OR prior achievement • Grade level OR age • Socioeconomic status

8. What characteristics of subgroups of participants are important (a) to have variation on and (b) to test within a study to determine whether an intervention is effective within these groups? What levels or labels capture this variation?	External Validity— Effects Tested Within Subgroups	Achievement labels applied to students
		  o Gifted, average, "at-risk," learning disabled, underachieving/below grade level, possessing a learning deficit
		• Grade levels
		  o K–12

(Continued)

Table 5.2 (Continued)

Contextual Question	Study DIAD Composite Question	Example of Answer to Questions for Evaluating Research on the Effects of Homework on Academic Achievement

a. Which of these characteristics of subgroups of participants are needed to conclude that a "limited" or "reasonable range" of characteristics have been included and tested?		• Socioeconomic levels
		  o Low
		  o Low-middle
		  o Middle
		  o Middle-upper middle
		  o Upper
		• Student sex
		• Any one characteristic for "limited"
		• Any three characteristics for "reasonable"

9. What characteristics of settings are important to test within a study to determine whether an intervention is effective within these groups?	External Validity— Effects Tested Within Subgroups	*In School*
		• Class size
		• Special vs. regular education classrooms
		• Classroom preparation
		  o Provision of materials
		  o Teacher-suggested approaches to work
		  o Teacher-provided links to the curriculum
		  o Start in class and finish at home
		• Feedback
		  o Written comments
		  o Grading
		  o Incentives
		  o Used as part of class grade

Contextual Question	Study DIAD Composite Question	Example of Answer to Questions for Evaluating Research on the Effects of Homework on Academic Achievement
		• Alignment with academic content • Use in classroom discussion *At Home* • Socioeconomic status of family • Number and type of siblings • Number of adults in the home
a. Which of these characteristics and settings are needed to conclude that a "full," "reasonable," or "limited" range of variations have been tested?		• All for "full" • Two from "school" and one from "home" for "reasonable" • Any one for "limited"
10. What is the appropriate interval for measuring the intervention's effect relative to the end of the intervention?	External Validity— Inclusive Sampling	• Any interval is appropriate
11. Considering the context of this study, for purposes of sampling, what constitutes the local pool of participants?	Internal Validity— Lack of Contamination	• Students attending the same school building at the same grade level
a. If participants are drawn from the same local pool, which groups of individuals (e.g., students, teachers, parents,		• Students in either group • Parents of students in either group • Teachers

(Continued)

Table 5.2 (Continued)

Contextual Question	Study DIAD Composite Question	Example of Answer to Questions for Evaluating Research on the Effects of Homework on Academic Achievement
administrators, caseworkers) might have been able to interfere with the fidelity of the comparison group if they knew who was in the intervention and comparison groups?		
12. For research on this topic, how would you define differential attrition from the intervention and control groups?	Internal Validity— Selection	• More than a 10% difference in attrition percentages between groups
13. For research on this topic, how would you define severe overall attrition?	Internal Validity— Selection	• More than 20% loss of the original sample
14. For research on this topic, what constitutes a minimal sample size that would permit a sufficiently precise estimate of the effect size?	Statistical Validity— Effect Size Estimation	• 50 students in each group
15. What percentage of important statistical information (i.e., sample size, direction of effect, effect size) is needed for the results of this study to be "fully," "largely," and "rarely" reported?	Statistical Validity— Reporting	• If full statistical results are known for all measured outcomes, results are "fully reported." • If full statistical results are known for 75–99% of measured outcomes, results are "largely reported."

Contextual Question	Study DIAD Composite Question	Example of Answer to Questions for Evaluating Research on the Effects of Homework on Academic Achievement
		• If full statistical results are known for less than 75% of measured outcomes, results are "rarely reported."
16. Considering the outcome measure and the context of this research question, what constitutes "overalignment" and "underalignment" of the intervention and outcome?	Fit Between Concepts— Outcome	• No outcomes are overaligned to the intervention for this research question. • If the homework assignments cover distinctly different subject matter than the assessment, then the outcomes are underaligned to the intervention.

SOURCE: Valentine and Cooper (2008, pp. 136–138). Copyright 2008 by the American Psychological Association. Reprinted by permission.

input from a broad sampling of social science researchers. So, there is greater consensus that these are the critical methodological features of studies to consider when judging a study's quality than is the case in other quality scales. Second, the fact that the Study DIAD requires that its users make explicit their definitions of important terms before it is applied (defined in Table 5.2) means that the meaning of these terms will be clear to people who read the synthesis. If there is disagreement about these definitions, then fruitful discussions can ensue about where the disagreement lies. Third, the algorithms are made explicit for combining the study design and implementation features into answers to the more abstract questions about quality (presented in Figure 5.1).

You can use the Study DIAD in several ways. Certainly, it is best to apply it in its full realization. But, as noted previously, you could also use the global and/or composite questions to guide you if you want to use a threats-to-validity approach. Or you could use the 30-odd design and implementation questions to guide your use of a methods-description approach. It is a simple task to transfer the 30-odd questions on to a coding sheet similar to the ones presented in Chapter 4. The definitions presented in Table 5.2 can be incorporated directly into the coding definitions.

Table 5.3   Algorithm for Combining Design and Implementation Questions to Arrive at an Answer to Composite Question 1.2: "Fit Between Concepts and Operations: Outcome Measure: Were the outcomes measured in a way that is consistent with the proposed effects of the intervention?"

	Response Pattern (read down columns to determine the answer to the question)		
1.2.1 Do items on the outcome measure appear to represent the content of interest (i.e., have face validity)?	Yes	Yes	Yes or No
1.2.2 Were the scores on the outcome measure acceptably reliable?	Yes	No	Yes or No
1.2.3 Was the outcome measure properly aligned to the intervention condition?	Yes	Yes	No
Answer to Composite Question 1.2 associated with this response pattern:	**Yes**	**Maybe No**	**No**

SOURCE: Valentine and Cooper (2008, Supplemental materials). Copyright 2008 by the American Psychological Association. Reprinted with permission.

What is most important is that when you are examining how a research synthesis handled the issue of evaluating the design and implementation of the constituent studies, you ask this question:

> *Were studies categorized so that important distinctions could be made among them regarding their research design and implementation?*

IDENTIFYING STATISTICAL OUTLIERS

Another aspect of evaluating studies cannot occur until after all of your data have been coded and entered into the computer and a first analysis of study results is ready to be run. At this point, the most extreme outcomes of the individual studies in your data set need to be examined to see if they are *statistical outliers*. You will want to discover if the most extreme outcomes are so discrepant from the other results that it is unlikely they are actually members of

Table 5.4 Example of Global and Composite Ratings for a Study of the Effects of Homework on Academic Achievement (McGrath, 1993)

Global Ratings		Composite Ratings	
Question	*Rating*	*Question*	*Rating*
1. Were the participants treated and the outcomes measured in a way that is consistent with the definition of the intervention and its proposed effects?	Yes	1.1 Were the participants treated in a way that is consistent with the definition of the intervention?	Yes
		1.2 Were the outcomes measured in a way that is consistent with the proposed effects of the intervention?	Yes
2. Did the research design permit an unambiguous conclusion about the intervention's effectiveness?	Maybe yes	2.1 Were the participants in the group receiving the intervention comparable to the participants in the comparison group?	Yes
		2.2 Was the study free of events that happened at the same time as the intervention that confused its effect?	Maybe yes
3. Was the intervention tested on participants, settings, and outcomes representative of its intended beneficiaries?	No	3.1 Did the study include variation on participants, settings, and outcomes representative of the intended beneficiaries?	No
		3.2 Was the intervention tested for its effect within important subgroupings of participants, settings, and outcomes?	No
4. Could accurate estimates of the intervention's impact be derived from the study report?	No	4.1 Were effect sizes and their standard errors accurately estimated?	No
		4.2 Were statistical tests adequately reported?	Yes

the same distribution of findings. For example, suppose you have a set of 60 correlations between the sex of the respondent to their attitude about rape. Suppose as well that 59 of the correlations range in value from −.05 to +.45, with positive values indicating that women are less accepting of rape than men. However, the 60th correlation is −.65. You can use statistical procedures and conventions to compare this most extreme data point to the overall sample distribution. You try to determine if this most extreme study outcome is too different from the overall distribution of outcomes to be considered a part of it.

Statistical outliers sometimes occur because of errors committed on your coding sheets or during data transfer. These you can correct. Or outliers can appear because these same types of errors were made by primary researchers. These you cannot correct. Sometimes the cause of a data point being a statistical outlier is unknown. Still, research synthesists agree that something needs to be done when a data point is so extreme that it is unlikely to be a member of the distribution of findings it is being compared to. One approach is simply to remove the study from your database. Another strategy is to reset the value of the outcome to three standard deviations above the mean or to its next nearest neighbor.

As an example, in the meta-analysis of the effects of choice on intrinsic motivation, we applied Grubbs' (1950) test to identify outliers separately for each outcome measure. These analyses identified none, one, or two outliers depending on the outcome. We could not discern the cause of the outliers but we set them to their nearest neighbor and retained the study for further analyses.

Barnett and Lewis (1984) provide a thorough examination of ways to identify statistical outliers and ways to treat them when found. *Whatever method you choose, it is good practice to look for statistical outliers and, when found, to address them in some manner.* This is the final step in evaluating the question of whether a particular study helps you get the best answer to the question that has motivated your research synthesis.

EXERCISES

1. Complete Table 5.2 for the topic of the synthesis you have chosen.

2. Pick a study that is relevant to your topic and answer the questions in Table 5.1.

3. Construct a method section of a coding frame for your research topic using Table 5.1 and your responses to the questions in Table 5.2. Pair up with a classmate and apply the coding frame to a study for each other's topic. What problems did you encounter? How would the problems change the way you would answer the questions in Table 5.2?

6

Step 5

Analyzing and Integrating
the Outcomes of Studies

What procedures should be used to condense and combine the research results?

Primary Function in Research Synthesis

To identify and apply procedures for (a) combining results across studies and (b) testing for differences in results between studies

Procedural Variation That Might Produce Differences in Conclusions

Variation in procedures used to analyze results of individual studies (e.g., narrative, vote count, averaged effect sizes) can lead to differences in cumulative results

Questions to Ask When Analyzing and Integrating the Results of Studies

1. Was an appropriate method used to combine and compare results across studies?

2. If a meta-analysis was performed, was an appropriate effect size metric used?

3. If a meta-analysis was performed, (a) were average effect sizes and confidence intervals reported and (b) was an appropriate model used to estimate the independent effects and the error in effect sizes?

4. If a meta-analysis was performed, was the homogeneity of effect sizes tested?

5. Were (a) study design and implementation features along with (b) other critical features of studies, including historical, theoretical, and practical variables, tested as potential moderators of study outcomes?

(Continued)

(Continued)

This chapter describes

- A rationale for the use of meta-analyses
- Statistical methods used to summarize research results including

  o Counting study outcomes
  o Averaging effect sizes
  o Examining the variability in effect sizes across studies

- Some practical issues in the application of meta-analytic procedures
- Some advanced meta-analytic procedures

D ata analysis involves reducing the separate data points collected by the inquirer into a unified statement about the research problem. It involves ordering, categorizing, and summarizing the data, as well as performing inference tests that attempt to relate data samples to the populations they arise from. Inferences made from data analysis require that decision rules be used to distinguish systematic data patterns from "noise," or chance fluctuation. Although different decision rules can be used, the rules involve assumptions about what the target population looks like (e.g., normally distributed) and what criteria (e.g., threshold probability for declaring a finding statistically significant) must be met before the existence of a pattern in the data is said to be reliable. The purpose of data analysis is to get the data into a form that permits valid interpretation.

DATA ANALYSIS IN PRIMARY
RESEARCH AND RESEARCH SYNTHESIS

Just as any scientific inquiry requires the leap from concrete operations to abstract concepts, both primary researchers and research synthesists must leap from patterns found in samples of data to more general conclusions about whether these patterns also exist in the target populations. However, until the mid-1970s, there had been almost no similarity in the analysis techniques used by primary researchers and research synthesists. Primary researchers were obligated to present sample statistics and to substantiate any inferences drawn from their data by providing the results of statistical tests. Most frequently, primary researchers (a) compared sampled means to one another or calculated other measures of relationship, (b) made the assumptions needed for conducting inference tests relating the sample results to populations, and (c) reported the probabilities associated with whether systematic differences in the sample could be inferred to hold in the target population as well.

Traditional statistical aids to primary data interpretation have not gone uncriticized. Some have argued that significance tests are not very informative since they only tell what the likelihood is of obtaining the observed results when the null hypothesis is true (e.g., Cohen, 1994; Kline, 2004). These critics argue that in a population of people, the null hypothesis is rarely if ever true and therefore the significance of a given test is mainly influenced by how many participants have been sampled. Also, critics who are skeptical about the value of null hypothesis significance testing point to limitations in the generalization of these findings to the target population. No matter how statistically significant a relation may be, the results of a study are generalizable only to people like those who participated in that particular research effort.

Skepticism about the value of statistics helps those who use them refine their procedures and keep their output in proper perspective. Nonetheless, most primary researchers use statistics and most would feel extremely uncomfortable about summarizing the results of their studies without some assistance (or credibility) supplied by statistical procedures.

In contrast to primary researchers, until recently, research synthesists were not obligated to apply any statistical techniques in the interpretation of cumulative results. Traditionally, synthesists interpreted data using intuitive rules of inference unknown even to themselves. Analysis methods were idiosyncratic to the perspective of that particular synthesist. Therefore, a description of the common rules of inference used in research syntheses was not possible.

The subjectivity in analysis of research literatures led to skepticism about the conclusions of many syntheses. To address the problem, methodologists introduced quantitative methods into the synthesis process. The methods use the research statistics contained in the individual studies as the primary data for the research synthesis.

META-ANALYSIS

I suggested in Chapter 1 that the two events that had the greatest influence on state-of-the-art research synthesis are the growth in the amount of research and the rapid advances in computerized research retrieval systems. A third major influence is the introduction of quantitative procedures, called *meta-analysis*, into the research synthesis process.

The explosion in social science research focused considerable attention on the lack of standardization in how synthesists arrived at general conclusions from series of related studies. For many topic areas, a separate verbal description of each relevant study was no longer possible. One traditional strategy was to focus on one or two studies chosen from dozens or hundreds. This strategy failed to portray accurately the accumulated state of knowledge. Certainly, in areas where dozens or hundreds of studies exist, synthesists must describe "prototype" studies so that readers understand the methods used by primary researchers.

However, relying on the *results* of prototype studies to represent the results of all studies may be seriously misleading. First, as we have seen, this type of selective attention is open to confirmatory bias: synthesists may highlight only studies that support their initial position. Second, selective attention to only a portion of all studies places little or imprecise weight on the volume of available tests. Presenting one or two studies without a cumulative analysis of the entire set of results gives the reader no estimate of the confidence that should be placed in a conclusion. Finally, selectively attending to evidence cannot give a good estimate of the strength of a relationship. As evidence on a topic accumulates, researchers become more interested in *how much* of a relationship exists between variables rather than simply *whether a relationship exists at all*.

Synthesists not employing meta-analysis also face problems when they consider the variation between the results of different studies. They will find distributions of results for studies sharing a particular procedural characteristic but varying on many other characteristics. Without meta-analysis, it is difficult to conclude accurately whether a procedural variation affected study outcomes; the variability in results obtained by any single method likely will overlap with the distributions of results of studies using a different method.

It seems, then, that there are many situations in which synthesists need to turn to meta-analytic techniques. The application of quantitative inference procedures to research synthesis was a necessary response to the expanding literature. If statistics are applied appropriately, they should enhance the validity of a synthesis' conclusions. Quantitative research synthesis is an extension of the same rules of inference required for rigorous data analysis in primary research. If primary researchers must specify quantitatively the relation of the data to their conclusions, the next users of the data should be required to do the same.

Meta-Analysis Comes of Age

Early on, meta-analysis was not without its critics, and some criticisms persist. The value of quantitative synthesis was questioned along lines similar to criticisms of primary data analysis (e.g., Barber, 1978; Mansfield & Bussey, 1977). However, much of the criticism stemmed less from issues in

meta-analysis than from more general inappropriate aggregation procedures, such as a lack of attention to moderating variables, that were incorrectly thought to be caused by the use of quantitative combining procedures
when they were really independent (and poor) decisions on the part of the
research synthesists.

Meta-analysis is now an accepted procedure and its application within the
social and medical sciences continues to grow. Today, literally thousands of
meta-analyses have been published, and the number published each year continues to grow larger. Figure 6.1 presents some evidence of this increasing
impact in the sciences and social sciences. The figure is based on entries in the
Science Citation Index Expanded and *Social Sciences Citation Index*,
according to the Web of Science reference database (retrieved August 20,
2008). It charts the growth in the number of citations to documents including
the terms "research synthesis," "systematic review," "research review," "literature
review," and/or "meta-analysis" in their title or topic during the years 1998 to
2007. The figure indicates that the total number of citations has risen every
year without exception. Clearly, the role that research syntheses and meta-
analysis play in our knowledge claims is large and growing larger.

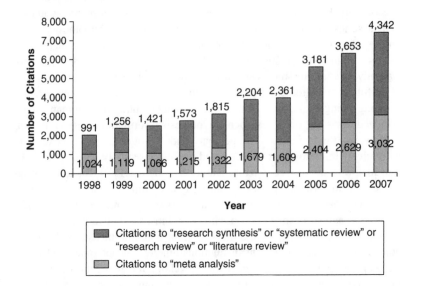

Figure 6.1   Web of Science Citations to "Research Synthesis" or "Systematic
Review" or "Research Review" or "Literature Review" or
"Meta-Analysis" for the Years 1998 to 2007

When Not to Do a Meta-Analysis

Much of this chapter will describe some basic meta-analysis procedures and how they are applied. However, it is important to state explicitly some circumstances for which the use of quantitative procedures in syntheses is *not* appropriate.

First, quantitative procedures are only applicable to research syntheses, not to literature reviews with other foci or goals (see Chapter 1). For instance, if a literature reviewer is interested in tracing the historical development of the concept "intrinsic motivation," it would not be necessary to do a quantitative synthesis. However, if the synthesist also intended to make inferences about whether different definitions of intrinsic motivation lead to different research results, then a quantitative summary of relevant research would be appropriate. Also, meta-analysis is not called for if the goal of the literature review is to critically or historically appraise the research study by study or to identify particular studies that are central to a field. In such instances, a proper integration likely would treat the results of studies as an emerging series of events, that is, it would use a historical approach to organizing the literature review rather than a statistical aggregation of the cumulative findings. However, if the synthesists are interested in whether the results of studies *change* over time, then meta-analysis would be appropriate.

Second, the basic premise behind the use of statistics in research syntheses is that a series of studies address an identical conceptual hypothesis. If the premises of a literature review do not include this assertion, then there is no need for cumulative statistics. Related to this point, a synthesist should not quantitatively combine studies at a broader conceptual level than readers would find useful. At an extreme, most social science research could be categorized as examining a single conceptual hypothesis—social stimuli affect human behavior. Indeed, for some purposes, such a hypothesis test might be very enlightening. However, the fact that "it can be done" should not be used as an excuse to quantitatively lump together concepts and hypotheses simply because methods are available to do so (see Kazdin, Durac, & Agteros, 1979, for a humorous treatment of this issue). Synthesists must pay attention to those distinctions in the literature that will be meaningful to the users of the synthesis. For example, in the meta-analysis of the effects of choice on intrinsic motivation, we did not combine study results across the nine different outcome measures. Doing so would have obscured important distinctions among the outcomes and might have been misleading. Instead, the highest level of data aggregation was within outcome types. Another instance of too much aggregation occurs when a hypothesis has been tested using different types of controls. For example, one study examining the effect of meeting weekly with a physical therapist on older adults' levels of activity might compare this treatment to a no-treatment control while another study compares it to a treatment in which participants receive written information. It might not be informative to statistically combine the results of these two studies. To what comparison does the combined effect relate? Synthesists might find that a distinction in the type of control group is important enough not to be obscured in a quantitative analysis (but separate meta-analyses might be done for each type of control group).

Third, under certain conditions, meta-analysis might not lead to the kinds of generalizations the synthesists wish to make. For example, cognitive psychologists or cognitive neuroscientists might argue that their methodologies typically afford good controls and reasonably secure findings because the things they study are not strongly affected by the context in which the study is conducted. Thus, the debate about effects in these areas of research usually occurs with reference to the choice of variables and their theoretical, or interpretive, significance. Under these circumstances, a synthesist might convincingly establish generalization using conceptual and theoretical bridges rather than statistical ones.

Finally, even if synthesists wish to summate statistical results across studies on the same topic, they may discover that only a few studies have been conducted and these use decidedly different methodologies, participants, and outcome measures. In circumstances where multiple methodological distinctions are confounded with one another and with differences in study results, the statistical combination of studies might mask important differences in research findings. In these instances, it may make the most sense not to use meta-analysis, or to conduct several discrete meta-analyses within the same synthesis, by combining only studies that share similar clusters of features, to make summary statements about relationships.

It is also important to point out that *the use of meta-analysis is no guarantee that the synthesist will be immune from all inferential errors.* The possibility always exists that the meta-analyst has incorrectly inferred a characteristic of the target population. As in the use of statistics in primary research, this can occur because the target population does not conform to the assumptions underlying the analysis techniques or because of the probabilistic nature of statistical findings. If you think that the population does not conform to the assumptions of the statistical test you have chosen, find a more appropriate test or eschew the use of meta-analysis altogether. In sum, then, an important question to ask when evaluating a research synthesis is,

Was an appropriate method used to combine and compare results across studies?

The Impact of Integrating Techniques on Synthesis Outcomes

In Chapter 1, I described a study I conducted with Robert Rosenthal (Cooper & Rosenthal, 1980) in which we demonstrated some of the differences in conclusions that might be drawn by nonquantitative synthesists and meta-analysts. In this study, graduate students and university faculty members were asked to evaluate the same set of studies, but half used quantitative procedures and half used whatever criteria appealed to them. We found that the meta-analysts thought there was more support for the sex-difference hypothesis and a larger relationship between variables than did the non-meta-analysts. Meta-analysts also tended to view future replications as less necessary than non-meta-analysts, although this finding did not reach statistical significance.

It is also likely that the different statistical procedures used by meta-analysts will create variance in synthesis conclusions. Several different paradigms have emerged for quantitatively integrating research with a traditional inference testing model (Hedges & Olkin, 1985; Hunter & Schmidt, 2004; Rosenthal, 1984), while others use a Bayesian perspective (Sutton, Abrams, Jones, Sheldon, & Song, 2000). The different techniques generate different output. Thus, the rules adopted to carry out quantitative analysis can differ from synthesist to synthesist and this may create differences in how synthesis results are interpreted. We can assume as well that the rules used by nonquantitative synthesists also vary but their inexplicit nature makes them difficult to compare formally.

MAIN EFFECTS AND
INTERACTIONS IN META-ANALYSIS

Before examining several of the quantitative techniques available to synthesists, it is important to take a closer look at some of the unique features of accumulated research results. In Chapter 2 on problem formulation, I pointed out that most research syntheses first focus on tests of main effects that were carried out in the primary studies. This is largely because conceptually related replications of main effects occur more frequently than tests of three or more interacting variables. So, for example, you are likely to find many more main-effect tests of whether choice influences intrinsic motivation than you are to find tests of interactions of whether this relationship is influenced by the number of choices given. Keep in mind that I am referring here to interaction tests within a single study, not your ability to test for the influence of number-of-choice at the synthesis level, because different studies have varied in the number of choices they provide in their test of the main effect.

It is not that interactions tested in primary studies cannot be combined. However, such replications are fewer and, we shall see in the next chapter, their interpretation can be a bit more complex. There are two different ways that interactions tested in primary research could be statistically combined across studies. First, the relationship strengths associated with each study's interaction test could be aggregated. An alternative strategy would be to aggregate separately the relationship of two of the interacting variables at each level of the third variable. For instance, assume there exists a set of studies in which the primary researchers tested whether the effect of choice in intrinsic motivation differed depending on the number of choices given to participants. The synthesists could generate an estimate of the difference in intrinsic motivation depending on the number of choices given by aggregating all motivation measures taken under conditions with one choice. They could do the same for measures taken after, say, two or three choices. This would probably be more useful and easily interpretable than a direct estimate of the magnitude of the interaction effect. However, in order to do this, the primary research reports must contain the information needed to isolate the different simple main effects. The synthesist might also have to group numbers of choices (say, three to five choices and six or more choices) in order to have enough tests to generate a good estimate.

Because main effects are most often the focus of meta-analysts and in many instances meta-analysts interested in interactions reduce them to simple effects, my discussion of the quantitative combining techniques will refer to main effects only. The generalization to meta-analyzing interactions is mathematically straightforward.

META-ANALYSIS AND
THE VARIATION AMONG STUDY RESULTS

In research syntheses, the most obvious feature of both main effects and interactions is that the results of the separate tests of the same relationship will vary from one study to the next. This variability is sometimes dramatic and requires us to ask where the variability comes from.

Sources of Variability in Research Findings

Differences in the outcomes of studies can be caused by two types of influences. The simplest cause is the one that is most often overlooked by nonquantitative synthesists—sampling variability. Even before the current interest in quantitative synthesis, Taveggia (1974) recognized this important influence:

A methodological principle overlooked by writers of . . . reviews is that research results are *probabilistic*. What this principle suggests is that, in and of themselves, the findings of any single research are meaningless—they may have occurred simply by chance. It also follows that if a large enough number of researches has been done on a particular topic, chance alone dictates that studies will exist that report inconsistent and contradictory findings! Thus, what appears to be contradictory may simply be the positive and negative details of a distribution of findings. (pp. 397–398)

Taveggia highlights one of the implications of using probability theory and sampling techniques to make inferences about populations.

As an example, suppose it was possible to measure the academic achievement of every American student. Also, suppose that if such a task were undertaken, it would be found that achievement was exactly equal for students who do and do not do homework—that is, exactly equal achievement test mean scores existed for the two subpopulations. Still, if 1000 samples of 50 homeworkers and 50 no-homeworkers were drawn from this population, very few comparisons between samples would reveal exactly equal group means. Further, if the sample means were compared statistically using a t-test and the $p < .05$ significance level (two-tailed), about 25 comparisons would show a significant difference favoring homeworkers while about 25 would favor no-homeworkers. This variation in results is an unavoidable consequence of the fact that the means estimated by sampling will vary somewhat from the true population values. And, just by chance alone, some comparisons will pair sample estimates that vary from their true population values by large amounts and in opposite directions.

In the example given, it is unlikely that you would be fooled into thinking anything but chance caused the result—after all, 950 comparisons would reveal nonsignificant differences and significant results would be distributed equally for both possible outcomes. However, in practice, the pattern of results is rarely this clear. As we discovered in the chapter on literature searching, you might not be aware of all null results because they are hard to find. Complicating matters further, even if an overall relation does exist between two variables (that is, the null hypothesis is false), some studies can still show significant results in a direction opposite to the relation in the population. To continue the example, if the average achievement of homeworkers is better than no-homeworkers, some comparisons of samples randomly drawn from the two subpopulations will still favor no-homeworkers, the number depending on the size of the relation, the size of the samples, and how many comparisons have been performed. In sum, then, one source of variance in the results of studies can be chance fluctuations due to the inexactness of estimates based on samples of people.

A second source of variance in study outcomes is of more interest to synthesists. This variance in results is created by differences in how studies are conducted. This variance is "added" to the variance due to sampling participants. Just as people are sampled, you can think of a set of studies as a sample of studies drawn from a population of all possible studies. And, because studies can be conducted in different ways (just as people can differ in personal attributes), a sample of studies also will exhibit chance variation from other possible samples of studies. For instance, the homework synthesists might find that studies comparing achievement among students who do and do not do homework have been conducted with students at different grade levels; with unit tests, class grades, or standardized tests as measures of achievement; and with an assortment of classes with different subject matters. Each of these differences in the studies' methods or contexts could create variation in study results and therefore could create results that differ randomly from another sample of studies drawn from the same population of studies. This variation will be "added to" the variation caused by the sampling of study participants from the population of participants.

It is also possible that this variation associated with study-level differences is systematically related to the variation in study results. For example, homework studies conducted with elementary school students might produce results that differ systematically from studies conducted with high school students. In Chapter 2, the notion of synthesis-generated evidence was introduced to describe what we learn when we find associations between study characteristics and study outcomes.

The existence of the two sources of variance in research results—that generated by sampling participants and that by sampling studies—raises an interesting dilemma. When contradictory findings occur within a set of studies, should you seek an explanation for them by attempting to identify systematic differences in results associated with differences in the methods used in studies? Or should you simply assume the contradictory findings were produced by variations due to sampling (of participants and/or study procedures)? Some tests have been devised to help you answer this question. In effect, these tests use *sampling error* as the null hypothesis. They estimate the amount of variance in findings that would be expected if sampling error alone were making the study findings different.[1] If the observed variation in results across studies is too great to be explained by sampling error alone, then the null hypothesis is rejected. It suggests that the notion that all the results were drawn from the same population of results can be rejected.

---

[1] And they permit you to choose whether you want the test to estimate sampling error based on participant variation alone or both participant and study variation. I will return to this choice later, when I discuss fixed-effect and random-effect models.

In the sections that follow, I will introduce some of the quantitative synthesis techniques that are available to you. I have chosen the techniques because they are relatively simple and broadly applicable. The treatment of each technique will be conceptual and introductory but detailed enough to permit you to perform a sound, if basic, meta-analysis. You can consult the primary sources cited in the text if (a) you want a more detailed description of these techniques and their variations, including how they are derived, and/or (b) your meta-analysis has some unique possibilities for exploring data in ways not covered here. For the discussion that follows, I have assumed you have a working knowledge of the basic inferential statistics employed in the social sciences.

Before I begin, though, there are three assumptions crucial to the validity of a conclusion based on an integration of statistical findings from individual studies. First and most obviously, *the individual findings that go into a cumulative analysis should all test the same comparison or estimate the same relationship.* Regardless of how conceptually broad or narrow your ideas might be, you should be comfortable with the assertion that the included statistical tests from the primary studies address the same question. Second, *the separate tests that go into the cumulative analysis must be independent of one another.* Identifying independent comparisons was discussed in Chapter 4, on gathering information from studies. You must take care to identify comparisons so that each one contains unique information about the hypothesis. Finally, you must believe that *the primary researchers made valid assumptions when they computed the results of their tests.* Thus, for example, if you want to combine the effect sizes resulting from comparisons between two means, you must assume that the observations in the two groups are independent and normally distributed, and that their variances are roughly equal to one another.

VOTE COUNTING

The simplest methods for combining independent statistical tests are the vote-counting methods. Vote counts can take into account the statistical significance of findings or focus only on the direction of the findings.

For the first method, the meta-analysts would take each finding[2] and place it into one of three categories: statistically significant findings in the expected direction (I will refer to these as positive findings), statistically significant

---

[2] Throughout this chapter and forward, I will use the terms *findings*, *studies*, and *comparisons* interchangeably to refer to the discrete, independent hypothesis tests or estimates of relationships that compose the input for a meta-analysis. I do this for exposition purposes, though sometimes these terms can have different meanings; for example, a study could contain more than one comparison between the same conditions.

findings in the unexpected (negative) direction, and nonsignificant findings, that is, ones that did not permit rejection of the null hypothesis. The meta-analysts then might establish the rule that the category with the largest number of findings tells what the direction of the relationship is in the target population.

This vote count of significant findings has much intuitive appeal and has been used quite often. However, the strategy is unacceptably conservative and often can lead to erroneous conclusions (Hedges & Olkin, 1980). The problem is that, using the traditional definition of statistical significance, chance alone should produce only about 5% of all findings, falsely indicating a significant effect. Therefore, much less than one-third positive and statistically significant findings might indicate a real difference exists in the target population. This vote-counting strategy requires that at least 34% of findings be positive and statistically significant before a result is declared a winner.

Let me illustrate just how conservative this approach is. Assume that a correlation of $r = .30$ exists between two variables in a population and 20 studies have been conducted with 40 people in each sample (this would not be an uncommon scenario in the social sciences). The probability that the vote count associated with this series of studies will conclude a positive relation exists—if the "plurality" decision rule described in the preceding is used—is less than 6 in 100. Thus, the vote count of significant findings could, and often does, lead vote counters to suggest accepting the null hypothesis, and perhaps abandoning fruitful theories or effective interventions when, in fact, no such conclusion is warranted.

Adjusting the frequencies of the three types of findings (positive, negative, and null) so that the true expected percentage of each finding (95% null and 2.5% significant in each direction) is taken into account solves one problem but it highlights another one. We have seen that null results are less likely to be reported by researchers and are less likely to be retrieved by synthesists. Therefore, if the appropriate expected values are used in a vote-count analysis, it could often occur that *both* positive and negative significant findings appear more frequently than would be expected by chance alone. Thus, it seems that using the frequency of nonsignificant findings in a vote count procedure is of dubious value.

An alternative vote-counting method is to compare the frequency of statistically significant positive findings against the frequency of significant negative ones. This procedure assumes that if the null hypothesis prevails in the population, then the frequency of significant positive and negative findings is expected to be equal. If the frequency of findings is found not to be equal, the null hypothesis can be rejected in favor of the prevailing direction. A problem with this vote-count approach is that the expected number of nonsignificant findings, even when the null hypothesis is not true, can still be much greater than the expected number of either positive or negative significant findings.

Therefore, this approach will ignore many findings (all nonsignificant ones) and will be very low in statistical power.

A final way to perform vote counts in research synthesis involves tallying the number of positive and negative findings regardless of their statistical significance. In this approach, the meta-analyst categorizes findings based solely on the direction of their outcome, ignoring their statistical significance. Again, if the null hypothesis is true—that is, if no relationship exists between the variables in the sampled population—we would expect the number of findings in each direction to be equal.

Once the number of results in each direction is counted, the meta-analyst can perform a simple sign test to discover if the cumulative result suggests that one direction occurs more frequently than would be expected by chance. The formula for computing the sign test is as follows:

$$Z_{vc} = \frac{(N_p) - (\frac{1}{2} N)}{\frac{1}{2} \sqrt{N}} \tag{1}$$

where

Z_{vc} = the standard normal deviate, or Z-score, for the overall series of findings;

N_p = the number of positive findings; and

N = the total number of findings (positive plus negative findings).

The Z_{vc} can be referred to a table of standard normal deviates to discover the probability (one-tailed) associated with the cumulative set of directional findings. If a two-tailed p-level is desired, the tabled p-value should be doubled. The values of Z associated with different p-levels are presented in Table 6.1. This sign test can be used in a vote count of either the simple direction of all findings or the direction of only significant findings, though using the direction of findings is recommended.

Suppose 25 of 36 comparisons find that older adults given an intervention to increase physical activity exhibited more subsequent activity than older adults in a no-intervention group. The probability that this many findings would be in one direction, given that in the target population (of intervention) there is equal activity exhibited by people in the two conditions, is $p < .02$ (two-tailed) associated with a Z_{vc} of 2.33. This result would lead the meta-analyst to conclude a positive intervention effect was supported by the series of findings.

The vote-count method that uses the direction of findings regardless of significance has the advantage of using information from all statistical findings.

Table 6.1   Standard Normal Deviation Distribution

Area z to −z	p-level 2-tailed	p-level 1-tailed	z-score
995	.005	.0025	2.807
.99	.01	.005	2.576
.985	.015	.0075	2.432
.98	.02	.01	2.326
.975	.025	.0125	2.241
.97	.03	.015	2.170
.965	.035	.0175	2.108
.96	.04	.02	2.054
.954	.046	.023	2.000
.95	.05	.025	1.960
.94	.06	.03	1.881
.92	.08	.04	1.751
.9	.1	.05	1.645
.85	.15	.075	1.440
.8	.2	.10	1.282
.75	.25	.125	1.150
.7	.3	.150	1.036
.6	.4	.20	0.842
.5	.5	.25	0.674
.4	.6	.30	0.524
.3	.7	.35	0.385
.2	.8	.40	0.253
.1	.9	.45	0.126

SOURCE: Noether (1971).

Still, it has some drawbacks. Similar to the other vote-count methods, it does not weight a finding's contribution to the overall result by its sample size. Thus, a finding based on 100 participants is given weight equal to one with 1000 participants. Further, the revealed magnitude of the relationship (for example, the impact of the treatment) in each finding is not considered—a finding showing a large increase in activity due to the intervention is given equal weight to one showing a small decrease in activity. Finally, a practical problem with the directional vote count is that primary researchers frequently do not report the direction of findings, especially if a comparison proved statistically nonsignificant.

Still, the vote count of directional findings can be an informative complement to other meta-analytic procedures, and can even be used to generate an estimate of the strength of a relationship. Bushman and Wang (2009) provide formulas and tables that can be used to estimate the size of a population relationship given that the meta-analysts know (a) the number of findings, (b) the direction of each finding, and (c) the sample size of each finding. For example, let's assume that each one of the 36 comparisons between an activity intervention and no-intervention group was based on a sample size of 50 participants. Using Bushman and Wang's technique, I find that when 25 of the 36 (69%) comparisons reveal more activity in the intervention group, the most likely population value for a correlation between group membership and activity is $r = .07$. Of course, this example is artificial because I assumed all the sample sizes were equal. The calculations are more complex in many circumstances, not only because sample sizes vary but also because you will have comparisons (votes) for which you have no direction. This complicates the estimating technique greatly. In the past, when we have used this technique (see Cooper, Charlton, Valentine, & Muhlenbruck, 2000), we conducted the analyses several times, using different sets of assumptions. In general, this technique should be used with caution and only in conjunction with other meta-analytic techniques that produce less tentative conclusions.

In sum, then, meta-analysts can perform vote counts to aggregate results across individual studies by comparing the number of directional findings and/or the number of significant directional findings. Both of these procedures will be very imprecise and conservative, that is, they will accept the null hypothesis when it should be rejected. The simple direction of results will not appear in many research reports in the first case, and nonsignificant findings cannot contribute to the analysis in the second case. Vote counts can be described in meta-analyses but should be used to draw inferences only in combination with more sensitive meta-analysis procedures.

Combining Significance Levels

One way to address the shortcomings of vote counts is to consider combining the exact probabilities associated with the results of each comparison. Rosenthal (1984) cataloged 16 methods for combining the results of inference tests so that an overall test of the null hypothesis can be obtained. By using the exact probabilities, the results of the combined analysis take into account the different sample sizes and relationship strengths found in each comparison. Thus, the combining-significance-levels procedure overcomes the improper weighting problems of the vote count. However, it has severe limitations of its own. First, as with vote counts, the combining-probability procedures answer the "yes or no?" questions but not the "how much?" question. Second, whereas the vote-count procedure is overly conservative, the combining-significance-levels procedure is extremely powerful. In fact, it is so powerful that for hypotheses or relationships that have generated a large number of findings, rejecting the null hypothesis is so likely that it becomes a rather uninformative exercise. For this reason, these procedures have largely fallen out of use.

MEASURING RELATIONSHIP STRENGTH

The primary function of the procedures described so far is to help meta-analysts accept or reject the null hypothesis. Until recently, most researchers interested in social theory and the impact of social interventions have been content to simply identify relations that have some explanatory value. The prevalence of this "yes or no" question was partly due to the relatively recent development of the social sciences. Social hypotheses were crudely stated first approximations to the truth. Social researchers rarely asked how potent theories or interventions were for explaining human behavior or how competing explanations compare with regard to their relative explanatory value. Today, as their theories and interventions are becoming more sophisticated, social scientists are more often making inquiries about the size of relationships.

Giving further impetus to the "how much?" question is a growing disenchantment with the null hypothesis significance test itself. As I noted earlier, whether or not a null hypothesis can be rejected is tied closely to the particular research project under scrutiny. If an ample number of participants are available or if a sensitive research design is employed, a rejection of the null hypothesis often is not surprising. This state of affairs becomes even more apparent in meta-analyses that include a combined significance level, where the power is great to detect even very small relations. A null hypothesis rejection, then, does not guarantee that an important social insight has been achieved.

Finally, when used in applied social research, the vote-count and combined-significance-level techniques give no information on whether the effect of a treatment or the relationship between variables is large or small, important or trivial. For example, if we find that the relationship between whether a participant (a) is a male and (b) believes that women share some culpability when a rape occurs is statistically significant and the correlation is $r = .01$, is this a strong enough relationship that it should influence how interventions are delivered? What if the result is statistically significant and the correlation is $r = .30$? This example suggests that the "yes or no?" question is often not the question of greatest importance. Instead, the important question is, "How much does the sex of the participant influence beliefs about rape?" The answer might be zero or it might suggest a small or large relationship. The answer to this question could help meta-analysts (and others) make recommendations about how best to construct rape-attitude interventions so they are most effective. Given these questions, meta-analysts would turn to the calculation of average effect sizes. Also, as we shall see shortly, the null hypothesis question, "Is the relationship different from zero?" can be answered by placing a confidence interval around the "how much?" estimate, removing the need for separate null hypothesis significance tests.

Definition of Effect Size

In order to answer meaningfully the "how much?" question, we must agree on definitions for the terms *magnitude of difference*, *relationship strength*, or what generally is called the *effect size*. Also, we need methods for quantitatively expressing these ideas once we have defined them. Jacob Cohen's (1988) book *Statistical Power Analysis for the Behavioral Sciences* presented what is now the standard definition of effect sizes. He defined an effect size as follows:

> Without intending any necessary implication of causality, it is convenient to use the phrase "effect size" to mean "*the degree* to which the phenomenon is present in the population," or "the degree to which the null hypothesis is false." By the above route it can now readily be clear that when the null hypothesis is false, it is false to some specific degree, i.e., *the effect size (ES) is some specific non-zero value in the population*. The larger this value, the greater the *degree* to which the phenomenon under study is manifested. (pp. 9–10)

Figure 6.2 presents three hypothetical relationships that illustrate Cohen's definition. Suppose the results come from three experiments comparing the effects of a physical activity intervention versus a no-treatment control on older adults' levels of activity. The top graph presents a null relationship. That is, the participants given the intervention have a mean and distribution of activity scores identical to the no-intervention participants. In the middle graph, the intervention group has a mean slightly higher than that of the no-intervention group, and in the bottom graph, the difference between intervention and no-intervention is even greater. A measure of effect size must express the three results so that greater departures from the null are associated with larger effect size values.

Cohen's (1988) book contains many different metrics for describing the strength of a relationship. Each effect size index is associated with a particular research design in a manner similar to *t*-tests being associated with two-group comparisons, *F*-tests associated with multiple-group designs, and chi-squares associated with frequency tables. Next, I will describe the three primary metrics used by the vast majority of meta-analysts. These metrics are generally useful— almost any research outcome can be expressed using one of them. For more detailed information on these effect-size metrics, as well as many others, the reader should consult Cohen's (1988) book or Kline (2004). However, Cohen describes several metrics that permit effect size estimates for multiple degree of freedom comparisons (e.g., a comparison involving more than two group means, such as three religious groups' attitudes toward rape), and these should not be used for reasons that will be discussed. Thus, my description of metrics is restricted to those commensurate with single degree of freedom tests.

The *d*-Index, or Standardized Mean Difference

The *d*-index, or *standardized mean difference* measure, of an effect size is appropriate to use when the difference between two means is being compared. The *d*-index is typically used in association with *t*-tests or *F*-tests based on a

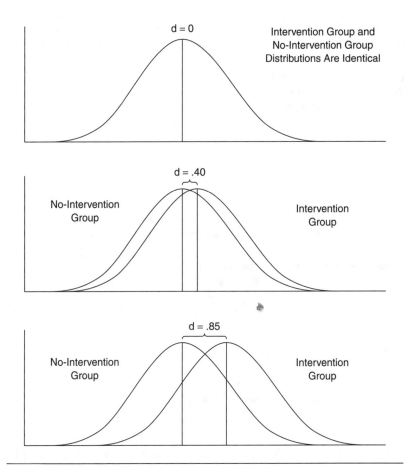

Figure 6.2 Three Hypothetical Relations Between an Exercise Intervention and a No-Intervention Group

comparison of two groups or experimental conditions. The d-index expresses the distance between the two group means in terms of their common standard deviation. By "common standard deviation," I mean that the assumption is made that if we could measure the standard deviations within the two subpopulations sampled into the two groups, we would find them to be equal.

The hypothetical research results for three studies presented in Figure 6.2 comparing an intervention meant to promote activity among older adults with a no-intervention condition illustrates the d-index. For the top graph, the research result supports the null hypothesis and the d-index equals zero. That is, there is no distance between the exercise intervention and no-intervention group means. The middle research result reveals a d-index of .40, that is, the mean of the intervention group lays 4/10ths of a standard deviation to the right of the no-intervention group's mean. In the third example, a d-index of .85 is portrayed. Here, the intervention group mean rests 85/100ths of a standard deviation to the right of the mean of the no-intervention group.

Calculating the d-index is simple. The formula is as follows:

$$d = \frac{\overline{X}_1 - \overline{X}_2}{SD_{\text{within}}} \tag{2}$$

where

X_1 and X_2 = the two group means; and

SD_{within} = the estimated common standard deviation of the two groups.

To estimate SD_{within}, you can use the formula

$$SD_{\text{within}} = \sqrt{\frac{(n_1 - 1)SD_1^2 + (n_2 - 1)SD_2^2}{n_1 + n_2 - 2}} \tag{3}$$

where

SD_1 and SD_2 = the standard deviations of Group X_1 and Group X_2, respectively, and

n_1 and n_2 = the sample sizes in Group X_1 and Group X_2, respectively.

The d-index is not only simple to compute but it is also scale free. That is, the standard deviation adjustment in the denominator of the formula means that studies using different measurement scales can be compared or combined. So, for example, if one study of the exercise intervention's effect used the number of times older adults went to the gym as the outcome measure and another study used their lung capacity as the outcome, it would make little sense to combine the two raw differences between the intervention and no-intervention group means—that is, combine the numerators of the d-index formula. However, it makes much sense to combine results if we first convert each to a standardized mean difference. Then, if we assume the two outcomes measure the same underlying *conceptual* variable (i.e., level of activity), the two outcomes have been transformed to a common metric.

The variance of the d-index can be closely approximated using the following formula:

$$v_d = \frac{n_1 + n_2}{n_1 n_2} + \frac{d^2}{2(n_1 + n_2)} \tag{4}$$

where

all variables are defined as above.

The 95% confidence interval for the d-index is then computed as $d - 1.95$ $\sqrt{v_d} \leq d \geq d + 1.95 \sqrt{v_d}$.

In many instances, meta-analysts will find that primary researchers do not report the means and standard deviations of the separate groups but do report the t-test or F-test associated with the difference in means, and the direction of their relationship. In such cases, Rosenthal (1984) has provided a computation formula that closely approximates the d-index and does not require the meta-analysts to have specific means and standard deviations. This formula is as follows:

$$d = \frac{2t}{\sqrt{df_{error}}} \tag{5}$$

where

t = the value of the t-test for the associated comparison, and

df_{error} = the degrees of freedom associated with the error term of the t-test ($n_1 + n_2 - 2$).

In instances where F-tests with a single degree of freedom in the numerator are reported, the square root of the F-value (i.e., $t = \sqrt{F}$) and its denominator degrees of freedom can be substituted in the above formula. Again, these approximations of the d-index assume the meta-analysts know the direction of the mean difference.

The r-Index, or Correlation Coefficient

A second effect size, the r-index, is simply the Pearson product-moment *correlation coefficient*. The r-index is the most appropriate metric for expressing an effect size when the researcher is interested in describing the relationship between two continuous variables. So, for example, if we are interested in the relationship between participants' amount of exposure to pornography and their degree of belief that women share culpability for rape, we would used the correlation coefficient to estimate this association.

The r-index is familiar to most social scientists but the formula for it requires both the variances and covariances of the two continuous variables, so it rarely can be computed from information typically presented in primary research reports. Luckily, primary researchers do report their r-indexes in most instances where they are applicable. However, if only the value of the t-test associated with the r-index is given, the r-index can be calculated using the following formula:

$$r = \sqrt{\frac{t^2}{t^2 + df_{\text{error}}}} \tag{6}$$

where

all terms are defined as above.

The variance of the r-index can be calculated using the following formula:

$$v_r = \frac{(1 - r^2)^2}{n - 1} \tag{7}$$

and can be used to calculate the 95% confidence interval as $r - 1.95 \sqrt{v_r} \leq r \geq r + 1.95 \sqrt{v_r}$.

OR, or the Odds Ratio

A third effect size metric is applicable when both variables are dichotomous, for example, when older adults either receive or do not receive a physical activity treatment and the outcome variable is whether or not they experience a heart problem within the next 5 years. This measure of effect, called an *odds ratio*, is used often in medical research, where researchers are frequently interested in the effect of a treatment on mortality or the appearance or disappearance of disease. It is used also in criminal justice research where the outcome variable might be recidivism or in education studies when, for example, high school graduation is the outcome of interest.

As its name implies, the odds ratio describes the relationship between two sets of odds. For example, suppose meta-analysts come across a study of the effects of an intervention promoting activity among older adults. Two hundred people either received or did not receive the intervention and 5 years later they were asked whether they had or had not experienced a problem with their heart. The results of the study were as follows:

	Intervention	No Intervention
No Heart Problem	75	60
Heart Problem	25	40

In order to calculate an odds ratio, the meta-analysts first determines that the odds of a participant in the intervention condition having a heart problem were 3 to 1 (75 to 25). The odds of having a heart problem in the no-intervention condition were 1.5 to 1 (60 to 40). In this case, the odds ratio is 2, meaning the odds of experiencing a heart problem in the no-intervention group were twice those in the intervention group. When the odds are the same in both conditions (that is, when the null hypothesis is true), the odds ratio will be 1. The odds ratio can be calculated more directly from the table by dividing the product of the main diagonal elements by the product of the off-diagonal elements, in our example (75×40)/(60×25).

Because the odds ratio is used less often in the social sciences, it will not be treated extensively in the next section. However, most of the techniques discussed in the next section are easily adapted to its use. There are many other metrics that can be used when two dichotomous variables are being related to one another; Fleiss and Berlin (2009) provide an overview of numerous effect size estimates gauging the relationship between two dichotomous variables.

Practical Issues in Estimating Effect Sizes

The formulas for calculating effect sizes are straightforward. In practice, however, meta-analysts face many technical issues when they attempt to calculate a magnitude of effect. The most important of these is missing data, which I discussed in Chapter 4 and will return to again in the next chapter. Other issues arise because different studies use somewhat different designs and because of some unique characteristics of the effect size metrics themselves. I will describe a few of these.

Choosing a metric when studies have different designs. Some primary researchers use parametric statistics (those that assume normal distributions) and others use nonparametric statistics (ones that make no assumptions about distributions) to test and express the same relationship. For instance, this would be the case if one researcher measured intrinsic motivation in a choice study by calculating the average time each participant spent on the chosen task during a free-play period (a continuous variable dictating the use of parametric tests), and another simply recorded whether each participant did or did not choose the task during a free-play period (a dichotomous variable dictating use of nonparametric tests). Most often, statistical techniques based on one set of assumptions will predominate greatly over the other. Then, the statistics from the lesser-used approach can be converted to their dominant-approach equivalents and aggregated as though they shared the dominant approach's assumptions. As long as the number of these conversions is small, there will be no great distortion of results. If there are substantive reasons to distinguish between the outcome variables or if the split between parametric and nonparametric tests is relatively even, the two sets of studies should be examined separately.

Related to the issues of studies that use different statistical procedures is that different primary researchers sometimes convert continuous variables to dichotomous ones. For instance, some primary researchers studying the relation between individual differences and attitudes toward rape might dichotomize personality scores into "high" and "low" groups. Then, they might use a *t*-test to determine if the "high" and "low" group means were different on a continuous measure of attitudes toward rape. This suggests that a *d*-index would be most appropriate to estimate the relation. However, other researchers might leave the same personality scale in its continuous form and report the correlate between them. Conveniently, the different effect size metrics are easily converted from one to the other. The *r*-index can be transformed into a *d*-index using the following formula:

$$d = \frac{2r}{\sqrt{1 - r^2}} \tag{8}$$

or the *d*-index into the *r*-index using

$$r = \frac{d}{\sqrt{d^2 + a}} \tag{9}$$

Table 6.2   Equivalences of the d-Index and r-Index

d	r
0	.000
.1	.050
.2	.100
.3	.148
.4	.196
.5	.243
.6	.287
.7	.330
.8	.371
.9	.410
1.0	.447
1.1	.482
1.2	.514
1.3	.545
1.4	.573
1.5	.600
1.6	.625
1.7	.648
1.8	.669
1.9	.689
2.0	.707
2.2	.740
2.4	.768
2.6	.793
2.8	.814
3.0	.832
3.2	.848
3.4	.862
3.6	.874
3.8	.885
4.0	.894

SOURCE: Adapted from Cohen (1988). Copyright 1988 by Taylor & Francis Group LLC, p. 22. Adapted with permission.

where

a = a correction factor to adjust for different sample sizes between the two groups.

This correction factor, a, can be calculated using this formula:

$$a = \frac{(n_1 + n_2)^2}{n_1 n_2} \qquad (10)$$

where

all variables are defined as above.

If the sample sizes are equal, the correction factor will always be 4. Table 6.2 provides the equivalences when the sample sizes are equal.

When a chi-square statistic associated with a 2×2 contingency table is given, the r-index can be estimated as follows:

$$r = \sqrt{\frac{\chi^2}{n}} \qquad (11)$$

where

χ^2 = the chi-square value associated with the comparison, and

n = the total number of observations in the comparison.

Cohen (1988) also gives an effect size (not an odds ratio), called the w-index, associated with chi-squares. This metric is identical to an r-index when $df = 1$.

Even though metrics can be converted easily, meta-analysts still must pick a single metric in which to describe their results. The choice of how to express the effect size should be determined by which metric best fits with the measurement and design characteristics of the variables under consideration. So, *the effect size metric used should be based on the characteristics of the conceptual variables.* Therefore, an important question to ask when evaluating a research synthesis is,

---

If a meta-analysis was performed, was an appropriate effect size metric used?

When we related individual differences to rape attitudes, the *r*-index was appropriate most often (e.g., when personality dimensions were of interest) because the two variables were conceptually continuous in nature. If a study created two "artificial" groups by dichotomizing the continuous individual difference measure into high and low scorers, we would calculate a *d*-index comparing the group means, then convert it to an *r*-index using formula (9).

Choosing an estimate for the standard deviation of the d-index. Clearly, an important influence on the *d*-index is the size of the standard deviation used to estimate the variance around group means. And I mentioned previously that the *d*-index formula is based on the assumption that the standard deviations are equal in the two groups. Many times, meta-analysts have no choice but to make this assumption because the *d*-index must be estimated from an associated *t*-test or *F*-test, which also makes this assumption. However, in instances where information about standard deviations is available and they appear to be unequal, the meta-analyst can choose one group's standard deviation to serve as the denominator in the *d*-index for purposes of standardizing the mean difference. For example, if an intervention and no-intervention group are being compared and the standard deviations appear to be different (perhaps because the intervention creates variance in outcomes as well as shifts the group mean), then the control group standard deviation should be used.

Estimating effect sizes when studies compare more than two groups. Suppose we find a study of interventions to promote physical activity that compared three groups, say, an exercise group, an information group, and a no-intervention group. In this instance, we likely would calculate two *d*-indexes, one comparing exercise to no-intervention and another comparing information to no-intervention (we could also consider comparing the two different interventions, if this were the focus of our meta-analysis). These two *d*-indexes are not statistically independent, since both rely on the means and standard deviations of the same no-intervention group. However, this complicating factor is preferable to the alternative strategy of using an effect size metric associated with a multiple-group inference test. Here is why.

One effect size metric that can be used when more than two groups are being compared simultaneously involves calculating the percentage of variance in the dependent variable explained by group membership. This effect size has the initially appealing characteristic that it can be used regardless of the number of groups in the study (indeed, it can be used with two continuous measures as well). So, it is very generally applicable. However, it has the unappealing characteristic that the resulting effect size tells us nothing about which of the multiple conditions has the highest mean, or more specifically, how the values of the means are ordered and how much each differs from the others. So, identical percentages of variance explained can result from lots of different rank ordering of, and distances between, the group means. It is then impossible for the meta-analysts to draw conclusions about how the different groups "stack up" relative to one another. In fact, the results might cancel one another out if we looked at single degree of freedom comparisons, suggesting no differences between groups. The percentage of variance explained would not catch this. This is why it is rarely, if ever, used by meta-analysts.

Estimating effect sizes from analyses including multiple predictor variables. Another way that research design influences effect sizes involves the number of factors employed in the primary data analysis procedures. For example, a primary researcher testing the effect of homework versus no-homework on achievement might also include individual difference variables—such as the sex or intelligence of the students, or even their pretest scores on the outcome measure—in a multifactored analysis of variance. The primary researcher also might not report the simple means and standard deviations for the homework and no-homework groups. Meta-analysts then are faced with two choices.

First, they can calculate an effect size estimate based on the F-test reported by the researchers. However, this test uses an error term that has been reduced by the inclusion of the extra factors. This will reduce the size of the estimate of S_{within} in the d-index formula. This approach creates the problem that different effect sizes going into the same quantitative synthesis are likely to be known to differ in a systematic way, that is, in how the within-group standard deviation has been calculated. Likely, if the additional factors in the analysis are associated with variance in the achievement outcome measure, then this study will produce a larger effect size for homework than a study that did not include these additional factors in the analysis, all else being equal.

A second approach is to attempt to retrieve the standard deviations that would have occurred had all the extraneous factors been ignored (i.e., not been included in the error term used to calculate the F-test). Whenever possible, this strategy should be used, that is, an attempt should be made to calculate the effect size as though the comparison of interest was the sole comparison in the analysis. The best way to do this is to contact the authors of the primary research and see if they will share the data you need. Perhaps a more realistic approach is to adjust the effect size by estimating the relationships between the additional variables and the outcome measure. Borenstein (2009) presents some ways to calculate these estimates. The problem here, of course, is that the resulting estimate of the effect size is only as good as the estimates of the relationships used to make adjustments.

Practically speaking, then, it is often difficult for meta-analysts to retrieve the unadjusted standard deviation estimates for the two groups if they are not given in the primary research report, nor is a simple t-test or 1 degree of freedom F-test. In such cases, when you look for influences on study outcomes, you should either (a) leave these estimates out, if they are few, or (b) examine whether or not the number of factors included in the analysis is associated with the size of the effect. If a relation is found, you should report separately the results obtained from analyses of studies that used only the single factor of interest. So, for example, in the meta-analysis of homework research, we found one experimental study that reported the effect of homework only in an analysis of covariance with several covariates. This study's results could not be combined with studies that did not adjust for covariates. We also found other studies that presented results regarding the relation between time spent on homework and achievement only in multiple regression analyses. These could not be combined with the studies that presented simple bivariate correlations.

Removing bias from small sample estimates of population values. A sample statistic—be it an effect size, a mean, or a standard deviation—typically is based on measurements taken on a small number of people drawn from a larger population. These sample statistics will differ in known ways from the values obtained if we could measure every person in the population. Meta-analysts have devised ways to adjust for the known biases that occur because effect size estimates based on samples are not always true reflections of their underlying population values.

Hedges (1980) showed that the d-index based on small samples may slightly overestimate the size of an effect in the population. However, the bias is minimal if the sample size is more than 20. If meta-analysts are calculating d-indexes from primary research based on samples smaller than 20, Hedges' (1980) correction factor should be applied. Some ways of calculating odds ratios also can lead to over- or underestimates (see Fleiss & Berlin, 2009).

In addition to the small sample bias in effect size estimates, meta-analysts should always be cautious in interpreting any effect size based on a small number of data points. When samples are small, a single extreme value can create an exceptionally large effect size estimate.

Normalizing the distribution of r-*indexes.* When r-indexes are large, that is, when they estimate population values very different from zero, they will exhibit nonnormal sampling distributions. This occurs because r-indexes are limited to values between +1.00 and −1.00. Therefore, as a population value approaches either of these limits, the range of possible values for a sample estimate will be restricted on the tail toward the approached limit (see Shadish & Haddock, 2009).

To adjust for this, most meta-analysts convert r-indexes to their associated z-scores before the effect size estimates are combined or tested for moderators. The z-scores have no limiting value and are normally distributed. In essence, the transformation "stretches" the restricted tail of the distribution and restores the bell shape of the curve. Once an average z-score has been calculated, it can be converted back to an r-index. An examination of the r-to-z transformations presented in Table 6.3 reveals that the two values are nearly identical until $r = .25$. However, when the r-index equals .50, the associated z-score equals .55, and when the r-index equals .8, the associated z-score equals 1.1.

Adjusting for the impact of methodological artifacts. The magnitude of an effect size will also be influenced by the presence of methodological artifacts in the primary data collection procedures. Hunter and Schmidt (2004) described many of these artifacts—including, for example, restrictions in the range of sampled values and lack of reliability in measurements—and how they can be addressed in meta-analyses.

In the case of less reliable measures, measures with more error are less sensitive for detecting relationships involving its conceptual variable. For example, assume two personality dimensions have equal "true" relationships with attitudes toward rape. However, if one personality variable is measured with more error than the other, this less reliable measure will produce a smaller correlation, all else being equal. So the meta-analysts might estimate the impact of the reliability of measures on effect sizes by obtaining the reliabilities (e.g., internal consistencies) of the various measures. Using procedures described by Hunter and Schmidt (2004), the meta-analyst could estimate what effect sizes would be if all measures were perfectly reliable. Or the reliabilities can be used in moderator analyses to see if effect sizes correlate with the reliability of the measures.

Table 6.3 r-to-z Transformations

r	z	r	z	r	z	r	z	r	z
.000	.000	.200	.203	.400	.424	.600	.693	.800	1.099
.005	.005	.205	.208	.405	.430	.605	.701	.805	1.113
.010	.010	.210	.213	.410	.436	.610	.709	.810	1.127
.015	.015	.215	.218	.415	.442	.615	.717	.815	1.142
.020	.020	.220	.224	.420	.448	.620	.725	.820	1.157
.025	.025	.225	.229	.425	.454	.625	.733	.825	1.172
.030	.030	.230	.234	.430	.460	.630	.741	.830	1.188
.035	.035	.235	.239	.435	.466	.635	.750	.835	1.204
.040	.040	.240	.245	.440	.472	.640	.758	.840	1.221
.045	.045	.245	.250	.445	.478	.645	.767	.845	1.238
.050	.050	.250	.255	.450	.485	.650	.775	.850	1.256
.055	.055	.255	.261	.455	.491	.655	.784	.855	1.274
.060	.060	.260	.266	.460	.497	.660	.793	.860	1.293
.065	.065	.265	.271	.465	.504	.665	.802	.865	1.313
.070	.070	.270	.277	.470	.510	.670	.811	.870	1.333
.075	.075	.275	.282	.475	.517	.675	.820	.875	1.354
.080	.080	.280	.288	.480	.523	.680	.829	.880	1.376
.085	.085	.285	.293	.485	.530	.685	.838	.885	1.398
.090	.090	.290	.299	.490	.536	.690	.848	.890	1.422
.095	.095	.295	.304	.495	.543	.695	.858	.895	1.447
.100	.100	.300	.310	.500	.549	.700	.867	.900	1.472
.105	.105	.305	.315	.505	.556	.705	.877	.905	1.499
.110	.110	.310	.321	.510	.563	.710	.887	.910	1.528
.115	.116	.315	.326	.515	.570	.715	.897	.915	1.557
.120	.121	.320	.332	.520	.576	.720	.908	.920	1.589

r	z	r	z	r	z	r	z	r	z
.125	.126	.325	.337	.525	.583	.725	.918	.925	1.623
.130	.131	.330	.343	.530	.590	.730	.929	.930	1.658
.135	.136	.335	.348	.535	.597	.735	.940	.935	1.697
.140	.141	.340	.354	.540	.604	.740	.950	.940	1.738
.145	.146	.345	.360	.545	.611	.745	.962	.945	1.783
.150	.151	.350	.365	.550	.618	.750	.973	.950	1.832
.155	.156	.355	.371	.555	.626	.755	.984	.955	1.886
.160	.161	.360	.377	.560	.633	.760	.996	.960	1.946
.165	.167	.365	.383	.565	.640	.765	1.008	.965	2.014
.170	.172	.370	.388	.570	.648	.770	1.020	.970	2.092
.175	.177	.375	.394	.575	.655	.775	1.033	.975	2.185
.180	.182	.380	.400	.580	.662	.780	1.045	.980	2.298
.185	.187	.385	.406	.585	.670	.785	1.058	.985	2.443
.190	.192	.390	.412	.590	.678	.790	1.071	.990	2.647
.195	.198	.395	.418	.595	.685	.795	1.085	.995	2.994

Coding Effect Sizes

The statistics you need to calculate effect sizes and all the other statistics described next should be collected as part of your more general coding procedures. For example, Table 6.4 provides a simple example of the information on the statistical results of studies that might be collected by study coders. Here, the example involves experimental studies of the effects of homework on achievement. Most meta-analyses in which two conditions are being compared (variations in task choice, participation versus no participation in an activity intervention) would look very similar. Coding sheets for correlational studies or studies relating two dichotomous variables would also be similar, but these might be even a bit simpler. Some of the information on the coding sheet may never be used and much of this information will be left blank. For example, when studies give the means and standard deviations, you may never use the information on the *t*-test. However, when means and/or standard deviations are

Table 6.4   An Example Coding Sheet for the Statistical Outcomes of Experimental
Studies on the Effects of Homework on Achievement

Effect Size Estimate	
E1. What was the effect of homework on the achievement measure? + = positive – = negative	___
E2. Information about each experimental group (Note. Leave blank if not reported. *M* = Mean. *SD* = standard deviation.)	
Homework Group	
a. Pretest *M* on outcome (if any)	___ ___ ___ . ___ ___
b. Pretest *SD*	___ ___ ___ . ___ ___
c. Posttest *M* on outcome	___ ___ ___ . ___ ___
d. Posttest *SD*	___ ___ ___ . ___ ___
e. Sample size	___ ___ ___
No-Homework Group	
f. Pretest *M* on outcome (if any)	___ ___ ___ . ___ ___
g. Pretest *SD*	___ ___ ___ . ___ ___
h. Posttest *M* on outcome	___ ___ ___ . ___ ___
i. Posttest *SD*	___ ___ ___ . ___ ___
j. Sample size	___ ___ ___
k. Total sample size (if not given for each group separately)	___ ___ ___
E3. Information about null hypothesis significance tests	
a. Independent *t*-statistic (or $\sqrt{}$ of *F*-test in one-factor ANOVA)	___ ___ . ___ ___
b. Degrees of freedom for test	___ ___ ___

Effect Size Estimate	
c. p-value from test	< .___ ___ ___
d. Dependent t-statistic	___ ___ . ___ ___
e. Degrees of freedom for test	___ ___ ___
f. p-value from test	< .___ ___ ___
g. F-statistic (when included in a multifactored ANOVA)	___ ___ . ___ ___
h. Degrees of freedom for denominator of F-test	___ ___ ___
i. p-value from F-test	< .___ ___ ___
j. # of variables in multifactored ANOVA	___

missing, you will need the information on the null hypothesis significance test to calculate the d-index. Or if you want to examine whether the standard deviations in the experimental and control group are roughly equal, you will need this regardless of how you calculate the d-index. So, you might not know exactly what information is important to you until after you have begun your analysis.

COMBINING EFFECT SIZES ACROSS STUDIES

Once each effect size has been calculated, the meta-analysts next average the effects that estimate the same comparison or relationship. It is generally accepted that these averages should weight the individual effect sizes based on the number of participants in their respective samples. This is because larger samples give more precise population estimates. For example, a d-index or r-index based on 500 participants will give a more precise estimate of its underlying population effect size than will an estimate based on 50 participants. The average effect size should reflect this fact. So, while unweighted average effect sizes are sometimes presented in meta-analyses, they are typically accompanied by weighted averages.

One way to take the precision of the effect size estimate into account when calculating an average effect size is to multiply each estimate by its sample size and then divide the sum of these products by the sum of the sample sizes. However, there is a more precise procedure, described in detail by Hedges and

Olkin (1985), which has many advantages but also involves more complicated calculations.

The d-Index

For the d-index, this procedure first requires the meta-analyst to calculate a weighting factor, w_i, which is the inverse of the variance associated with each d-index estimate. It can be calculated taking the inverse of the result of formula (4), or more directly by using the following formula:

$$w_i = \frac{2(n_{i1} + n_{i2})n_{i1}n_{i2}}{2(n_{i1} + n_{i2})^2 + n_{i1}n_{i2}d_i^2} \qquad (12)$$

where

n_{i1} and n_{i2} = the number of data points in Group 1 and Group 2 of Study i; and

d_i = the d-index of the comparison under consideration.

While the formula for w_i looks imposing, it is really a simple arithmetic manipulation of three numbers available whenever a d-index is calculated. It also is easy to program a statistical software package to perform the necessary calculation. Programs designed to perform meta-analysis will do it for you routinely.

Table 6.5 presents the group sample sizes, d-indexes, and weighting factors (the w_is) associated with the results of seven hypothetical comparisons. Let us assume the seven comparisons come from experiments that compared the effects of homework versus no homework on a measure of academic achievement. All seven of the experiments produced results favoring homework assignments.

To further demystify the weighting factor, note in Table 6.5 that its values equal approximately half the average sample size in a group (it becomes less similar to half the average sample size as the sample sizes in the two groups become more different). It should not be surprising, then, that the next step in obtaining a weighted average effect size involves multiplying each d-index by its associated w_i and dividing the sum of these products by the sum of the weights. This is done using the following formula:

$$d. = \frac{\sum_{i=1}^{k} d_i w_i}{\sum_{i=1}^{k} w_i} \qquad (13)$$

where

k = the total number of comparisons and all other terms are defined as above.

Table 6.5 shows the average weighted d-index for the seven comparisons is $d = .115$.

Table 6.5 An Example of d-Index Estimation and Tests of Homogeneity

Study	n_{i1}	n_{i2}	d_i	w_i	$d_i^2 w_i$	$d_i w_i$	Q_b Grouping
1	259	265	.02	130.98	.052	2.619	A
2	57	62	.07	29.68	.145	2.078	A
3	43	50	.24	22.95	1.322	5.509	A
4	230	228	.11	114.32	1.383	12.576	A
5	296	291	.09	146.59	1.187	13.193	B
6	129	131	.32	64.17	6.571	20.536	B
7	69	74	.17	35.58	1.028	6.048	B
Σ	1083	1101	1.02	544.27	11.69	62.56	

NOTE: Weighted average $d. = 62.56/544.27 = +.115$;

$CI_{d.95\%} = .115 \pm 1.96 \sqrt{\dfrac{1}{544.27}} = .115 \pm .084$;

$Q_t = 11.69 - \dfrac{62.56^2}{544.27} = 4.5$;

$Q_w = 1.16 + 2.36 = 3.52$;

$Q_b = 4.5 - 3.52 = .98$.

One advantage of using the w_is as weights, rather than sample sizes, is that the w_is can also be used to generate a confidence interval around the average effect size estimate. To do this, an estimated variance for the average effect size must be calculated. First, the inverse of the sum of the w_is is found. Then, the square root of this variance is multiplied by the Z-score associated with the confidence interval of interest. Thus, the formula for a 95% confidence interval is

$$CI_{d.95\%} = d. \pm \sqrt{\dfrac{1}{\sum\limits_{i=1}^{k} w_i}} \qquad (14)$$

where all terms are defined as above.

Table 6.5 reveals that the 95% confidence interval for the seven homework comparisons encompasses values of the d-index .084 above and below the average d-index. Thus, we expect 95% of estimates of this effect to fall between $d = .031$ and $d = .199$. Note that this interval does not contain the value $d = 0$. It is this information that can be taken as a test of the null hypothesis that no relation exists in the population, in place of directly combining the significance levels of null hypothesis tests. In this example, we would reject the null hypothesis that there was no difference in achievement between students who did and did not do homework.

The r-Index

The procedure for finding the average weighted r-index and its associated confidence interval is similar. Here, I will illustrate how to do this when each r-index is first transformed to its corresponding z-score, z_i. In this case, the following formula is applied:

$$z. = \frac{\sum_{i=1}^{k} (n_i - 3)z_i}{\sum_{i=1}^{k} (n_i - 3)} \qquad (15)$$

where

n_i = the total sample size for the ith comparison and

all other terms are defined as above.

Notice that formulas for calculating average effect sizes all follow the same form: multiply the effect size by a weight, sum the products, and divide by the sum of the weights. So, to combine the r-indexes directly, multiply each by its weighting factor—in this case, like the d-index, it is the inverse of its variance (formula [7])—and divide the sum of this product by the sum of the weights, just as was done for the d-index.

To obtain a confidence interval for the average z-score, the formula is

$$CIz_{95\%} = z. \pm \frac{1.96}{\sqrt{\sum_{i=1}^{k} (n_i - 3)}} \qquad (16)$$

To obtain a confidence interval for the r-indexes combined directly, simply substitute the sum of the weights in the denominator of the formula [16]. Table 6.3 presents the r-to-z transformations. Once the confidence interval has been established, meta-analysts can refer back to Table 6.3 to retrieve the r-indexes corresponding to the average r-index and the limits of the confidence interval.

Table 6.6 presents an example of how average r-indexes are calculated. For example, the six correlations might come from studies relating the amount of time students report spending on homework and their score on an achievement test. The average z_i was .207 with the 95% confidence interval ranging from .195 to .219. Note that this confidence interval is quite narrow. This is because the effect size estimates are based on large samples. Note also that the r-to-z transformations result in only minor changes in two of the r-index values. This would not be the case had the r-indexes been larger. As with the earlier example, $z_i = 0$ is not contained in the confidence interval. Therefore, we can reject the null hypothesis that there is no relation between the amount of time students reported spending on homework and their level of achievement.

Table 6.6   An Example of r-Index (Transformed to z) Estimation and Tests of Homogeneity

Study	n_i	r_i	z_i	$n_i - 3$	$(n_i - 3)z_i$	$(n_i - 3)z_i^2$	Q_b Grouping
1	3,505	.06	.06	3,502	210.12	12.61	A
2	3,606	.12	.12	3,603	432.36	51.88	A
3	4,157	.22	.22	4,154	913.88	201.05	A
4	1,021	.08	.08	1,018	81.44	6.52	B
5	1,955	.27	.28	1,952	546.56	153.04	B
6	12,146	.26	.27	12,143	3278.61	885.22	B
Σ	26,390	1.01	1.03	26,372	5462.97	1310.32	

NOTE: Weighted average $z. = \dfrac{5462.97}{26,372} = .207$;

$CI_{z.95\%} = .207 \pm 1.96/\sqrt{26,372} = .207 \pm .012$;

$Q_t = 1310.32 - \dfrac{(5462.97)^2}{26,372} = 178.66$;

$Q_w = 34.95 + 50.40 = 85.35$;

$Q_b = 178.66 - 85.35 = 93.31$.

In sum, each of the effect size metrics can be averaged across studies and confidence intervals can be placed around these mean estimates. Therefore, when evaluating a research synthesis, it is important to ask,

> *If a meta-analysis was performed, (a) were average effect sizes and confidence intervals reported and (b) was an appropriate model used to estimate the independent effects and the error in effect sizes?*

The Synthesis Examples

Both the standardized mean difference and the correlation coefficient were used in the synthesis examples. In the synthesis of the effects of homework, the d-index was used to express the findings from comparisons that purposively manipulated homework and then measured the difference in terms of unit test scores. The weighted average d-index across five studies was $d. = .60$, with a 95% confidence interval encompassing values from $d = .38$ to $d = .82$. Clearly, then, the null hypothesis could be rejected. The homework research synthesis also used correlation coefficients to estimate the relationship between student or parent reports of the amount of time spent on homework and a variety of measures of achievement. Of 69 such correlations, 50 were positive and 19 were negative. The weighted average correlation was $r = .24$ with a very narrow 95% confidence interval, encompassing the values between .24 and .25. The confidence interval was so small because of the large number of participants in these studies; the adjusted mean sample size in the studies was 7,742.

The meta-analysis of individual differences and attitudes toward rape also used correlation coefficients as the measure of the strength of relationships. Among the many correlations involving individual differences, we found, for example, that across 15 correlations, older participants were more accepting of rape than younger ones, average $r. = .12$ (95% CI $= .10–.14$).

The meta-analyses on (a) interventions to increase physical activity among older adults and (b) the effects of choice on intrinsic motivation used the standardized mean difference to measure effects. The weighted average d-index across 43 studies indicated that older adults who participated in the interventions were more likely to engage in subsequent physical activity than nonparticipants, $d. = .26$ (95% CI $= .21–.31$). The average weighted effect size for the 47 estimates of the impact of choice on measures of intrinsic motivation was $d. = .30$ (95% CI $= .25–.35$), indicating choice led to greater intrinsic motivation.

ANALYZING VARIANCE
IN EFFECT SIZES ACROSS FINDINGS

The analytic procedures described thus far have illustrated how to estimate effect sizes, average them, and use the confidence interval surrounding the average to test the null hypothesis that the difference between two means or the size of a correlation is 0. Another set of statistical techniques helps meta-analysts discover why effect sizes vary from one comparison to another. In these analyses, the effect sizes found in the separate comparisons are the *dependent* or predicted variables and the characteristics of the comparisons are the predictor variables. The meta-analysts ask whether the magnitude of relation between two variables in a comparison is affected by the way the study was designed or carried out.

One obvious feature of the effect sizes in Table 6.5 and 6.6 is that they vary from comparison to comparison. An explanation for this variability is not only important but it also represents the most unique contribution of research synthesis. By performing an analysis of differences in effect sizes, the meta-analyst can gain insight into the factors that affect the strengths of relationships even though these factors may have never been studied in a single experiment. For instance, assume that the first four studies listed in Table 6.5 were conducted in elementary schools while the last three studies were conducted in high schools. Is the effect of homework different for students at different grades? This question could be addressed through the use of the analytic techniques described next, even though no single study included both elementary and high school students and tested to see if the grade level of students moderated the effect of homework.

The techniques that follow are a few examples of many procedures for analyzing variance in effect sizes. I do not cover some of the more complex synthesis techniques. In particular, I have omitted the Confidence Profile Method (Eddy, Hasselblad, & Schacter, 1992) and the Bayesian approach (Sutton et al., 2000). These require knowledge of more advanced statistical concepts and formulas. The descriptions I do present are conceptual and brief. My intent is to give you a basic understanding of what meta-analysts do and provide you with the skills needed to conduct your own basic meta-analysis. If you are interested in more complex questions and techniques, you should first examine these in more detailed treatments, especially those given in Cooper, Hedges, and Valentine (2009).

Traditional Inferential Statistics

One way to analyze the variance in effect sizes is to apply the traditional inference procedures that are used by primary researchers. Meta-analysts interested in whether an intervention's effects on older adults' activity levels were stronger for males than females might do a t-test on the difference between effect sizes found in comparisons using exclusively males versus comparisons using exclusively females. Or, if the meta-analysts were interested in whether the intervention effect size was influenced by the length of delay between the intervention and the measurement of activity, the meta-analysts might correlate the length of delay in each comparison with its effect size. In this instance, the predictor and dependent variables are continuous, so the significance test associated with the correlation coefficient would be the appropriate inferential statistic. For more complex questions, a synthesist might categorize effect sizes into multifactor groupings—for instance, according to the gender and age of participants—and perform an analysis of variance or multiple regression on effect sizes. For Table 6.5, if a one-way analysis of variance were conducted comparing the first four d-indexes with the last three d-indexes, the result would not be statistically significant.

Standard inference procedures were the techniques initially used by some meta-analysts for examining variance in effects. Glass et al. (1981) detailed how this approach is carried out. However, at least two problems arise with the use of traditional inference procedures in meta-analysis. The first is that traditional inference procedures do not test the hypothesis that the variability in effect sizes is due solely to sampling error (recall the discussion earlier in this chapter). Therefore, the traditional inference procedures can reveal associations between design characteristics and effect sizes without determining first whether the overall variance in effects is greater than that expected by sampling error alone.

Also, because effect sizes can be based on different numbers of data points (sample sizes), they can have different sampling variances associated with them—that is, they are measured with different amounts of error. If this is the case (and it often is), then the effect sizes violate the assumption of homogeneity of variance that underlies traditional inference tests. For these two reasons, traditional inferential statistics are no longer used when performing a meta-analysis.

Comparing Observed to Expected Variance

In place of traditional procedures, several approaches have gained acceptance. One approach was proposed by Hunter and Schmidt (2004). It compares the variation in the observed effect sizes with the variation expected if only sampling error were causing differences in effect size estimates. This approach involves calculating (a) the observed variance in the effect sizes from the known findings and (b) the expected variance in these effect sizes given that all are estimating the same underlying population value. Sampling theory allows us to calculate precise estimates of how much sampling variation to expect in a group of effect sizes. This expected value is a function of the average effect size estimate, the number of estimates, and their sample sizes. The meta-analysts then compare the observed with the expected variance. Hunter and Schmidt (2004) suggest that meta-analysts refrain from formal tests to judge whether a significant difference exists between the observed and expected variances. Instead, they suggest that if the observed variance is twice as large as the expected sampling variance, then we should assume the two are reliably different. Whatever the criteria, if the variance estimates are deemed not to differ, then sampling error is the simplest explanation for the variance in effect sizes. If they are deemed different, that is, if the observed variance is much greater than that expected due to sampling error, then the meta-analysts begin the search for systematic influences on effect sizes.

Hunter and Schmidt (2004) also suggest that meta-analysts adjust effect size estimates to account for methodological artifacts. Earlier, I gave some examples of these when I discussed factors that influence effect size estimates.

Homogeneity Analyses

A homogeneity analysis also compares the observed variance to that expected from sampling error. However, unlike the first approach, it includes a calculation of how probable it is that the variance exhibited by the effect sizes would be observed if only sampling error was making them different. This is the approach used most often by meta-analysts, so I will provide a few more of its details.

Homogeneity analysis first asks the question, "Is the observed variance in effect sizes statistically significantly different from that expected by sampling error alone?" If the answer is no, then some statisticians advise that the meta-analysts stop the analysis there. After all, chance or sampling error is the simplest and most parsimonious explanation for why the effect sizes differ. If the answer is yes, that is, if the effect sizes display significantly greater variability than expected by chance, the meta-analysts then begin to examine whether study characteristics are systematically associated with variance in effect sizes. Some meta-analysts feel that the search for moderators should proceed regardless of whether sampling error is rejected as a plausible sole cause of variability in effect sizes *if* there are good theoretical or practical reasons for choosing moderators. This is the approach I usually take. Regardless of the approach you prefer, when evaluating a research synthesis, it is important to ask,

If a meta-analysis was performed, was the homogeneity of effect sizes tested?

Suppose a meta-analysis reveals a homogeneity statistic that has an associated p-value of .05. This means that only 5 times in 100 would sampling error create this amount of variance in effect sizes. Thus, the meta-analysts would reject the null hypothesis that sampling error alone explains the variance in effect sizes and they would begin the search for additional influences. They would then test whether study characteristics explain variation in effect sizes. Studies would be grouped by common features, and the average effect sizes for groups would be tested for homogeneity in the same way as the overall average effect size.

An approach to homogeneity analysis will be described that was introduced simultaneously by Rosenthal and Rubin (1982) and Hedges (1982). The formula presented by Hedges and Olkin (1985; also see Hedges, 1994) will be given here and the procedures using d-indexes will be described first.

The d-index. In order to test whether a set of d-indexes is homogeneous, the meta-analysts must calculate a statistic Hedges and Olkin (1985) called Q_t. The formula is as follows:

$$Q_t = \sum_{i=1}^{k} w_i d_i^2 - \frac{\left(\sum_{i=1}^{k} w_i d_i \right)^2}{\sum_{i=1}^{k} w_i} \tag{17}$$

where all terms are defined as above.

The Q-statistic has a chi-square distribution with $k - 1$ degrees of freedom, or, one less than the number of comparisons. The meta-analysts refer the obtained value of Q_t to a table of (upper tail) chi-square values. If the obtained value is greater than the critical value for the upper tail of a chi-square at the chosen level of significance, the meta-analysts reject the hypothesis that the variance in effect sizes was produced by sampling error alone. Table 6.7 presents the critical values of chi-square for selected probability levels.

For the set of comparisons given in Table 6.5, the value of Q_t equals 4.5. The critical value for chi-square at $p < .05$ based on 6 degrees of freedom is 12.6. Therefore, the hypothesis that sampling error explains the differences in these d-indexes cannot be rejected.

The procedure to test whether a methodological or conceptual distinction between studies explains variance in effect sizes involves three steps. First, a Q-statistic is calculated separately for each subgroup of comparisons. For instance, to compare the first four d-indexes in Table 6.5 with the last three, a separate Q-statistic is calculated for each grouping. Then, the values of these

Q-statistics are summed to form a value called Q_w. This value is then subtracted from Q_t to obtain Q_b:

$$Q_b = Q_t - Q_w \qquad (18)$$

where all terms are defined as above.

The statistic Q_b is used to test whether the *average* effects from the two groupings are homogenous. It is referred to a chi-square table using as degrees of freedom one less than the number of groupings. If the average d-indexes are homogeneous, then the grouping factor does not explain variance in effects beyond that associated with sampling error. If Q_b exceeds the critical value, then the grouping factor is a significant contributor to variance in effect sizes.

In Table 6.5, the Q_b comparing the first four and last three d-indexes is .98. This result is not significant with 1 degree of freedom. So, if the first four effect sizes were taken from studies of the effect of homework on achievement using elementary school students and the last three using high school students, we could not reject the null hypothesis that effect sizes were equal in the two populations of students.

The r-index. The analogous procedure for performing a homogeneity analysis on r-indexes transformed to z-scores involves the following formula:

$$Q_t = \sum_{i=1}^{k} (n_i - 3) z_i^2 - \frac{\left[\sum_{i=1}^{k} (n_i - 3) z_i \right]^2}{\sum_{i=1}^{k} (n_i - 3)} \qquad (19)$$

where all terms are defined as above.

To compare groups of r-indexes, Formula [19] is applied to each grouping separately, and the sum of these results, Q_w, is subtracted from Q_t to obtain Q_b.

The results of a homogeneity analysis using the z-transforms of the r-indexes are presented in Table 6.6. The Q_t value of 178.66 is highly significant, based on a chi-square test with 5 degrees of freedom. While it seems that a range of r-indexes from .06 to .27 is not terribly large, Q_t tells us that, given the sizes of the samples on which these estimates are based, the variation in effect sizes is too great to be explained by sampling error alone. Something other than sampling error likely is contributing to the variance in r-indexes.

Suppose we know that the first three correlations in Table 6.6 are from samples of high school students and the last three are from elementary school

Table 6.7   Critical Values of Chi-Square for Given Probability Levels

	Upper Tail Probabilities					
DF	*.500*	*.250*	*.100*	*.050*	*.025*	*.010*
1	.455	1.32	2.71	3.84	5.02	6.63
2	1.39	2.77	4.61	5.99	7.38	9.21
3	2.37	4.11	6.25	7.81	9.35	11.3
4	3.36	5.39	7.78	9.49	11.1	13.3
5	4.35	6.63	9.24	11.1	12.8	15.1
6	5.35	7.84	10.6	12.6	14.4	16.8
7	6.35	9.04	12.0	14.1	16.0	18.5
8	7.34	10.2	13.4	15.5	17.5	20.1
9	8.34	11.4	14.7	16.9	19.0	21.7
10	9.34	12.5	16.0	18.3	20.5	23.2
11	10.3	13.7	17.3	19.7	21.9	24.7
12	11.3	14.8	18.5	21.0	23.3	26.2
13	12.3	16.0	19.8	22.4	24.7	27.7
14	13.3	17.1	21.1	23.7	26.1	29.1
15	14.3	18.2	22.3	25.0	27.5	30.6
16	15.3	19.4	23.5	26.3	28.8	32.0
17	16.3	20.5	24.8	27.6	30.2	33.4
18	17.3	21.6	26.0	28.9	31.5	34.8
19	18.3	22.7	27.2	30.1	32.9	36.2
20	19.3	23.8	28.4	31.4	34.2	37.6
21	20.3	24.9	29.6	32.7	35.5	33.9

22	21.3	26.0	30.8	33.9	36.8	40.3
23	22.3	27.1	32.0	35.2	38.1	41.6
24	23.3	28.2	33.2	36.4	39.4	43.0
25	24.3	29.3	34.4	37.7	40.6	44.3
26	25.3	30.4	35.6	38.9	41.9	45.6
27	26.3	31.5	36.7	40.1	43.2	47.0
28	27.3	32.6	37.9	41.3	44.5	48.3
29	28.3	33.7	39.1	42.6	45.7	49.6
30	29.3	34.8	40.3	43.8	47.0	50.9
40	49.3	45.6	51.8	55.8	59.3	63.7
60	59.3	67.0	74.4	79.1	83.3	88.4
	.500	*.750*	*.900*	*.950*	*.975*	*.990*

Lower Tail Probabilities

students. A homogeneity analysis testing the effect of grade level on the magnitude of r-indexes reveals a Q_b of 93.31. This value is highly statistically significant, based on a chi-square test with 1 degree of freedom. For high school students, the average weighted r-index is .253, whereas for elementary school students it is $r = .136$. Thus, the null hypothesis can be rejected and the grade level of the student is one potential explanation for the variation in r-indexes.

Using computer statistical packages. Calculating average weighted effect sizes and homogeneity statistics by hand is time-consuming and prone to error. Today, it is rare for meta-analysts to compute statistics for themselves, as I have done in the previous examples. Conveniently, the major computer statistics packages, such as SAS (Wang & Bushman, 1999), SPSS (1990), and STATA can be used to do the calculations. Even better, there are stand-alone meta-analysis packages such as Comprehensive Meta-Analysis (Borenstein, Hedges,

Higgins, & Rothstein, 2005) that will produce all the results for you, and give you many options for how to carry out your analyses. Regardless of how the statistics are calculated, when evaluating a research synthesis, you should ask,

> *Were (a) study design and implementation features along with (b) other critical features of studies, including historical, theoretical, and practical variables, tested as potential moderators of study outcomes?*

ISSUES IN META-ANALYSIS

Choosing Between Different Models of Error

An important decision you will make when conducting a meta-analysis involves whether a fixed-effect or random-effect model of error should be used to calculate the variability in effect size estimates averaged across studies. As I discussed above, fixed-effect models calculate error that only reflects variation in studies' outcomes due to the sampling of participants. However, other features of studies also can be viewed as random influences on outcomes. In many cases, it may be most appropriate to treat studies as randomly sampled from a population of all studies. The variation that might be added to the estimate of error due to variations in study methods is ignored when a fixed-effect model is used. In a random-effect model, study-level variance is assumed to be present as an additional source of random influence.

The question you must answer, then, is whether you believe the effect sizes in your data set are noticeably affected by study-level random influences. Regrettably, there are no hard and fast rules for making this determination. It is rarely clear-cut which model—fixed effect or random effect—is most appropriate for a particular set of effect sizes. In practice, many meta-analysts opt for the fixed-effect assumption because it is analytically easier to manage. But some meta-analysts argue that fixed-effect models are used too often when random-effect models are more appropriate (and conservative). Others counter this argument by claiming that a fixed-effect model can be applied if a thorough, appropriate search for moderators of effect sizes is part of the analytic strategy—that is, if the meta-analysts examine the systematic effects of study-level influences—and in this way make moot the issue of random effects at the study level.

What should your decision be based on? One approach is to decide based on the outcome of the test of homogeneity of effects using a fixed-effect model; if the hypothesis of homogeneous effects is rejected under the fixed-effect assumption, then you switch to a random-effect model. Or many researchers interested in evaluating applied interventions (such as activity-promoting programs for older adults) often choose the random-effect model because they feel the random sampling of studies is more descriptive of their real-world circumstances and also will lead to a more conservative conclusion about the range of impacts the intervention might have. So, if you suspect a large influence of study-level sources of random error, then a random-effect model is most appropriate in order to take these sources of variance into account. Other researchers studying basic social processes—ones that likely do not change greatly due to the contexts in which they are being studied (such as, perhaps, tests of cognitive functioning)—tend to favor fixed-effect models. Hedges and Vevea (1998, p. 3) state that fixed-effect models of error are most appropriate when the goal of the research is "to make inferences only about the effect size parameters in the set of studies that are observed (or a set of studies identical to the observed studies except for uncertainty associated with the sampling of subjects)." In studies of basic processes, this type of inference might suffice, because you make the extrastatistical assumption that the relationship you are studying is largely insensitive to its context. A further consideration is that in the search for moderators, fixed-effect models may seriously underestimate error variance and random-effect models may seriously overestimate error variance when their assumptions are violated (Overton, 1998).

In view of these competing sets of concerns, you might also consider applying both models. Specifically, all analyses could be conducted twice, once employing fixed-effect assumptions and once using random-effect assumptions. Differences in results based on which set of assumptions is used can then be incorporated into the interpretation and discussion of your findings. I will return to the issue of interpreting fixed-effect and random-effect models in Chapter 7.

Calculating random-effect estimates of the mean effect size, confidence intervals, homogeneity statistics, and moderator analyses is complex and involves a two-stage process where first the meta-analysts must estimate the between-study variance and then this estimate is added to the variance of each study before the set of studies is combined statistically. Because of this complexity, the formulas I have provided in this chapter are for fixed-effect models. If you are interested in the mechanics of calculating random-effect models, you can find them in Hedges and Olkin (1985) or Raudenbush (2009). Thankfully, the statistical packages developed specifically for meta-analysis and the program macros for more general statistical packages allow you to conduct analyses using both fixed-effect and random-effect assumptions.

Combining Slopes From Multiple Regressions

Up to this point, the procedures for combining and comparing study results have assumed that the measure of effect is a difference between means, a correlation, or an odds ratio. However, regression analysis is a commonly used technique in the social sciences, particularly in nonexperimental studies where many variables are used to predict a single criterion. Similar to the standardized mean difference or correlation coefficient, the regression coefficient, b, or the standardized regression coefficient, β, are also measures of effect size. β will typically be of most interest to meta-analysts because, like the d-index and r-index, it standardizes effect size estimates when different measures of the same conceptual variable are used in different studies. β, represents the change in a standardized predictor variable, controlling for all other predictors, given one standard unit change in the criterion variable.

Meta-analyses of regression coefficients are difficult to conduct for a variety of reasons. First, with regard to using the unstandardized b-weight, this is like using raw score differences as measures of effect—the scales of the predictor and outcome of interest typically vary across studies. Directly combining them can lead to uninterpretable results. This problem can be overcome by using β, the fully standardized estimate of the slope for a particular predictor.[3] But still, the other variables included in models using multiple regression generally differ from study to study (note the related earlier discussion about multifactored analyses of variance). Each study may include different predictors in the regression model and, therefore, the slope for the predictor of interest will represent a different partial relationship in each study (Becker & Wu, 2007). For example, in our meta-analysis of homework and achievement, we found numerous studies that performed analyses of the relationship between time spent on homework and achievement that reported β. However, each was based on a regression model that included different additional variables. This made it questionable that the βs should be directly combined. So, rather than average them, we described these studies' individual βs and the range of β-values across the studies. These were overwhelmingly positive, were generally based on very large samples, and used a variety of achievement outcome measures. As such,

---

[3] *Half-standardizing* is an alternative way to create similar slopes when only outcomes are dissimilar (see Greenwald, Hedges, & Laine, 1996).

they strengthened our claim about the positive effects of homework on achievement that was based on the few small studies that purposively manipulated homework and tested its effect on a single limited outcome measure, unit test scores.

Regression slopes can be directly combined when (a) the outcome and predictor of interest are measured in a similar fashion across studies, (b) the other predictors in the model are the same across studies, and (c) the predictor and outcome scores are similarly distributed (Becker, 2005). It is rare that all three of these assumptions are met; typically, measures differ across studies and regression models are diverse in terms of which additional variables are included in them.

Considering Multiple
Moderators Simultaneously or Sequentially

Homogeneity statistics can become unreliable and difficult to interpret when the meta-analysts wish to test more than one moderator of effect sizes at a time. Hedges and Olkin (1985) present one technique for testing multiple moderators. The model uses simultaneous or sequential tests for homogeneity. It removes the variance in effect sizes due to one moderator and then removes from the remaining variance any additional variance due to the next moderator. So, for example, if we were interested in whether the sex of the student influenced the effect of homework on achievement after controlling for the student's grade level, we would first test grade level as a moderator, then test the student's sex as a moderator *within* each grade level category.

This procedure is often difficult to apply because characteristics of studies are often correlated with one another and the number of effect sizes in categories of interest rapidly becomes small. For example, suppose we wanted to test whether the effect of homework on achievement is influenced by both the grade level of students and the type of achievement measure. We might find that these two study characteristics are often confounded—more studies of high school students used standardized tests while more studies of elementary school students used class grades. Studies of homework with elementary school students using standardized tests may be rare. The problem would get even worse if yet a third variable was added to the mix.

Finally, another statistical approach to testing multiple moderators of effect sizes simultaneously or sequentially is called *meta-regression*. As the name implies, this approach is the meta-analysis analog to multiple regression. In meta-regression, the effect sizes are the criterion variables and the study characteristics are the predictors (Hartung, Knapp, & Sinha, 2008). Meta-regression shares with multiple regression all the problems regarding the interpretation of the analysis' output when the predictors are intercorrelated (a likely characteristic of research synthesis data) and when the number of data points (effect sizes in meta-regression) are small. Meta-regression has been used more frequently in the medical than social sciences. I suspect it will become more familiar to social scientists as it becomes available in meta-analysis software packages.

Another approach to addressing the intercorrelation of study characteristics is to first generate homogeneity statistics for each characteristic separately, by repeating the calculation of Q-statistics. Then, when the results concerning moderators of effect sizes are interpreted, the meta-analysts also examine a matrix of intercorrelations among the moderators. This way, the meta-analyst can alert readers to study characteristics that may be confounded and draw inferences with these relations in mind. For example, we followed this procedure in the meta-analysis of the effects of choice on intrinsic motivation. We found that the effect of giving choices influenced children's intrinsic motivation more positively than adults' motivation. But we found also that the age of the participant was associated with the setting in which the choice experiment was conducted; studies with adults were more likely to be conducted in a traditional lab setting than studies with children. This means that the different effect of choice on motivation for children and adults might not be due to the participants' age but to where the study was conducted.

In sum, then, you need to make many practical decisions when conducting a meta-analysis, and the guidelines for making these are not as clear as we would like. While it is clear that a formal analysis of the variance in effect sizes is an essential part of any research synthesis containing large numbers of comparisons, it is also clear that you must take great care in the application of these statistics and in the description of how they were applied.

SOME ADVANCED
TECHNIQUES IN META-ANALYSIS

Model-Based Meta-Analysis

The statistical procedures for meta-analysis described so far apply to synthesizing two-variable relationships from experimental and descriptive research. Meta-analysis methodologists are working to extend statistical synthesis procedures to more complex ways to express the relations between variables. Previously, I discussed the difficulties in synthesizing the effect sizes associated with a variable that was included in a multiple regression. But what if the question of interest involves integrating the output of *entire* regression equations? For example, suppose we were interested in how five personality variables (perhaps those in the five-factor model) jointly predicted attitudes toward rape? Here, we would want to develop from a meta-analysis a regression equation, or perhaps a structural equation model, based on the results of a set of studies. To do so, we would need to integrate results of studies concerning not one correlation between the variables but rather an entire matrix of correlations relating all the variables in the model of interest to us. It is this correlation matrix that forms the basis of the multiple regression model. The techniques used to do this are still being explored, as are the problems meta-analysts face in using them. For example, can we simply conduct separate meta-analyses for each correlation coefficient in the matrix and then use the resulting matrix to generate the regression equation? The answer is "probably not." The individual correlations would then be based on different samples of participants and a regression analysis using them can produce nonsensical results, such as prediction equations that explain more than 100% of the variance in the criterion variable. Still, there are circumstances under which these applications of meta-analysis to complex questions can produce highly informative results. Becker (2009) presents an in-depth examination of the promise and problems involved in model-driven meta-analysis.

Meta-Analysis Using Individual Participant Data

The most desirable technique for combining results of independent studies is to have available and to integrate the raw data from each relevant comparison or estimate of a relationship (Cooper & Patall, in press). Then, the individual participant data (IPD) can be placed into a new primary data analysis that employs the comparison that generated the data as a blocking variable. When IPD is available, the meta-analysis can

- perform subgroup analyses that were not conducted by the initial data collectors,
- check data in the original studies,
- ensure that the original analyses were conducted properly,
- add new information to the data sets,
- test with greater power variables that moderate effect sizes, and
- test for both between-study and within-study moderators.

Obviously, instances in which the integration of IPD can be achieved are rare. IPD are seldom included in research reports, and attempts to obtain raw data from researchers often end in failure. If they were retrievable, the use of different metrics in different studies would limit the ability to statistically combine the results. Also, meta-analyses using IPD can be very expensive because of the recoding involved in getting the data sets into similar form and content. So it is unlikely that meta-analyses using IPD will be replacing the meta-analysis techniques described previously any time soon. Still, meta-analysis of IPD is an attractive alternative, one that has received considerable attention in the medical literature, and likely will become more attractive as the availability of raw data sets improves.

EXERCISES

Finding	n_{i1}	n_{i2}	d_i
1	193	173	−.08
2	54	42	.35
3	120	160	.47
4	62	60	.00
5	70	84	.33
6	60	60	.41
7	72	72	−.28

1. For the findings in this table, what is the average weighted d-index?

2. Are the effect sizes of the seven studies homogeneous? Calculate your answer both by hand and by using a computer statistical package.

7

Step 6

Interpreting the Evidence

What conclusions can be drawn about the cumulative state of the research evidence?

Primary Function in Research Synthesis

To summarize the cumulative research evidence with regard to its conclusiveness, generalizability, and limitations

Procedural Variation That Might Produce Differences in Conclusions

Variation in (a) criteria for labeling results as "important" and (b) attention to details of studies might lead to differences in interpretation of findings

Questions to Ask When Interpreting the Cumulative Evidence

1. Were analyses carried out that tested whether results were sensitive to statistical assumptions and, if so, were these analyses used to help interpret the evidence?

2. Did the research synthesists (a) discuss the extent of missing data in the evidence base and (b) examine its potential impact on the findings of the synthesis?

3. Did the research synthesists discuss the generality and limitations of the synthesis' findings?

4. Did the synthesists make the appropriate distinction between study-generated and synthesis-generated evidence when interpreting the synthesis' results?

5. If a meta-analysis was performed, did the synthesists (a) contrast the magnitude of effects with other related effect sizes and/or (b) present a practical interpretation of the significance of the effects?

(Continued)

(Continued)

This chapter describes

- How to account for missing data
- Statistical sensitivity analysis
- Generalization and specification of findings
- Study-generated and synthesis-generated evidence
- Substantive interpretation of effect sizes

Properly interpreting the results of your research synthesis will require you to carefully (a) state the claims you want to make based on the evidence, (b) specify what results warrant each claim, and (c) make explicit any appropriate qualifications to claims that need to be made. In this chapter, I discuss five important issues related to the interpretation of results in research synthesis:

- The impact of missing data on conclusions
- The sensitivity of your conclusions to changes in assumptions about the statistical characteristics of your data
- Your ability to generalize your conclusions to people and circumstances not included in the constituent studies
- Whether conclusions are based on study-generated or synthesis-generated evidence
- The substantive interpretation of effect sizes

MISSING DATA

Even after the careful planning, searching, and coding of research reports, missing data can influence the conclusions drawn from research syntheses. When data are systematically missing, not only is the amount of evidence you gathered reduced, but the representativeness of your results may be compromised. In Chapter 4, I discussed the issue of missing data and suggested a few ways to address the problem when you code studies. But even these techniques for estimating missing data do not solve the problem entirely. You do not have an equal chance of retrieving every study, so there might be some studies completely missing from your data set. Also, in some instances, studies you do have may have collected data on an outcome and tested them but then failed to give any indication of this in the report. These completely missing results cannot be estimated by the procedures described in Chapter 4. Compounding the problem is the fact that in many instances a disproportionate number of completely missing cases will be associated with statistically nonsignificant effect sizes. As such, they would tend to be the smaller effect sizes in the distribution of estimates. This means the effect sizes you do find may overestimate the true population value.

Yet, there are some things you can do. *A number of graphical and statistical techniques can be used to assess the possible existence of completely missing data and its implications for the interpretation of your results, and it is good practice to apply at least one of these to your data.* These techniques include regression methods such as the Rank Correlation Test (Begg & Mazumdar, 1994) and Egger's Test (Egger, Davey Smith, Schneider, & Minder, 1997). A method we have found especially useful is the *trim-and-fill method* (Duval & Tweedie, 2000a, 2000b).

Though not perfect, the trim-and-fill method makes reasonable assumptions about the missing data, is intuitively appealing, and is easy to understand. The trim-and-fill method tests whether the distribution of effect sizes used in the analyses is consistent with the distribution that would be predicted if the estimates were symmetrically distributed around their mean. If the distribution of observed effect sizes is found to be asymmetric in some way—indicating possible missing effect sizes caused by a search limitation or by data censoring on the part of primary researchers—the trim-and-fill method provides ways to estimate the values from missing studies that would improve the symmetry of the distribution. Then, after imputing these values, it permits you to estimate the impact of data censoring on the observed mean and variance of effect sizes. Duval (2005) gives a good introduction to how to carry out the trim-and-fill analysis.

In our homework meta-analysis, we conducted trim-and-fill analyses using the five effect sizes we found for studies that manipulated whether or not students received homework. Figure 7.1 shows the results of the analyses using a funnel plot. You can see that the trim-and-fill analysis suggested that, if the distribution of effect sizes were truly symmetrical, two studies might be missing from the left side of the funnel plot. Methods are provided to calculate what these values might be (under both fixed-effect and random-effect models), and then recalculate average effect sizes and confidence intervals. In this case, recalculating the average homework effects produced a smaller average effect size ($d = .48$) but one that was still highly statistically significant. Thus, this technique for estimating completely missing effect sizes leaves us more confident that our results would not change substantively had the missing data been found.

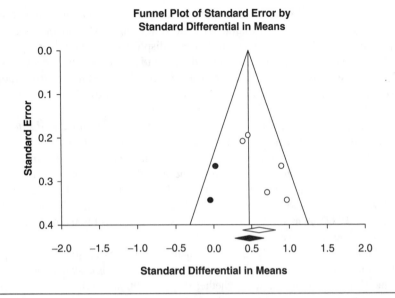

Figure 7.1   Example of a Trim-and-Fill Funnel Plot

Regardless of the techniques you use, *you are obligated to discuss how much of the data were missing from the individual study reports, how you handled it, and why you chose to treat the missing data the way you did.* Thus, an important question to ask about missing data when evaluating research syntheses is,

> *Did the research synthesists (a) discuss the extent of missing data in the evidence base and (b) examine its potential impact on the synthesis' findings?*

STATISTICAL SENSITIVITY ANALYSES

The next important step in the interpretation of data from meta-analyses also is undertaken as part of data analysis: the performance of statistical sensitivity analyses. Statistical sensitivity analyses are used to determine whether and how the conclusions of your analyses might differ if they were conducted using different statistical procedures or different assumptions about the data. There are numerous decisions you make about how to analyze your data that are candidates for sensitivity analysis. For example, the calculation of weighted and unweighted effect sizes can be considered a form of sensitivity analysis. When you present these measures of central tendency calculated differently, in essence, you are answering the question, "Do I come to a different conclusion about the average effect size when I ignore the precision of the individual effect size estimates than when I take their precision into account?"

You might also consider, as we did in our meta-analysis of the association between the time students spend on homework and achievement, conducting your analyses twice, once using a fixed-effect model and once using a random-effect model. Rather than choosing a single model for error, we chose to apply both models to our data. By employing this sensitivity analysis, differences in results based on which set of assumptions about error was used could then be part of our interpretation of results. If an analysis revealed a finding was significant under fixed-effect assumptions but not under random-effect assumptions, this result suggests that the finding relates only to what past studies have found but not necessarily to the likely results of a broader universe of similar studies. For example, we found that a small but significant negative association between time on homework and achievement for elementary school students was statistically significant using a fixed-effect model, but the association was not significant using a random-effect model. A similar set of results occurred for this association when parents reported time on homework. Also, we found that of four moderator variables that produced significant effects using a fixed-effect model, two were also significant using a random-effect model (the association was stronger for high school than elementary school students and when students reported time on homework than when parents were reporters), while two were not significant using the random-effects model (the type of outcome measure and the subject matter).

Each time you do a sensitivity analysis, you are seeking to determine whether a particular finding is robust across analyses conducted with different sets of statistical assumptions. In the interpretation of evidence, a finding that conclusions do not change using different statistical tests or assumptions means greater confidence can be placed in the conclusion. *If results are different under different assumptions, this suggests a caution, or different interpretation, is needed when you share your results with the users of your synthesis.* So, another question to ask when you evaluate the interpretation of results in research synthesis is,

---

Were analyses carried out that tested whether results were sensitive to statistical assumptions and, if so, were these analyses used to help interpret the evidence?

SPECIFICATION AND GENERALIZATION

Research synthesis, like any research, involves specifying the targeted participants, program or intervention types, occasions, settings, and outcomes. *When you interpret your results, you must assess whether and how well each of the target elements is represented in the evidence base.* For example, if you were interested in making claims about the effectiveness of a program to promote physical activity among older adults, you would need to note whether important targeted groups were included or missing from the samples of participants.

The trustworthiness of any claim about the generality of a research finding will be compromised if the elements in the accessed samples are not representative of the target elements, be they targeted people, programs, settings, times, or outcomes. Thus, you may find you need to respecify your covered elements once your data analysis is complete. For example, if only older adults with heart disease were used in studies of activity-promoting programs, then any claims about the effectiveness of these programs either must be restricted to this particular type of participant or the rationale for extrapolation beyond the included types of participants must be provided in your interpretation of the data.

Your influence on permissible generalizations is constrained by the types of elements sampled by primary researchers. Still, generalization in research synthesis injects a note of optimism into the discussion. There is good reason to believe research syntheses will pertain more directly to the target participants, programs, settings, times, and outcomes—or to more subgroups within these targets—than will the separate primary studies. The cumulative literature can contain studies conducted on participants and programs with different characteristics at different times and in different settings using different outcome measures. For certain topics containing numerous replications, participants and circumstances accessible to the synthesists may more closely approximate the targeted elements than does any individual primary study. For example, if some studies of activity-promoting programs contain only heart patients and others excluded individuals with cardiovascular disease, then the synthesist can ask whether program effects were similar or different across the two types of participants, a question unanswerable by any individual study.

Integrating Interaction Results Across Studies

A problem in interpreting the results of research syntheses that is related to the issue of generalization concerns the interpretation of interactions. Often, the integration of interaction results in research synthesis is not as simple as averaging the effect sizes from each study. Figure 7.2 illustrates the problem by presenting the results of two hypothetical studies comparing the effects of homework versus in-school study on students' ability to retrieve the covered material from memory. These two studies tested whether the effect of the two instructional strategies was mediated by the delay between when the instruction occurred and when the measure of retention was taken. In Study 1, retention was compared across students at both 1 and 8 weeks after the intervention. In Study 2, the intervals of delay were 1 and 4 weeks. Study 1 might have produced no significant main effect but a significant interaction involving the measurement interval while Study 2 might have reported a significant main effect only.

If you uncovered these two studies and did not examine the precise form of the data, you might be tempted to conclude that they produced inconsistent results. However, an examination of the two figures illustrates why this might not be an appropriate interpretation. The results of Study 2 would have closely approximated those of Study 1 had the measurement delay in Study 2 been the same as that in Study 1. Note that the slopes for the lines for the two groups in Study 1 and Study 2 are nearly identical.

This example demonstrates that synthesists should not assume that different strengths of interaction uncovered by different studies necessarily imply inconsistent results. *Synthesists need to examine the differing ranges of values of the variables employed in different studies, be they measured or manipulated. If*

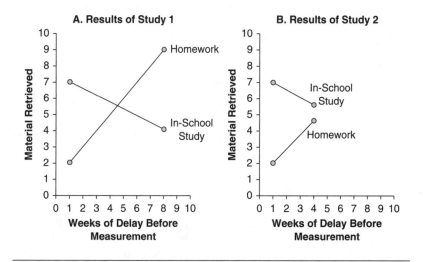

Figure 7.2   Results of Two Hypothetical Studies Comparing the Effects of
Homework and In-School Study on Retention

possible, you should chart results taking the different levels into account. In this manner, one of the benefits of research synthesis is realized. While one study's authors might conclude that measurement delay has no effect on the ability to retrieve information from memory when homework and in-school study are compared and a second study's authors might conclude such an interaction exists, a research synthesist could discover that the two results are in fact perfectly consistent.

This benefit of research synthesis also highlights the importance of primary researchers presenting detailed information concerning the levels of variables used in their studies. Research synthesists cannot conduct an across-study analysis similar to our example without this information. If the researchers in Study 1 and Study 2 neglected to specify their range of measurement delays—perhaps they simply said they compared "short" delays with "longer" delays—the commensurability of the results would have been impossible to demonstrate.

I should mention that variations in ranges of values for variables also can produce discrepancies in results involving two-variable or main effect relationships. For example, had Study 1 included a retention measurement at one week, Study 2 at 4 weeks, and a third study at 8 weeks, the three studies would have produced three different results. In such a case, we would hope that the research synthesists would examine measurement delay as a moderator variable and reveal the influence it had on study results. I mention here the impact of ranges in values in the case of interactions because this is the circumstance under which the problem is least likely to be recognized and is most difficult to remedy when it is discovered.

In general then, the next question to ask when evaluating the interpretation of a research synthesis is,

> *Did the research synthesists discuss the generality and limitations of the synthesis findings?*

STUDY-GENERATED AND
SYNTHESIS-GENERATED EVIDENCE

In Chapter 2, I made the important point that research syntheses can contain two different sources of evidence about the research problem or hypothesis. Study-generated evidence is present when a single study contains results that directly test the relation being considered. Synthesis-generated evidence does not come from individual studies but rather from the variations in procedures across studies. I noted that only study-generated evidence based on experimental research allows you to make statements concerning causality. I return to the point here to emphasize that *making the distinction between what evidence in your synthesis supports causal relationships and what evidence does not is an important aspect of proper interpretation of your results.* Therefore, the next important question to ask when evaluating the interpretation of evidence in a research synthesis is,

---

Did the synthesists make the appropriate distinction between study-generated and synthesis-generated evidence when interpreting the synthesis' results?

THE SUBSTANTIVE
INTERPRETATION OF EFFECT SIZE

In quantitative syntheses, one function of a discussion section is the interpretation of the size of reported effects, be they the magnitudes of group differences or correlations. Once you have calculated effect sizes, how do you know if they are large or small, meaningful or trivial? Since statistical significance cannot be used as a benchmark—small effects can be statistically significant and large effects nonsignificant—a set of rules must be established for determining the explanatory or practical "value" of a given effect magnitude.[1]

The Size of the Relationship

To help interpret effect sizes, social scientists have applied labels that describe the size of the relationship between two variables. Jacob Cohen provided the first guides to interpreting effect sizes in this way in the 1977 edition of his book on statistical power analysis (reprinted as Cohen, 1988). He proposed a set of values to serve as definitions of small, medium, and large effects. Cohen recognized that judgments of "largeness" and "smallness" are relative. In order to make them, a comparison between two items is required, and the choice of a contrasting element for an observed effect could be governed by

---

[1] Portions of this discussion include minor modifications of a similar discussion I provided in Cooper (2009).

many different rules. Interestingly, however, Cohen did not intend his labels to serve as guides for substantive interpretation by social scientists. Rather, he intended his rules to assist with power analyses in planning future studies, a very different objective. However, since they have been used so often for substantive interpretation, we should look at their characteristics.

In defining the adjectives for magnitude, Cohen compared different average effect sizes he had encountered in the behavioral sciences. He defined a small effect as $d = .2$ or $r = .1$ (equivalent values), which his experience suggested were typical of those found in personality, social, and clinical psychology research. A large effect of $d = .8$ or $r = .5$ was more likely to be found in sociology, economics, and experimental or physiological psychology. Medium effects, $d = .5$ and $r = .3$, fell between these extremes. According to Cohen, then, a social psychologist studying the impact of choice on intrinsic motivation might interpret an effect size of $d = .2$ to be small when compared with all behavioral science effects but about average when compared with all other effects in social psychology.

Cohen (1988) was careful to stress that his conventions were to be used "only when no better basis for estimating the ES [effect size] is available" (p. 25). Today, with so many meta-analytic estimates of effects available, other more closely related contrasting effects often can be found. So, when you interpret the magnitude of effects, it is most informative to use contrasting elements that are more closely related to your topic than to use Cohen's benchmarks.

For example, our meta-analysis of interventions to increase physical activity among older adults found that the average effect of such interventions was $d = .26$, indicating that on average, participants scored about one quarter of a standard deviation higher than nonparticipants on subsequent measures of activity. Using Cohen's guide, we would label this effect "small." However, other contrasting elements might be available to us. These might come from other meta-analyses that looked at entirely different ways to promote activity in older adults, such as drug treatments. Thus, one way to interpret the effect of activity-promoting interventions would be to ask whether they revealed smaller or larger effects than other types of interventions on how much activity older adults reported.

Alternatively, other meta-analyses might share the same treatment but vary in outcome measure. For example, some studies of activity-promoting interventions may have examined participants' ratings of the quality of their life rather than their subsequent activity level. Then, a good interpretation would consider whether activity-promoting interventions have a smaller or larger effect on subsequent activity than on perceived quality of life. (Of course, these types of interpretations could occur among results within the same research synthesis.)

When you cannot find meta-analyses this closely aligned with your topic, you might be able to find compendia of meta-analyses on more distant but related topics that are still closer to your topic than Cohen's benchmarks. For example, Lipsey and Wilson (1993) compiled the results of 302 meta-analyses across the fields of education, mental health, and organizational psychology. In education, the authors cataloged 181 average effect sizes. The middle one fifth of these ranged from $d = .35$ to $d = .49$. The top one fifth of effect size estimates were above $d = .70$, and the bottom one fifth were below $d = .20$. So, in our meta-analysis of experimental studies examining the effects of homework on student's grades on unit tests, we reported an average d-index of about .60. Comparing this to Lipsey and Wilson's estimates, we might label the homework effect as "above average."

Effect sizes also need to be interpreted in relation to the methodology used in the primary research. Cohen (1988) acknowledged this when he pointed out that field studies should expect smaller effects than laboratory studies (p. 25). In addition, studies that provide an intervention in greater frequency and intensity (for example, more frequent meetings with older adult participants) would have greater likelihood of showing a large effect than more conscribed versions of another intervention, even if the interventions were equally effective when tested under comparable conditions. Or studies that remove more error from the measurement of the outcome (perhaps by using a more reliable measure) should produce larger effects than studies that allow more extraneous influences on outcomes. Therefore, research design differences must be considered when drawing a conclusion about the relative size of effects; more sensitive research designs and measures with less random error can be expected to reveal larger effect sizes, all else being equal.

In sum, then, the choice of contrasting elements is critical in interpreting the magnitude of an effect. In fact, almost any effect can be deemed large or small depending on the chosen contrast. In addition, contrasting elements often vary on dimensions other than the impact of the manipulations or predictor variables they are "sizing up." *It is essential that (a) contrasting elements be chosen that hold constant those aspects of research design that are known to influence effect size estimates but are not inherent to the intervention itself or (b) differences in research design be considered when the contrast between effects is interpreted.*

Using Adjectives to Convey the "Significance" of Effects

Researchers are well aware that the term "significant effect" has a different meaning for statisticians than for the broader public. To those who calculate social science statistics, a significant effect typically means it is one that permits the rejection of the null hypothesis with some minimal potential for error, usually 1 chance in 20. To the general public, however, the meaning of "significant" is different. The *New Shorter Oxford English Dictionary* (1993) defines *significance* first as "meaning" and second as "importance, consequence." Most researchers recognize this distinction between colloquial and scientific usage, and when they use the term "significant effect" in public conversations, they typically use it to mean important, notable, or consequential, rather than in the statistical sense.

The question becomes, then, when can you use terms such as "significant," "important," "notable," or "consequential" (or their antonyms) to describe effect sizes? At least two organizations set this bar at $d = .25$ (Promising Practices Network, 2007; What Works Clearinghouse, 2007). In contrast, after comparing the results of psychoeducational meta-analyses with results from the field of medicine, Lipsey and Wilson (1993) conclude that "we cannot arbitrarily dismiss statistically modest values (even 0.10 or 0.20 SDs) as obviously trivial" (p. 1199).

You also can assess how much *any* relation might be valued by consumers of your synthesis. This assessment involves the difficult task of making practical judgments about significance. So, for example, an effect size of $d = .26$ on activity among older adults may be "small" when compared to Cohen's benchmarks and other contrasting elements. Still, we might argue that this improvement translates into an equivalent measure suggesting that a practically important number of older adults will remain healthy until later in life (see Rosenthal, 1990, for a similar argument). It might then be argued that the cost of the intervention was minimal relative to its change in life satisfaction, or even the cost of health care saved by participants. Levin (2002) has laid out some ground rules for conducting this type of cost-effectiveness analysis for educational programs.

In a similar vein relating to the impact of afterschool programs, Kane (2004) made the case that the interpretation of an effect also needs to be influenced by what a reasonable expectation might be for the impact of the intervention or manipulation. His assessment of valuations of afterschool programs led Kane to use a threshold even lower than that suggested by Lipsey and Wilson. He pointed out that the national samples used to norm the Stanford 9 achievement test suggested that test scores of fifth graders in the spring were one-third a standard deviation higher in reading and one-half a standard deviation higher in math than they were in the spring of fourth grade. This effect is the result of "everything that happens to a student between the end of fourth grade and the end of fifth grade" (p. 3). Given this effect, Kane argued it would be unreasonable to expect an effect size of even $d = .20$ (Cohen's definition of a small effect) from the added instruction made available through afterschool programs. He went on to argue that a more reasonable expectation for interventions such as afterschool programs could be set by calculating (a) the fraction of school-year time students spend in such programs or (b) the gain in earnings in later life needed to offset the cost of the program. Kane suggested that in both cases, the more reasonable expectation for a consequential effect of afterschool programs would be between $d = .05$ and $.07$.

Thus, it appears that criteria labeling an effect size as practically significant, important, or consequential also vary, and a case can be made that developing such criteria requires a contextualization of the effect little different from that involved in applying labels on the size of an effect relative to other effects.

Using Adjectives to Convey "Proven" and "Promising" Findings

Two other descriptors of research results related to program evaluations that have recently garnered attention among some social scientists are "proven" and "promising." For example, the Promising Practices Network (PPN, 2007) requires that for a program or practice to be labeled "proven," the associated evidence must meet the following criteria:

- The program must directly affect one of the indicators of interest.
- At least one outcome is changed by 20%, $d = 0.25$, or more.
- At least one outcome with a substantial effect size is statistically significant at the 5% level.
- The study design used a convincing comparison group to identify program impacts, including studies that used random assignment or some quasi-experimental designs.
- The sample size of the evaluation exceeds 30 in both the treatment and comparison groups.
- The report is publicly available.

These criteria appear to refer to as few as one study.

To claim that anything is "proven" through research is always problematic, as most philosophers of science accept the notion that a rejection of the null hypothesis at any statistical level is not an affirmation of any specific alternative hypothesis (Popper, 2002). Of course, there are different levels of uncertainty about alternative hypotheses depending on the number and nature of other explanations that fit the data.

The PPN goes on to define "promising" as follows:

- The program may affect an intermediary outcome for which there is evidence that it is associated with one of the indicators of interest.
- There is an associated change in outcome of more than 1%.
- Outcome change is significant at the 10% level.
- The study has a comparison group, but it may exhibit some weaknesses; for example, the groups lack comparability on preexisting variables or the analysis does not employ appropriate statistical controls.
- The sample size exceeds 10 in both the program and comparison groups.
- The report is publicly available.

The *Shorter Oxford English Dictionary* (1993) defines *promising* as "likely to turn out well; full of promise; hopeful." Thus, there is some correspondence between the PPN definition and common parlance, if we assume that having an impact on mediating variables and using less-than-optimal research designs can provide hope that the practice will produce positive results in future studies that test the intervention more directly and rigorously. However, the PPN definitions of both "proven" and "promising" also include reference to the magnitude of the program's effect. So, it appears that a program would be labeled "promising" even if it measured the outcomes of most interest and used more rigorous designs but revealed a smaller effect size than PPN requires for a program to be considered "proven" (that is, at least one outcome is changed by 20%, $d = 0.25$, or more). This confounding of the trustworthiness of the evidence and the magnitude of the effect may be a divergence from the everyday understanding of what both *proven* and *promising* mean.

Should Researchers Supply Labels at All?

Cohen (1988) cautioned that magnitude labels applied to effect sizes would involve an arbitrary choice of contrasting elements. To serve your audience best then, *it is best practice to present multiple contrasting elements, perhaps picking some contrasting elements that make the effect of interest look relatively small and other elements that make it look relatively large.* The search for definitions of "significance" has revealed that effects of small magnitude, relatively speaking, may not be inconsequential. And, effects that are even smaller than small may be all we can reasonably expect with some interventions. Trying to provide such benchmarks are valiant and instructive efforts that, at the least, caution you *not to apply labels for effects without providing your audience with much additional context, even multiple contexts.*

Further, I am skeptical of efforts to define terms such as "proven" and "promising" by associating them with different clusters of research characteristics and results, whether these clusters are based on the number of studies and participants, the research designs used, the statistical significance of results, the size of effects, and so on, in various combinations. Efforts to define these labels seem destined to always come up short, lead to a lack of consensus concerning what cluster of evidence justifies what label, and, perhaps of most concern, provide esoteric definitions of commonly used words that simply do not map onto the ways these terms are understood in everyday language.

METRICS THAT ARE MEANINGFUL TO GENERAL AUDIENCES

One way you can get around providing qualitative labels is to try to express the quantitative results of your meta-analysis in metrics that have meaning for your audience. If this can be accomplished, the audience should be able to apply their own qualitative labels to the quantitative result and perhaps debate the appropriateness of different labels they have applied. Put simply, if you can convey a clear understanding of what constitutes "an ounce," then audiences should be able to determine, or debate, whether an 8-ounce glass containing 4 ounces of liquid is half empty or half full. Next I describe a few ways to translate effect size metrics into specific contexts that have enough intuitive meaning that general audiences can apply, and debate, the appropriateness of different labels.

Raw and Familiar Transformed Scores

Many metrics are familiar enough to be understood implicitly by audiences not steeped in statistical training. These include some metrics in their raw form, such as a person's blood pressure. So, if you tell your audience that an activity-promotion intervention for older adults led to a 10-point reduction in systolic blood pressure and a 5-point reduction in diastolic blood pressure, your audience might be able to interpret this finding as "important" or "trivial" without you supplying a label, though you might still want to present the effects of some other interventions meant to accomplish the same type of result and, perhaps, a relative cost-benefit analysis. Other scores are familiar transformations of raw scores. These would include, for example, IQ and SAT scores. You can report the change in these familiar transformed scores as a function of being exposed to an intervention (e.g., intervention X led to a 50-point improvement in SAT scores) and be fairly confident that the results will be understood by a general audience.

One shortcoming of presenting effect sizes in terms of raw and familiar transformed scores is that the scores cannot be combined across different types of measures. For example, effects expressed as changes in SAT scores cannot be directly combined with changes in ACT scores. Thus, the results associated with each type of measure must be reported separately. This is not necessarily a bad thing if you consider it important to maintain these distinctions among outcomes, even if all measures relate to the same broader construct. If you want to describe an intervention's general effect on standardized achievement test scores, these effects will have to be standardized before you do so.

Translations of the Standardized Mean Difference

The three effect size metrics used most frequently in meta-analysis—the d-index, r-index, and odds ratio—are examples of standardized measures of effect. However, describing them to general audiences without additional explanation leaves most people scratching their heads.

For standardized mean differences, I have developed two ways to express the d-index for general audiences that are helpful in interpreting an intervention's effect on achievement (see Cooper, 2007a). Both are based on a metric associated with the d-index that Cohen (1988) called U_3. U_3 represents the percentage of the units in the group with the lower mean that is exceeded by 50% of the scores in the higher-meaned group. Table 7.1 presents the equivalent values for the d-index and U_3. Thus, U_3 answers the question, "What percentage of the scores in the lower-meaned group was surpassed by the average score in the higher-meaned group?" For example, consider a randomly assigned group of middle-school students, one half of whom received instruction in how to study for an algebra exam and the other half of whom received no instruction. An end-of-unit test in algebra is the principal outcome measure. If the study found a d-index of .30, it would be associated with a U_3 value of 61.8%. This means that the average student receiving study skills instruction (50th percentile) scored higher on the unit test than 61.8% of students who received no instruction.

But there is no need to stop with U_3. It is still quite abstract and not necessarily more intuitive than the d-index itself. U_3 can also be used to express the change in achievement associated with an intervention when achievement is graded on a curve. Here, you must begin by proposing the grade curve. In this case, the researcher reveals the effect by showing how the average student's grade would change only if that student received the intervention. Figure 7.3 presents one such grade curve. It also illustrates the effect that hypothetical instruction in algebra

Table 7.1 Equivalents for d-Index and U_3 Effect Size Metrics

d	U_3 (%)
0	50.0
.1	54.0
.2	57.9
.3	61.8
.4	65.5
.5	69.1
.6	72.6
.7	75.8
.8	78.8
.9	81.6
1.0	84.1
1.1	86.4
1.2	88.5
1.3	90.3
1.4	91.9
1.5	93.3
1.6	94.5
1.7	95.5
1.8	96.4
1.9	97.1
2.0	97.7
2.2	98.6
2.4	99.2
2.6	99.5
2.8	99.7
3.0	99.9
3.2	99.9
3.4	[a]
3.6	[a]
3.8	[a]
4.0	[a]

SOURCE: Cohen (1988, p. 22). Copyright 1988 by Taylor & Francis Group LLC. Reprinted with permission.

a. >99.9.

study skills would have on the unit test grade received by the average student (had instruction not occurred). As shown in Figure 7.3, the average student in a class of students receiving study skill instruction would receive the middle C. If that student were the only student in class getting study skills instruction (and all else was unchanged), the intervention would improve the student's grade to a C+, graded on the proposed curve.

It is critical that you point out to your audience that you have supplied the grade curve and that other curves could be more or less sensitive to changes in the outcome measure. Therefore, the grade curve used in Figure 7.3 might be considered very tough by today's standards; the average student gets a C and only 9% of students get an A or A–. Had a "softer" curve been used, the middle grade could be higher than C and the discrimination of scores on the top half of the curve would be diminished. The result would suggest a lesser change in grade as a function of study skills instruction.

Why is offering an arbitrary grade curve better than providing an arbitrary yardstick, such as Cohen's adjectives, for the magnitude and significance of effects? First, the grade curve metric is perfectly transparent. All its assumptions are known and are easily displayed. All its values are familiar to most audiences. Second, because it is familiar, audiences can evaluate the appropriateness of the curve and adjust the effect of the intervention on grades for themselves, if they wish. Finally, the audience does not need special expertise—that is, knowledge of which other research outcomes might

Grading on a curve, the student who would have received the middle C grade
on the algebra test in a class receiving study skills instruction would move
up to a C+ grade had he or she been graded in a class in which
no one else received instruction

When only the average student gets study skills instruction, her or his grade moves	Grade	% of Scores
	A	4
	A-	5
	B+	6.5
	B	7
	B-	8.5
... to here >	**C+**	**11.5**
... from here >	**C**	**15**
	C-	11.5
	D+	8.5
	D	7
	D-	6.5
	F+	5
	F	4

Figure 7.3 "Grading" a Hypothetical Study Skills Intervention on a Curve

SOURCE: Cooper (2009). Copyright 2008 by Blackwell Publishing. Reprinted with permission.

have been used as yardsticks—to translate findings to other curves they find
more legitimate.

My second use of U_3 gets around the problem of choosing one grade curve
among the many. It shows how a student's class rank might change as a function of the intervention. For example, assume that an intervention provides a
randomly chosen group of ninth graders with a course in general study skills,
and the outcome measure is students' cumulative grade point average upon

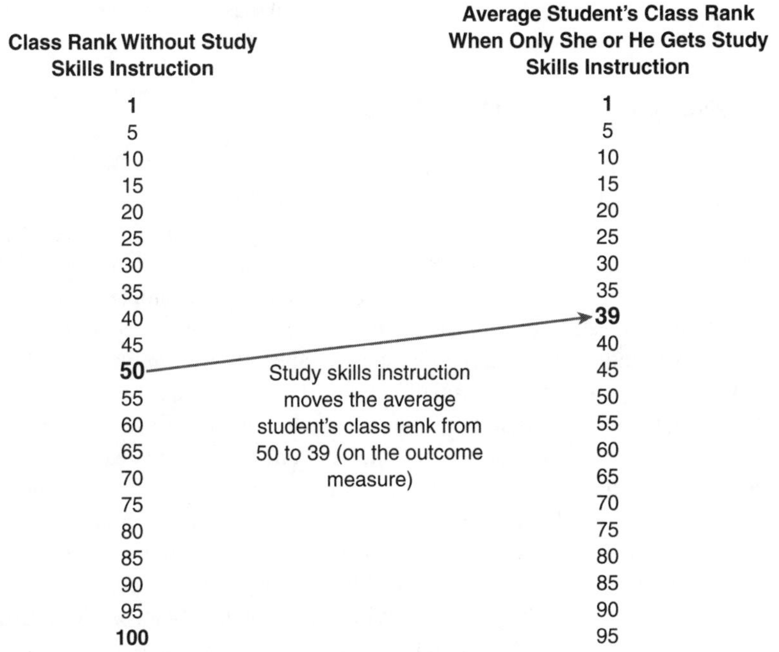

Class Rank Without Study Skills Instruction	Average Student's Class Rank When Only She or He Gets Study Skills Instruction
1	1
5	5
10	10
15	15
20	20
25	25
30	30
35	35
40	**39**
45	40
50 Study skills instruction	45
55 moves the average	50
60 student's class rank from	55
65 50 to 39 (on the outcome	60
70 measure)	65
75	70
80	75
85	80
90	85
95	90
100	95

Figure 7.4   Hypothetical Change in a Student's Class Rank Due to Study Skills Instruction

SOURCE: Cooper (2009). Copyright 2008 by Blackwell Publishing. Reprinted with permission.

graduation. Assume as well that the effect of the intervention is again $d = .3$ and $U_3 = 61.8\%$. In this scenario, the student who would have placed in the middle of the final class ranking would surpass 11% of students if he or she were the only student to receive instruction. (Eleven percent is the rounded difference between the 50th percentile student and the 61.8th percentile student.) Figure 7.4 presents this result visually for a graduating class with 100 students.

These are just two examples of how standardized effect sizes can be contextualized to convey greater intuitive meaning to general audiences. The grade curve translation is most meaningful when applied to outcome measures that are natural candidates for grading on a curve, such as class exams. However, the need to provide a grading curve is a drawback to its use. The class rank translation is most meaningful in the context of high school interventions that are meant to have general effects on achievement, as measured by cumulative grade point averages, and class rank has meaning because of its use in college admissions.

Translations of Binomial Effect Size Display

Rosenthal and Rubin (1982) provide a translation of the effects of discrete interventions on dichotomous outcomes, called the binomial effect size display (BESD). They suggest it could be used for other effect size metrics as well. The BESD transforms a d-index and r-index into a 2 × 2 table with the marginals assumed to be equal for both rows and columns. In their examples, Rosenthal and Rubin assume 100 participants, with 50 in each of the two conditions and 50 outcomes indicating intervention success and 50 indicating failure. They show that Cohen's relatively "small" effect of $d = .20$ (equivalent to $r = .1$, explaining 1% of the variance) is associated with an increase in success rates from 45% to 55%. For example, an intervention meant to increase students' reading scores above a proficiency threshold and with this effect size would mean that 10 more children in every 100 would meet the minimum requirement. This should be a metric that most general audiences will understand.

The BESD is not without its critics (little is in this area), especially because of its assumptions regarding marginal values (Randolph & Shawn, 2005). Even so, it seems that the BESD is an intuitively appealing expression of effect when the intervention outcome is dichotomous, and even more so when the observed marginals can be retrieved. Indeed, when this information is available, the BESD reduces to a display of raw score results. Its application is more difficult when it requires the audience to mentally convert continuous outcome measures into dichotomous ones.

Translations of Effects
Involving Two Continuous Measures

Providing translations for associations between two continuous variables—ß-weights and r-indexes—requires knowledge of the raw scales and the standard deviations of the predictor and outcome. With this information, you can describe the change in outcome associated with a specified additional amount of exposure to the intervention. For example, assume a predictor variable is the number of minutes a child with a behavior problem spends in counseling each week, and the standard deviation for this variable is 30 minutes. The outcome variable is the number of absences from school, and its standard deviation is 4. Both are measured across a full school year. In such case, a ß-weight or r-index of −.50 would mean that, on average, students in the sample who spent 30 more minutes in counseling each week also had two fewer absences that year.

CONCLUSION

To conclude, then, along with analyses that examine the impact of missing data and varying assumptions for the statistical analyses, the next question you should ask when evaluating the interpretation of effect sizes in meta-analysis is,

Did the synthesists (a) contrast the magnitude of effects with other related effect sizes and/or (b) present a practical interpretation of the significance of the effects?

A complete and careful assessment of the generality of the synthesis' findings and the confidence with which you can draw causal inferences from it are also critical parts of how you will interpret the findings of a research synthesis.

EXERCISES

Find two primary research reports on the same topic that vary in method. Then

1. calculate the effect sizes reported in each;

2. compare the effect sizes to one another, taking into account the influences of their different methods; and

3. decide whether you consider the magnitude of the effect sizes to be

   a. large, medium, or small and
   b. important or not important.

4. Justify your decision.

8

Step 7

Presenting the Results

What information should be included in the report of the synthesis?

Primary Function in Research Synthesis

To identify the aspects of methods and results readers of the report will need to know to evaluate the synthesis

Procedural Variation That Might Produce Differences in Conclusions

Variation in reporting might (a) lead readers to place more or less trust in synthesis outcomes and (b) influence others' ability to replicate results

Question to Ask When Presenting the Research Synthesis Methods and Results

Were the procedures and results of the research synthesis documented clearly and completely?

This chapter describes

- A format for research syntheses reports
- How to present tabulated data in syntheses

The transformation of your notes, printouts, and coding forms into a cohesive public document describing your research synthesis is a task with profound implications for the accumulation of knowledge. All your efforts to conduct a trustworthy and convincing integration of the research literature will be for naught unless you pay careful attention to how your synthesis is described in the report.

REPORT WRITING IN SOCIAL SCIENCE RESEARCH

The codified guidelines used by many social science disciplines for reporting primary research are contained in The American Psychological Association's *Publication Manual* (2001). The *Publication Manual* is quite specific about the style and format of reports, and it even gives some guidance concerning grammar and the clear expression of ideas. It tells researchers how to set up a manuscript page, what the major section headings should be, and what conventions to use when reporting the results of statistical analyses, among many other details of report preparation. Naturally, however, it is much less explicit in guiding judgments about what makes a finding important to readers. It would be impossible to explicate a general set of rules for defining the scientific importance of results. Hopefully, the previous chapter has provided you with some guidance on how to interpret the findings of your research synthesis.

Because the integration of research results has grown in importance, several attempts have been made to develop standards for the reporting of research syntheses, especially those that contain meta-analyses. Four proposals regarding what information should be included in the report of a meta-analysis come from researchers and statisticians in the medical sciences. These include the QUOROM Statement (Quality of Reporting of Meta-analysis; Moher et al., 1999) and its revision, PRISMA (Preferred Reporting Items for Systematic Reviews and Meta-analyses; Moher, Tetzlaff, Altman, & the PRISMA Group, 2008); MOOSE (Meta-analysis of Observational Studies in Epidemiology; Stroup et al., 2000); and the Potsdam consultation on meta-analysis (Cook, Sackett, & Spitzer, 1995). In the social sciences, a task force of the American Psychological Association proposed a set of reporting standards for meta-analysis, called MARS (Meta-Analysis Reporting Standards; APA Publications and Communications Board Working Group on Journal Article Reporting Standards, 2008).[1] The MARS was constructed by, first, comparing the content of the aforementioned four sets of standards and developing a list of elements contained in any of these. Second, the items on this list were rewritten to make the terms used in them more familiar to social science audiences. Third, the members of the working group added some items of their own. Then, this set of items was shared with members of the Society for Research Synthesis Methodology, who were asked to make suggestions about the inclusion of other items or the removal of

---

[1] In the interest of full disclosure, I should mention that I served as chair of this committee.

items that seemed unnecessary. Finally, the Publications and Communications Board of the American Psychological Association reacted to the items. After receiving these reactions, the working group arrived at the list of recommendations contained in Table 8.1. The emergence of these reporting guidelines is critical to progress in the social sciences because they will promote the complete and transparent reporting of methods and results for meta-analyses. Next, I will provide a bit more context and detail regarding the items in the MARS.

META-ANALYSIS
REPORTING STANDARDS (MARS)

As Table 8.1 reveals, the format for reporting meta-analyses has evolved to look a lot like that of reports of primary research, with an introduction, method section, results section, and discussion. If a research synthesis does not include a meta-analysis, there is still much sound advice for preparing a report in Table 8.1, though many of the items listed under the method and results sections would be irrelevant. In the following, I will assume that your report is describing the results of a research synthesis that employed meta-analytic techniques.

Title

It is important that the title of your report include the term "meta-analysis," if one was conducted, or "research synthesis," "research review," or a related term, if a meta-analysis was not performed. These terms are very informative about what is contained in your report. Also, people who are searching the literature for documents on your topic using a computerized reference database may use one of these terms if they are interested in finding only documents that contain summaries of the literature. If your title does not contain one of these terms and a search is conducted on titles only, your report will not be included in the search results. So, for example, our title "A Meta-Analysis on the Effect of Choice on Intrinsic Motivation and Related Outcomes" includes the three terms most likely to be used in a search by someone interested in finding documents like ours.

Abstract

The abstract for a research synthesis follows the same rules as abstracts for primary research. Because an abstract is short, you can only spend a sentence or two on stating the problem, the kinds of studies that were included in the meta-analysis, your method and results, and major conclusions. As with the title, it is important to think about people doing literature searches when writing your abstract. Remember to include the terms you think searchers who are interested in your topic are likely to pick when they construct their computer searches. Also, remember that many people will read only your abstract, so you must tell them the most important things about your meta-analysis.

The Introduction Section

The introduction to a research synthesis sets the stage for the empirical results that follow. It should contain a conceptual presentation of the research problem and a statement of the problem's significance. Introductions are typically short in primary research reports. In research syntheses, introductions should be considerably more detailed. You should attempt to present a complete overview of the research question, including its theoretical, practical, and methodological history. Where do the concepts involved in the research come from? Are they grounded in theory—as is, for example, the notion of intrinsic motivation—or in practical circumstances—as is the notion of homework? Are there theoretical debates surrounding the meaning or utility of the concepts? How do theories predict that the concepts will be related to one another? Are there conflicting predictions associated with different theories? What variables do different theories, scholars, or practitioners suggest might influence the strength of the relation?

The introduction to a research synthesis must contextualize the problem under consideration. Especially when the synthesist intends to report a meta-analysis, it is crucial that ample attention be paid to the qualitative and historical debates surrounding the research question. Otherwise, you will be open to the criticism that numbers have been crunched together without ample appreciation for the conceptual and contextual underpinnings that give empirical data their meaning.

Once the context of the problem has been laid out, the introduction then should describe how the important issues you have identified have guided your decisions about how the meta-analysis was conducted. How did you translate the theoretical, practical, and historical issues and debates into your choices about what moderator variables to explore? Were there issues of concern regarding how studies were designed and implemented, and were these represented in your meta-analysis?

The introduction to a research synthesis is also where you should discuss previous efforts to integrate the research on the topic. This description of past syntheses should highlight what has been learned from these efforts as well as point out their inconsistencies and methodological strengths and weaknesses. The

Table 8.1   Meta-Analysis Reporting Standards

Paper Section and Topic	Description
Title	• Make it clear that the report describes a research synthesis and include "meta-analysis," if applicable • Footnote funding source(s)
Abstract	• The problem or relation(s) under investigation • Study eligibility criteria • Type(s) of participants included in primary studies • Meta-analysis methods (indicating whether a fixed or random model was used) • Main results (including the more important effect sizes and any important moderators of these effect sizes) • Conclusions (including limitations) • Implications for theory, policy, and/or practice

Introduction	• Clear statement of the question or relation(s) under investigation
	  o Historical background
	  o Theoretical, policy, and/or practical issues related to the question or relation(s) of interest
	  o Rationale for the selection and coding of potential moderators and mediators of results
	  o Types of study designs used in the primary research, their strengths and weaknesses
	  o Types of predictor and outcome measures used, their psychometric characteristics
	  o Populations to which the question or relation is relevant
	  o Hypotheses, if any

Method	
Inclusion and Exclusion Criteria	• Operational characteristics of independent (predictor) and dependent (outcome) variable(s) • Eligible participant populations • Eligible research design features (e.g., random assignment only, minimal sample size) • Time period in which studies needed to be conducted • Geographical and/or cultural restrictions
Moderator and Mediator Analyses	• Definition of all coding categories used to test moderators or mediators of the relation(s) of interest

Paper Section and Topic	Description

Search Strategies	• Reference and citation databases searched
	• Registries (including prospective registries) searched
	  o Keywords used to enter databases and registries
	  o Search software used and version
	• Time period in which studies needed to be conducted, if applicable
	• Other efforts to retrieve all available studies, e.g.,
	  o Listservs queried
	  o Contacts made with authors (and how authors were chosen)
	  o Reference lists of reports examined
	• Method of addressing reports in languages other than English
	• Process for determining study eligibility
	• Aspects of reports examined (i.e., title, abstract, and/or full text)
	  o Number and qualifications of relevance judges
	  o Indication of agreement
	  o How disagreements were resolved
	• Treatment of unpublished studies

Coding Procedures	• Number and qualifications of coders (e.g., level of expertise in the area, training)
	• Intercoder reliability or agreement
	• Whether each report was coded by more than one coder and, if so, how disagreements were resolved
	• Assessment of study quality
	  o If a quality scale was employed, a description of criteria and the procedures for application
	  o If study design features were coded, what these were
	• How missing data were handled

Statistical Methods	• Effect size metric(s)
	  o Effect sizes calculating formulas (e.g., means and SDs, use of univariate F-to-r transform, etc.)
	  o Corrections made to effect sizes (e.g., small sample bias, correction for unequal sample sizes, etc.)
	• Effect size averaging and/or weighting method(s)

(Continued)

Table 8.1 (Continued)

Paper Section and Topic	Description
Statistical Methods	• How effect size confidence intervals (or standard errors) were calculated • How effect size credibility intervals were calculated, if used • How studies with more than one effect size were handled • Whether fixed- and/or random-effects models were used and the model choice justification • How heterogeneity in effect sizes was assessed or estimated • Means and SDs for measurement artifacts, if construct-level relationships were the focus • Tests and any adjustments for data censoring (e.g., publication bias, selective reporting) • Tests for statistical outliers • Statistical power of the meta-analysis • Statistical programs or software packages used to conduct statistical analyses

Results	• Number of citations examined for relevance
	• List of citations included in the synthesis
	• Number of citations relevant on many but not all inclusion criteria excluded from the meta-analysis
	• Number of exclusions for each exclusion criteria (e.g., effect size could not be calculated), with examples
	• Table giving descriptive information for each included study, including effect size and sample size
	• Assessment of study quality, if any
	• Tables and/or graphic summaries
	  o Overall characteristics of the database (e.g., number of studies with different research designs)
	  o Overall effect size estimates, including measures of uncertainty (e.g., confidence and/or credibility intervals)
	• Results of moderator and mediator analyses (analyses of subsets of studies)
	  o Number of studies and total sample sizes for each moderator analysis
	  o Assessment of interrelations among variables used for moderator and mediator analyses
	• Assessment of bias including possible data censoring

Paper Section and Topic	Description

Discussion	• Statement of major findings
	• Consideration of alternative explanations for observed results
	  o Impact of data censoring
	• Generalizability of conclusions, e.g.,
	  o Relevant populations
	  o Treatment variations
	  o Dependent (outcome) variables
	  o Research designs, etc.
	• General limitations (including assessment of the quality of studies included)
	• Implications and interpretation for theory, policy, or practice
	• Guidelines for future research

SOURCE: APA Publications and Communications Board Working Group on Journal Article Reporting Standards (2008).

contribution of your new effort should be emphasized by a clear statement of the unresolved empirical questions and controversies addressed by your new work.

In sum, the introduction to a research synthesis should present a complete overview of the theoretical, conceptual, and/or practical issues surrounding the research problem. It should present the controversies in the topic area still to be resolved, and which of these were the focus of the new synthesis effort. It should present a description of prior syntheses, what their contribution and shortcomings were, and why your synthesis is innovative and important.

The Method Section

The purpose of a method section is to describe operationally how the research was conducted. The method section of a research synthesis will be considerably different from that of a primary research report. The MARS suggests that a meta-analysis method section will need to address five separate sets of questions—inclusion and exclusion criteria, moderator and mediator analysis, search strategies, coding procedures, and statistical methods. The order in which they are presented can vary, but you should consider using these topics as subheadings in the report.

Inclusion and exclusion criteria. The method section should address the criteria for relevance that were applied to the studies uncovered by the literature search. What characteristics of studies were used to determine whether a particular effort was relevant to the topic of interest? For example, in the synthesis of research on the effects of choice on intrinsic motivation, three criteria had to be met by every study included in the synthesis: (a) the study had to include an experimental manipulation of choice (not a naturalistic measure of choice); (b) the study had to use a measure of intrinsic motivation or a related outcome, such as effort, task performance, subsequent learning, or perceived competence; and (c) the study had to present enough information to allow us to compute an effect size.

Next, you need to describe what characteristics of studies would have led to their exclusion from the synthesis, even if they otherwise met the inclusion criteria. You should also state how many studies were excluded for any given reason. For example, the meta-analysis of the effect of choice on intrinsic motivation excluded studies that met the three inclusion criteria but were not conducted on normal populations in the United States or Canada. This led to the exclusion of two studies conducted on children with learning disabilities or behavior disorders and eight studies conducted outside North America.

When readers examine the relevance criteria employed in a synthesis, they will be critically evaluating your notions about how concepts and operations fit together. Considerable debate about the outcomes of a particular synthesis may focus on these decisions. Some readers may find that your relevance criteria were too broad—operational definitions of concepts were included that they feel were irrelevant. Of course, you can anticipate these concerns and use the debatable criteria as distinctions between studies and then analyze them as potential moderators of study results. Other readers may find that your operational definitions were too narrow. For example, some readers might think that we should have included samples from countries outside North America in our synthesis on choice and intrinsic motivation. However, we justified our decision by pointing out that very few studies were found that used non–North American samples and only a few countries were represented among these. Therefore, we felt that including these studies still would not have warranted generalizing our conclusions to people other than those living in North America. Moderator analyses could have been used to determine whether the effect of choice varied depending on the country sampled, but we felt there were too few studies to reliably conduct such an analysis. Still, these exclusion criteria might lead readers to examine excluded studies to determine if including their findings would affect the synthesis outcome.

In addition to this general description of the included and excluded evidence, this subsection is a good place to describe the typical methodologies found in primary research. The presentation of prototype studies is a good way to present methods that are used in many studies. You can choose several studies that exemplify the methods used in many other studies and present the specific details of these investigations. In instances where only a few studies are found to be relevant, this exercise may not be necessary—the description of the methods used in each study can be combined with the description of the study's results. In our meta-analysis of homework, we took this approach to describing the methods and results of the few studies that used experimental manipulations of homework.

Moderator and mediator analyses. Similar to the inclusion and exclusion criteria, the descriptions you give of the variables you tested as moderators or mediators of study results let readers know how you defined these variables and, especially, how you chose to distinguish among studies based on their different status on these variables. So, for example, the meta-analysis on choice and intrinsic motivation identified "the number of options per choice" as a potential variable that might mediate the effect of choice. Our method section defined this variable and told readers that we grouped the studies into those that provided (a) two options per choice, (b) three to five options, or (c) more than five options.

Searching strategies. Information on the sources, keywords, and years covered by the literature search allows the reader to assess the thoroughness of your search and therefore how much credibility to place in the conclusions of the synthesis. In terms of attempted replication, it is the description of the literature search that first would be examined when other scholars attempt to understand why different syntheses on the same topic have come to similar or conflicting conclusions. It is also good to include a rationale for the choice of sources, especially with regard to how different sources were used to complement one another in order to reduce bias in the sample of studies.

Coding procedures. A third subsection of methods should describe the characteristics of the people who retrieved information from the studies, the procedures used to train them, and how the reliability of the retrieved information was assessed, as well as what this assessment revealed. It is also important to discuss here how missing data were handled. For example, in our meta-analysis of choice and intrinsic motivation, we used our ability to calculate an effect size as an inclusion criterion. So studies were examined to determine whether an effect size could be calculated from them before the process of coding other information began. If no effect size was available, no further coding occurred. In other meta-analyses, estimation procedures might be used to fill in these blanks. The same is true for other missing study characteristics. For example, if a study lacks information on whether random assignment was used, the study might be represented as giving no such information. Other times, you might develop a convention that says if the use of random assignment was not mentioned, it was assumed the study did not use random assignment. These kinds of rules should be described in this section of your report.

The coding section also can be where you described how you made judgments about study quality. The decision about where to put information on study quality really can fit in several sections, so it is best placed where it provides for the clearest exposition. If studies were excluded based on features of their design or implementation, this would be reported with other inclusion and exclusion criteria.

Statistical methods. The final topics described in the method section of a research synthesis are the procedures and conventions used to carry out any quantitative analysis of results. Why was a particular effect size metric chosen and how was it calculated? What analyses techniques were used to combine results of separate tests of a hypothesis and to examine the variability in findings across tests? This section should contain a rationale for each procedural choice and convention you use and should describe what the expected impact of each choice might be on the outcomes of the research synthesis.

Another important topic to cover in this subsection concerns how you identified independent findings (see Chapter 4). You should carefully spell out the criteria used to determine whether you considered as independent or dependent multiple hypothesis tests from the same laboratory, report, or study.

The Results Section

The results section should present a summary description of the literature and the findings of the meta-analysis. It should also present any results of the synthesis used to test the implications of different assumptions about the data, such as different models of error and different patterns of missing data. While the results sections of syntheses will vary considerably depending on the nature of the research topic and evidence, the MARS provides a good general strategy for presenting results. Next, I suggest some possible subsections for organizing the presentation of results, along with some suggestions regarding how to visually display your findings in tables and figures. Additional suggestions regarding the presentation of data in meta-analysis can be found in Borman and Grigg (2009).

Results of the literature search. Often, synthesists will present a table that lists all the studies included in the meta-analysis. This table will also describe a few critical characteristics of each study. For example, Table 8.2 reproduces the table we used in the synthesis of homework research to describe the six studies that tested the effects of homework using an experimental manipulation. We decided that the most important information to include in the table, along with the name of the first author and year of report appearance, was the research design, the number of classes and students included in the study, the students' grade level, the subject matter of the homework assignment, the achievement outcome measure, and the effect size. Nearly all tables of this sort include information on author and year, sample size, and effect size, so this is a pretty simple example. Sometimes the information you want to present in this table will be extensive. If so, you may want to use abbreviations. Table 8.3 presents such a table reproduced from our meta-analysis on choice and intrinsic motivation. In this case, we resorted to an extensive footnote to describe the abbreviations.

In some instances, you may also want to provide a table that describes the studies that were potentially relevant but were excluded. The MARS refers to these as studies "relevant on many but not all inclusion criteria." This table might look like Table 8.2 or 8.3; it is usually not as extensive and contains columns that identify the relevance criteria or at least a column that explains the criteria that led to the study's exclusion.

Table 8.3 contains only a small portion of the studies that appeared in the actual table. Because tables that describe the studies that went into a meta-analysis can be quite long, journals are now providing auxiliary websites on which this and other material can be placed, rather than including it in the printed version of the manuscript. In electronic versions of articles, the tables may reside on separate web pages but be linked to the article at the point in the report that they would otherwise appear. When you submit your report for publication, you should be sure to include these tables (in the report or in a separate document), and when your paper is accepted, you and the editor will decide what the best strategy is to present your results.

Assessment of study quality. If you conducted an assessment of the quality of each study, this can be included in the described tables. Or, if the judgments were complex, you might consider presenting them in a table of their own. For example, the information in Table 5.3 could be presented in a table in which the quality dimensions are presented in columns and quality ratings (the "yes" and "no" in Table 5.3) are given in separate rows devoted to each study.

Aggregate description of the literature. Certain aggregate descriptive statistics about the literature should be reported as well. Table 8.4 presents the section of our homework meta-analysis that presented the aggregate results for studies that correlated a measure of the amount of homework a student did and the student's achievement. This subsection includes the following elements:

- The number of studies, effect sizes, and samples that went into the meta-analysis
- A description of studies that caused any differences in these numbers, that is, studies with more than one sample and/or outcome measure
- The range of years that reports appeared[2]
- The total number of participants across all studies and the range, median, mean, and variance of sample sizes within studies
- A test for statistical outliers among the sample sizes
- The variables that could not be tested as moderators because either (a) too many studies were missing this information or (b) there was insufficient variation across studies
- The number of positive and negative effect sizes
- The range of and median effect size
- The unweighted and weighted mean effect size and the confidence interval for the weighted mean
- A test for statistical outliers among the effect sizes
- The results of a test for missing data and how adjusting for missing data affected the cumulative results

You may consider putting some of this information in a table, but in the homework example, we felt some of the nuances in the data and the rationales for our choices needed explanation that might be lost in a tabular presentation.

Graphic presentation of results. A good way to present the results of your meta-analysis is to use what is called a Forrest Plot. Figure 8.1 presents a Forrest Plot of the results of the hypothetical meta-analysis I used in Chapter 6

---

[2] In the meta-analysis of individual differences in rape attitudes, a chart was presented that illustrated the frequency of reports on rape attitudes because we wanted to show how interest in the topic was growing.

Table 8.2 Studies That Manipulated Homework Versus No-Homework Conditions

Author (Year)	Research Design	Classes Students ESS[a]	Grade Level	Subject Matter	Type of Achievement Measure	Effect Size
Finstad (1987)	Nonequivalent control with no pretest differences	2 39 5.2	2	Places to 100	Unit test developed by Harcourt Brace Jovanovich	+.97
Foyle (1984)	• Randomized by class • Analyzed by student	6 131 15.8	9–12	American history	Unit test developed by the teacher	+.46
Foyle (1990)	• Randomized by class • Analyzed by student	4 64 10.2	5	Social studies	Unit test developed by the teacher	+.90
McGrath (1992)	• Randomized within class • Analyzed by student	3 94 8.0	12	Shakespeare	Unit test developed by Harcourt Brace Jovanovich	+.39
Meloy (1987)	Unlucky random assignment followed by nonequivalent control with pretest	5 70 12.6 3 36 7.4	3 4	English skills	• Unit test developed by McDougal Littell • Researcher-shortened version of the Iowa Test of Basic Skills Language subtest • Unit test developed by McDougal Littell • Researcher-shortened version of the Iowa Test of Basic Skills Language subtest	+ – + –
Townsend (1995)	Nonequivalent control without equating	2 40 5.2	3	Vocabulary	Unit test developed by the teacher	+.71

SOURCE: Cooper, Robinson, and Patall (2006, p. 18). Copyright 2006 by the American Educational Research Association. Reprinted with permission.
a. ESS stands for effective sample size based on an assumed intraclass correlation of .35.

Table 8.3 Characteristics of Selected Experimental Studies Examining the Effects of Choice on Intrinsic Motivation

Author (Year)	Type of Document	Sample	Number of Choices	Options	Choice Type	Control Group Type	Knowledge of Alternatives	Design	Setting	Reward Condition	Outcome	Measure Type	Effect Size
Abrahams 1 (1988)	D	48a A	4 SC	IND	IR	RAC	UAW	Y	TUL	NRW	FCTS	B	+.90
											I/E/L	S	+.84
											TP	B	+.18
Abrahams 2 (1988)	D	42b A	4 SC	IND	IR	RAC	UAW	Y	TUL	NRW	FCTS	B	+.51
											I/E	S	+.12
											WTE	S	+.41
Amabile & Gitomer (1984)	J	28 C	5 MC	10	IR	NSOC	AW	Y	LNS	NRW	FCTS	B	+.79
											CR	S	+1.06
Bartleme (1983)	D	104 A	8 MC	IND	IR	RAC	UAW	Y	TUL	CLPSD	E/L	S	+.07
											E/L	S	–.11
											E/L	S	+.08
											WTE	S	–.16
											TP	B	–.05
											SL	B	–.22
		34 A								NRW	E/L	S	+.46
											E/L	S	–.53
											E/L	S	+.15
											WTE	S	+.10
											TP	B	+.17
											SL	B	–.22

Becker (1997)	J	41 A	1	2	IR	NSOC	UAW	M	NS	RWd NRW	E/L	S	–.17
		70 A									E/L	S	–.05
											E/L	S	+.10
											WTE	S	–.56
											TP	B	–.17
											SL	B	–.17
											GIMe	S	+.58
											TP	B	+1.25

SOURCE: Patall, Cooper, and Robinson (2008, 281–286). Copyright 2008 by the American Psychological Association. Adapted with permission.

NOTE: D = Dissertation, J = Journal article, MT = Master's thesis, R = Report, A = Adults, C = Children, MC = Multiple choices from a list of options, SC = Successive choices, IND = Indeterminate number of options, ACT = Choice of activities, V = Choice of versions, IR = Instructionally relevant choice, IIR = Instructionally irrelevant choice, CRW = Choice of rewards, MX = Mixed, SOC = Significant other control, NSOC = Nonsignificant other control, RAC = Random assignment control, DC = Denied choice, SGC = Suggested choice control, SMC = Some choice control, AW = Aware of alternatives, UAW = Unaware of alternatives, Y = Yoked, M = Matched, NYM = No yoking or matching, TUL = Traditional university laboratory, LNS = Laboratory within a natural setting, NS = Natural setting, NRW = No reward, RW = Reward, FCTS = free choice time spent, FCE = Free choice to engage in activity, I = interest, E/L = enjoyment/liking, WTE = Willingness to engage in task again, I/E/L = Interest/Enjoyment/Liking, GIM = General intrinsic motivation, CIM = Combined intrinsic motivation measure, TP = Task performance, EF = Effort, SL = Subsequent learning, CR = Creativity, PFC = Preference for challenge, PC = Perceived choice, P/T = Pressure/tension, SF = Satisfaction, B = Behavioral, S = Self-report, NA = Not applicable, NR = Not reported, VRD = Varied, CLPSD = Collapsed condition. For studies in which there were a number of subgroups, both subgroup effect sizes and overall effect sizes collapsed across subgroups are presented. The overall effect sizes collapsed across subgroups appear in the top of a row for every study with multiple subgroups. Note that overall effect sizes are not equal to taking an average of the subgroup effects. This is because overall effect sizes were computed using means, standard deviations, t- or F-tests provided in original paper rather than computed by averaging across the effect sizes of subgroups.

Table 8.4   An Example of a Text Summary of Aggregate Meta-Analysis Results

---

The literature search uncovered 32 studies that described the correlations between the time that a student spent on homework, as reported by either the student or a parent, and a measure of academic achievement. These studies are listed in Table 8. The 32 studies reported 69 separate correlations based on 35 separate samples of students. Cooper et al. (1998) reported 8 correlations, separating out effects for elementary and secondary students (two independent samples) on both class grades and standardized tests with time-on-homework reported by either students or parents. Drazen (1992) reported 12 correlations, for reading, math, and multiple subjects for three national surveys (three independent samples). Bents-Hill (1988) reported 8 correlations, for language arts, math, reading, and multiple subjects for both class grades and for a standardized test of achievement. Epstein (1988), Olson (1988), and Walker (2002) each reported two effect sizes, one for math and one for reading. Fehrmann et al. (1992), Wynn (1996), and Keith and Benson (1992) each reported two correlations, one involving class grades and one involving achievement test results. Hendrix et al. (1990) reported three correlations, one for multiple subjects, one for verbal ability, and one for nonverbal ability. Mau & Lynn (2000) reported three correlations, one for math, one for reading, and one for science. Singh et al. (2002) reported two correlations for math and one for science.

The 32 studies appeared between the years 1987 and 2004. The sample sizes ranged from 55 to approximately 58,000 with a median size of 1,584. The mean sample size was 8,598 with a standard deviation of 12,856, suggesting a non-normal distribution. The Grubbs test revealed a significant outlier, $p < .05$. This sample was the largest in the dataset, reported by Drazen (1992) for six correlations obtained from the 1980 High School and Beyond longitudinal study. As a result, we replaced these six sample sizes with the next largest sample size in the dataset, 28,051. The mean sample size for the adjusted dataset was 7,742 with a standard deviation of 10,192. We then presented the results of a test of whether any of these sample sizes were statistical outliers.

Only three studies specifically mentioned that students were drawn from regular education classrooms and one of these studies included learning disabled students as well (Deslandes, 1999). The remaining studies did not report information on the students' achievement or ability level. Seventeen studies did not report information on the socioeconomic status of students, 11 reported that the sample's SES was "mixed, 3 described the sample as middle SES, and 1 as lower SES. Seventeen studies did not report the sex make-up of the sample while 14 reports said the sample was comprised of both sexes. Only one study reported correlations separately for males and females. Because of a lack of reporting or variation across categories, no analyses were conducted on these variables.[1]

Of the 69 correlations, 50 were in a positive direction and 19 in a negative direction. The mean unweighted correlation across the 35 samples (averaging multiple correlations within each sample) was $r = .14$, the median was $r = .17$, and the correlations ranged from $-.25$ to $.65$.

The weighted average correlation was $r = .24$ using a fixed-error model with a 95% confidence interval (95% CI) from $.24$ to $.25$. The weighted average correlation was $r = .16$ using a random-error model with a 95% confidence interval from $.13$ to $.19$. Clearly then, the hypothesis that the relationship between homework and achievement is $r = 0$ can be rejected under either error model. There were no significant outliers among the correlations so all were retained for further analysis.

The trim-and-fill analyses were conducted in several different ways. We performed the analyses looking for asymmetry using both fixed and random error models to impute the mean correlation and creating graphs using both fixed and random models (see Borenstein et al., 2005) while searching for possible missing correlations on the left side of the distribution (those that would reduce the size of the positive correlation). None of the analyses produced results different from those described above. Using a random error model, there was evidence that three effect sizes might have been missing and imputing them would lower the mean correlation to $r = .23$ (95% CI = $.22/.23$). The random error results of this analysis were $r = .14$ (95% CI = $.11/.17$).

SOURCE: Cooper, Robinson, and Patall (2006, pp. 29, 37, 40). Copyright 2006 by the American Educational Research Association. Adapted with permission.

to illustrate the mechanics of the calculations (Table 6.5). This figure was generated by the Comprehensive Meta-Analysis software package (Borenstein, Hedges, Higgins, & Rothstein, 2005).The first three columns of the figure present the study number, whether it was a member of Moderator Group A or B, and its total sample size.[3] The next three columns give each study's correlation and the lower and upper limits of its 95% confidence interval. The Comprehensive Meta-Analysis program would let me report other statistics here as well. The Forrest Plot part of the figure is on the right. This graph presents each correlation in a "box and whiskers" display. The box is centered on the value of the study's correlation. The size of the box is proportional to the study's sample size relative to the other studies in the meta-analysis.

[3] Had this been an actual meta-analysis, I would have substituted the first author's name and the year of the report for the study number.

Model	Study name	Group by	Statistics for each study			Correlation and 95% CI
		Moderator	Total	Correlation	Lower limit	Upper limit
	1.000	A	3505	0.06	0.03	0.09
	2.000	A	3606	0.12	0.09	0.15
	3.000	A	4157	0.22	0.19	0.25
Fixed		A		0.14	0.12	0.16
	4.000	B	1021	0.08	0.02	0.14
	5.000	B		0.27	0.23	0.31
	6.000	B	1955	0.26	0.25	0.28
Fixed		B	12146	0.25	0.24	0.27
Fixed		Overall		0.20	0.19	0.22

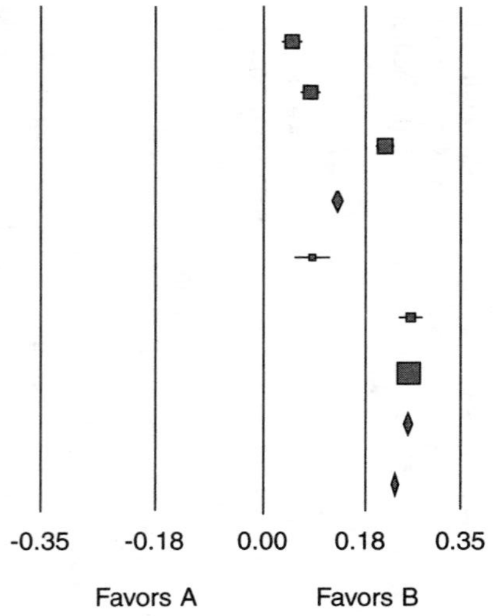

Figure 8.1 Forrest Plot of Hypothetical Meta-Analysis Conducted in Chapter 6

NOTE: This figure was generated using *Comprehensive Meta-Analysis*, V. 2 (Borenstein et al., 2005).

The length of the whiskers depicts the correlation's confidence interval. Note as well that the figure includes the weighted average correlations and confidence intervals for the Group A and B studies and for the overall set of studies (using a fixed-effect model; a random-effect model could also have been requested). These averages are depicted on the Forrest Plot as diamonds rather than boxes and whiskers.[4] This type of figure is growing in popularity for the presentation of meta-analytic results.

Another good way to present graphically the effect sizes that contribute to a meta-analytic database is in the form of a stem-and-leaf display. In a simple stem-and-leaf display, the first decimal place of each effect size acts as the stem, which is placed on the left side of a vertical line. The second decimal place acts as the leaf, placed on the right side of the vertical line. Leaves of effect sizes sharing the same stems are placed on the same line.

Our example meta-analyses on homework used a stem-and-leaf display, so I have reproduced it here in Figure 8.2. This is a somewhat more complex stem-and-leaf display. Here, we used this graphic to present the results of 33 studies that correlated the amount of homework students reported doing each night with a measure of their achievement. The stems are the first digit of the correlations and are presented in the middle column of the figure. The leaves are the second digit of each correlation. In the left side of the center column, we have represented each of the 10 correlations we found that were calculated based on responses from children in elementary school, grades 1 through 6. On the right side of the center column, we represented the 23 correlations based on secondary school samples. So, with no loss in the precision of the information presented, this figure allows the reader to see the shape and dispersion of the 33 correlations and to note that the correlations are most often positive. But they can also visually detect a relationship between the magnitude of correlations and the grade level of students.

In general, then, the subsection that describes the aggregate results of the meta-analysis should give the reader a broad quantitative overview of the literature. This should complement the qualitative overviews contained in the introduction and method sections. It should provide the reader with a sense of the kinds of people, procedures, and circumstances contained in the studies. This subsection of results gives readers an opportunity to assess for themselves the representativeness of the sampled people and circumstances relative to the target populations. Also, it provides the broad overview of the findings regarding the main hypothesis under investigation.

---

[4] The calculations in Figure 8.1 are based on r-indexes transformed to z-scores then transformed back to rs. So, the results differ very slightly from those in Table 6.5.

Lower Grades	Stem	Upper Grades
5	+.6	
	+.3	00
6	+.2	998665
1	+.2	32200000
5	+.1	877
1	+.1	
	+.0	4
689	-.0	38
1	-.1	
5	-.2	3

Figure 8.2 Distribution of Correlations Between Time on Homework and Achievement as a Function of Grade Level

SOURCE: Cooper, Robinson, and Patall (2006, p. 43). Copyright 2006 by the American Educational Research Association. Reprinted with permission.

NOTE: Lower grades represent grades 1 through 6. Upper grades represent grades 7 through 12 or samples that were described as middle or high school.

Analyses of moderators of study results. Another subsection should describe the results of analyses meant to uncover study characteristics that might have influenced their outcomes. For each moderator tested, the report should present results on whether the study characteristic was statistically significantly associated with variance in effect sizes. If the moderator proved significant, the report should present an average effect size and confidence interval for each grouping of studies. For example, we used a table to report the results from our search for moderators of the effects of choice on intrinsic motivation. This table is partially reproduced here as Table 8.5. Note that the number of findings differed slightly for each moderator variable we tested due to our use of a shifting unit of analysis.

Finally, the section describing moderator and mediator analyses should give readers some idea of the interrelationships among the different predictors of effect sizes. So, for example, in the report of our meta-analysis on the effects of choice on intrinsic motivation, we included a table that presented a matrix of the relationships between each pair of moderator variables. These interrelationships were used in the discussion of results to caution readers about possible confounds among our results.

In sum, the results section should contain your overall quantitative description of the covered literature, a description of the overall findings regarding the hypotheses or relationships of primary interest, and the outcomes of the search for moderators and mediators of relationships. This lays the groundwork for the substantive discussion that follows.

The Discussion Section

The discussion section of a research synthesis serves the same functions served by discussions in primary research. Discussions typically contain at least five components.

First, your discussion should present a summary of the major findings of the synthesis. This should not be too long and should focus primarily on the results you will spend time interpreting.

Second, you should interpret the major findings. The interpretation should describe the magnitude of the important effect sizes and their substantive meaning. This will involve examining the results in relation to the predictions you made in the introduction. Also, you need to examine the results for what they tell us about the theories and theoretical debates presented in the introduction.

Third, your discussion should consider alternative explanations for your data. Typically, these will include, at a minimum, consideration of the possible impact of (a) missing data, (b) correlations among moderator variables, and (c) issues arising from methodological artifacts shared by the studies going into the meta-analysis.

Fourth, you will need to examine the generalizability of your findings. This will require you to consider (a) whether participants from all the relevant sub-populations have been included in the studies that make up your meta-analytic database, (b) whether important variations in independent or predictor variables and dependent or outcome variables are represented (or not) in the studies, and (c) the match between the research designs used in the individual studies and the inferences you wish to draw.

Finally, you should include a discussion of topics that need to be examined in future research. These should include new questions raised by the outcomes of the synthesis, and old questions left unresolved because of ambiguous synthesis results or a lack of prior primary research.

In general, then, the discussion section of a research synthesis report is used to make substantive interpretation of findings, to assess the generalizability of findings, to appraise whether past controversies have been resolved, and to suggest fruitful directions for future research.

I have rarely, if ever, seen a report of a research synthesis that included everything I have mentioned and everything listed in the MARS. Sometimes this is understandable; the relevance of the information is minimal given the nature of the literature being described. Other times, the omission is more concerning. It leaves the reader wondering how to interpret the results and, ultimately, whether the results are to be trusted. So, it is important to ask, when you consider the report of the results of a research synthesis,

Were the procedures and results of the research synthesis documented clearly and completely?

Table 8.5 Table of Results of Moderator Analyses Examining the Effect of Choice on Intrinsic Motivation

Moderators	k	d	95% Confidence Interval		Q_b
			Low Estimate	High Estimate	
Publication type					14.98**(4.04)*
Published	28	$.41^{**}(.46)^{**}$	.33(.31)	.48(.60)	
Unpublished	18	$.20^{**}(.26)^{**}$	.13(.14)	.28(.38)	
Choice type					21.61**(5.63)
Choice of activities	11	$.16^{**}(.20)^{**}$	.06(.04)	.26(.35)	
Choice of versions	8	$.27^{**}(.26)^{**}$	.15(.06)	.38(.46)	
Instructionally irrelevant	8	$.59^{**}(.61)^{**}$	.43(.29)	.74(.94)	
Instructionally relevant	9	$.24^{**}(.33)^{**}$	.14(.14)	.34(.51)	
Choice of reward	3	$.35^{**}(.34)$	.09(−.03)	.60(.71)	
Number of options per choice					5.62$^+$(3.29)
Two	10	$.20^{**}(.19)^{**}$	.10(.05)	.29(.33)	
Three to five	13	$.38^{**}(.43)^{**}$	.26(.16)	.50(.69)	
More than five	18	$.26^{**}(.34)^{**}$	.18(.19)	.34(.49)	

Moderators	k	d	95% Confidence Interval		Q_b
			Low Estimate	High Estimate	
Number of choices					32.01**(11.15)**
One choice	21	$.21^{**}(.23)^{**}$	.14(.12)	.28(.33)	
Multiple choices	5	$.18^{**}(.25)$	.04(-.02)	.31(.53)	
Successive choices	18	$.54^{**}(.58)^{**}$	.44(.40)	.64(.77)	
Number of choices					27.66**(10.28)**
One choice	21	$.21^{**}(.23)^{**}$	.14(.12)	.28(.33)	
Two to four choices	12	$.61^{**}(.63)^{**}$	.48(.38)	.75(.88)	
More than five choices	12	$.32^{**}(.45)^{**}$	.22(.23)	.43(.66)	
Reward					24.41**(12.16)**
No reward	40	$.35^{**}(.40)^{**}$	.29(.27)	.41(.52)	
Reward internal to choice manipulation	5	.35**(.36)**	.16(.08)	.54(.64)	
Reward external to choice manipulation	5	-.01(-.02)	-.15(-.22)	.12(.18)	

SOURCE: Patall, Cooper, and Robinson (2008, p. 289). Copyright 2008 by the American Psychological Association. Adapted with permission.

NOTE: Random effects Q values and point estimates are presented in parentheses. $+p < .10$, $*p < .05$, $**p < .01$.

EXERCISES

Find a report of a meta-analysis that interests you. As you read it, check off the items in the MARS that are included in the report. What items are missing? Are they important to how you might interpret the findings? If so, how might their omission change your confidence in the conclusions of the synthesis?

9

Conclusion

Threats to the Validity of
Research Synthesis Conclusions

This chapter describes

For each stage of a research synthesis,

- The general validity issues associated with the methodological choices made during that stage
- The specific threats to validity
- What synthesists can do to lessen the chances that the threats will be plausible alternative explanations to their conclusions
- The cost and feasibility of conducting research syntheses
- The value of disconfirmation in science
- Creativity in the research synthesis process

In order to help you keep in mind the implications of decisions you make as you carry out your research synthesis, in this chapter I present some of the major threats to validity you will encounter at each stage of your project. I also summarize some of the practices you can implement to lessen the plausibility of these threats. Also, there are several issues related to research synthesis that involve more general and philosophical considerations in applying the guidelines set forth in the previous chapters. I end the chapter, and the text, by briefly addressing these issues.

VALIDITY ISSUES

Recall that Campbell and Stanley's (1963) list of validity threats to primary research was expanded and rearranged by Bracht and Glass (1968), Campbell

(1969), Cook and Campbell (1979), and, most recently, by Shadish, Cook, and Campbell (2002). This same expansion and rearranging of threats to validity has also occurred for research synthesis. In 1984, the first edition of this book (Cooper, 1984) suggested 11 threats to validity. Matt and Cook (1994) expanded this list to 21 threats; Shadish, Cook, and Campbell (2002) expanded the list to 29 threats; and then Matt and Cook (2009) pared the list back to 28 threats. Not only does the list of threats expand and contract, but list providers also differ somewhat in their construal of the general class of validity (construct, internal, external, or statistical) each specific threat might be related to. This is not a bad thing but a good one. It serves to emphasize that what we are working with here is a dynamic theory of evidence. As such, it is okay for theorists to disagree. It is a sign of vitality and suggests the future will hold even more progress and refinement in thinking.

In Tables 9.1 through 9.7, I provide a summary of the validity issues associated with each step in research synthesis. At the top of each table are general statements about the threats to validity associated with that step. Next, I provide a list of more specific threats to validity taken from Matt and Cook (2009; also found in Shadish et al., 2002) that I have tried to align with the seven steps. Just as these previous list makers disagreed somewhat about the placement of these threats into different broader classes, I am certain that others will disagree with my classification (I moved several into different steps myself before settling on final resting places). Also, I have listed only 24 of the threats proffered by previous list makers. I found that some of the threats appeared to be at least partially redundant in the concerns they covered.

Several of the threats to validity cataloged by Matt and Cook (1994, 2009) and by Shadish et al. (2002) that arise in the course of research synthesis are simply holdovers that represent pervasive problems in primary research. For instance, two threats to the validity of a synthesis' conclusions when data are being collected are that (a) the data from studies might not support conclusions about causal relations and (b) the people sampled in the covered studies might not be representative of the target population. This suggests that any threat associated with a particular primary research design is applicable to a synthesis' conclusions if the design characteristic appears in a substantial portion of the covered research. So, research designs should be examined carefully as potential moderators of study results. The creation of these "nomological nets" (Cronbach & Meehl, 1955) can be one of your synthesis' most valuable contributions. However, if an assortment of research designs (and participants, settings, and outcomes) is not contained in a synthesis, then threats associated with weaknesses in the dominant design features also threaten the synthesis' conclusions.

The last entries in Tables 9.1 through 9.7 summarize many of the good practices I mentioned in the previous chapters. Here, they are phrased in a way which shows how the practice will help protect your synthesis from the threats listed above them. You can use these tables along with Table 1.3, which lists the questions to ask about how a research synthesis was conducted, as summary guides to help you as you plan and execute your project.

Table 9.1 Questions Concerning the Validity of Research Synthesis Conclusions: Defining the Problem

---

General validity issues:

1. Poorly defined (a) constructs (both abstractly and operationally) and (b) relationships between constructs can lead to ambiguity in and/or misapplication of results to circumstances to which they are not relevant.

Specific validity threats:

Unreliability (of treatments and/or measures) of primary studies
Explanation: If individual studies are poorly implemented, it will be difficult to accurately define their treatments and outcomes.
Underrepresentation of prototypical attributes
Explanation: Synthesists may define their concepts in ways that suggest greater generality than the operations actually used in studies would warrant.

Protecting validity:

1. Undertake your literature searches with the broadest possible conceptual definitions in mind. Begin with a few central operations but remain open to the possibility that other relevant operations will be discovered in the literature. When operations of questionable relevance are encountered, err toward making overly inclusive decisions, at least in the early stages of your project.

2. As the literature is being searched, reevaluate the fit between your conceptual definitions and the operations you are finding. Adjust the conceptual definitions accordingly, so they accurately reflect what operations have been used in studies.

3. To complement conceptual broadness, be thorough in your attention to distinctions in study characteristics. Any suggestion that a difference in study results is associated with a distinction in study characteristics should receive some testing, if only in a preliminary analysis.

SOURCE: Validity threats in italics are taken from Shadish et al. (2002) and Matt and Cook (2009).

Table 9.2   Questions Concerning the Validity of Research Synthesis Conclusions: Searching the Literature

---

General validity issues:
1. Studies found by the literature search might be different in methods and results from the entire population of studies and therefore might lead to inaccurate portrayals of the cumulative evidence.

Specific validity threats:
  Publication bias
  Explanation: If only published studies are used in the meta-analysis, the findings may overestimate the strength of the relationship.

Protecting validity:
1. Conduct a broad and exhaustive search of the literature. A complete literature search has to include at least a search of reference databases, a perusal of relevant journals, an examination of references in related past primary research and research syntheses, and contact with active and interested researchers. The more exhaustive a search, the more confident you can be that another synthesist using similar, but perhaps not identical, sources of information will reach the same conclusions.

2. Present indices of potential retrieval bias, if they are available. For instance, many research syntheses examine whether any difference exists in the results of studies that are published versus those that are unpublished.

SOURCE: Validity threat in italics is taken from Shadish et al. (2002) and Matt and Cook (2009).

FEASIBILITY AND COST

It is considerably more expensive, in terms of both time and money, for synthesists to undertake a project using the guidelines set forth in this book than to conduct syntheses in a less rigorous manner. More people are involved who need to be compensated for their time. More time and resources are needed to search the literature, develop coding frames, run analyses, and prepare reports.

Given these costs, should a potential synthesist with limited resources be discouraged from undertaking such a project? Certainly not; just as the

Table 9.3   Questions Concerning the Validity of Research Synthesis Conclusions: Gathering Information From Studies

---

General validity issues:

1. Coders might incorrectly retrieve information from study reports that then misrepresent the studies in the cumulative analysis.

Specific validity threats:

Unreliability of coding in meta-analysis
Explanation: Unreliable coding can attenuate meta-analytic effect size estimates.
Rater drift
Explanation: Coders change their criteria for codes from one study to another (because of practice effects, fatigue, etc.)
Biased effect size sampling
Explanation: Only some of the plausibly relevant effect sizes are coded, and these favor one direction of findings.

Protecting validity:

1. Training and assessment procedures should be used to minimize unreliable retrieval of information from studies.
2. Intercoder agreement should be quantified and training should be continued until an acceptable level of agreement is reached.
3. Codes that lead to disagreement or low confidence should be discussed by multiple parties.
4. When possible, more than one coder should examine each study.

SOURCE: Validity threats in italics are taken from Shadish et al. (2002) and Matt and Cook (2009).

perfect, irrefutable primary study has never been conducted, so, too, the perfect synthesis remains an ideal. My guidelines represent more a yardstick for evaluating syntheses than a set of absolute requirements. In fact, you should be aware of several instances in which the syntheses I used as examples fell short of complete adherence to the guidelines. You should not hold the guidelines as absolute criteria that must be met but rather as targets that help you refine procedures until you strike a good balance between rigor and feasibility.

Table 9.4   Questions Concerning the Validity of Research Synthesis Conclusions: Evaluating the Correspondence Between the Methods and Implementation of Individual Studies and the Desired Inferences of the Synthesis

---

General validity issues:

1. Causal relationships are inferred when they are not supported by the evidence.

2. The use of nonquality factors to evaluate studies might result in the biased exclusion of studies or the improper weighting of studies in cumulative results.

Specific validity threats:

> *Absence of studies with successful random assignment*
> *Primary study attrition*
> Explanation: These two threats to validity occur within each study, so there is little the research synthesists can do to address them. If they are present in all or most studies, they create the threat that the synthesist may infer causal relationships that are not supported by the evidence.
> *Reactivity effects*
> Explanation: Coders are influenced by the expectations of the principal investigators.

Protecting validity:

1. Make every effort to ensure that only *a priori* conceptual and methodological judgments influence the decision to include or exclude studies from your synthesis, and not the results of the study.

2. If studies are to be weighted differently, your weighting scheme should be explicit and justifiable.

3. The approach used to categorize study methods should exhaust as many design characteristics as possible. Detail each design distinction that was related to study results and describe the outcome of the analysis.

SOURCE: Validity threats in italics are taken from Shadish et al. (2002) and Matt and Cook (2009).

THE SCIENTIFIC METHOD AND DISCONFIRMATION

While the practical aspects of conducting research syntheses may mean the investigator must settle for a less-than-perfect product, the ideals of science

Table 9.5 Questions Concerning the Validity of Research Synthesis Conclusions: Summarizing and Integrating the Evidence From Individual Studies

---

General validity issues:

1. Rules for summarizing and integrating data from the individual studies might be inappropriate and lead to incorrect cumulative results.

Specific validity threats:

Capitalization on chance
Explanation: Meta-analysts can test many relationships. If they do not adjust significance levels accordingly, they can inflate the likelihood that chance findings will appear statistically significant.

Lack of statistical independence among effect sizes
Explanation: If meta-analysts treat nonindependent effect sizes as if they were independent, they will overestimate the precision and power of their analyses.

Failure to weight study-level effect sizes proportional to their precision
Explanation: Meta-analysts who do not weight effect sizes (by the inverse of their sampling error) introduce imprecision into their estimates of average effect sizes

Inaccurate (low power) homogeneity tests
Explanation: Meta-analysts may conduct homogeneity tests that suffer from low statistical power

Underjustified use of fixed-error models
Explanation: Meta-analysts may use a fixed-effect model when the heterogeneity in effect sizes suggests a random-effect model is more appropriate.

Protecting validity:

Recommendations concerning what assumptions are appropriate for synthesists to make about their data will depend on the data in a particular problem area and the purposes of a synthesis. Therefore,

1. Be as explicit as possible about the assumptions that guided your analyses when you convey your conclusions and inferences to readers.

2. Your decision about the proper unit of analysis for your synthesis should be based both on statistical considerations and the nature of the particular problem under study. The approach you choose should be carefully described and justified.

3. If there is any evidence bearing on the validity of your interpretation rules, it should be presented.

SOURCE: Validity threats in italics are taken from Shadish et al. (2002) and Matt and Cook (2009).

Table 9.6   Questions Concerning the Validity of Research Synthesis Conclusions: Interpreting the Cumulative Evidence

---

General validity issues:

1. Cumulative results might be different if different statistical assumptions are used.
2. Missing data might cause results to be different than if all data were available.
3. Synthesis-generated evidence might be used to infer that moderator variables have a causal effect when a causal inference is not warranted.
4. The generality, magnitude, and/or importance of cumulative findings might be misrepresented.

Specific validity threats:

Missing effect sizes in primary studies

Bias in computing effect sizes (that must be estimated from other statistics)

Explanation: When data are missing, meta-analysts must omit or approximate effect sizes, and these approximation procedures can vary in accuracy.

Restricted range in primary studies

Explanation: If there is a restricted range of outcomes in the primary studies, these will attenuate the effect size estimates when they are combined in meta-analysis.

Moderator variable confounding

Explanation: Meta-analysts make claims about the causal relationship between a moderator and effect sizes when the moderator is correlated with other moderators.

Sampling biases associated with the persons, settings, treatments, outcomes, and times entering a meta-analysis

Restricted heterogeneity of substantively irrelevant third variables

Explanation: The above two threats occur because meta-analysts may overgeneralize to persons, settings, treatments, outcomes, and times not contained in the study samples.

Failure to test for heterogeneity in effect sizes

Explanation: Meta-analysts may not test moderator variables that account for systematic variation in effect sizes.

Lack of statistical power for homogeneity tests

Lack of statistical power for studying disaggregated groups

Explanation: When meta-analysts test for differences in effect sizes (a) averaged across subgroups of studies or (b) within subgroups of studies, they may not have sufficient statistical power to uncover important findings.

Restricted heterogeneity of irrelevancies

Explanation: A threat to the generality of the findings of a meta-analysis occurs when there is not enough variation in study attributes that are irrelevant to the relationship of interest, meaning the meta-analysts cannot test whether the effect holds across many situational variations.

Protecting validity:

1. State explicitly what conventions you used when incomplete or erroneous research reports were encountered.

2. Whenever possible, analyze your data using multiple procedures that require different assumptions. (Much greater confidence can be placed in results that do not vary across different analyses based on different assumptions.)

3. Summarize the sample characteristics of individuals used in the separate studies. Note important missing samples that may restrict generality.

SOURCE: Validity threats in italics are taken from Shadish et al. (2002) and Matt and Cook (2009).

Table 9.7 Questions Concerning the Validity of Research Synthesis Conclusions: Presenting the Research Synthesis Methods and Results

---

General validity issues:

1. Omission of synthesis procedures might make conclusions hard to evaluate with regard to plausible threats to validity, and difficult to reproduce.

Specific validity threats:

None

Protecting validity:

1. When writing your report, employ the Meta-Analysis Reporting Standards (MARS) presented in Table 8.1.

SOURCE: Validity threats in italics are taken from Shadish et al. (2002) and Matt and Cook (2009).

still must be strictly applied to the research synthesis process. The most crucial scientific element missing from haphazard synthesis procedures is the potential for the disconfirmation of the synthesist's prior beliefs. In most instances, primary researchers undertake their work with some recognition that the results of their study may alter their belief system. By extending the scientific method to research syntheses, we also expand the potential for disconfirmation. Ross and Lepper (1980) have stated this position nicely:

> We know all too well that the scientific method is not immune to the diseases of biased assimilation, causal explanation, and a host of other nagging afflictions; scientists can be blind, sometimes deliberately so, to unanticipated or uncongenial interpretations of their data and recalcitrant in their theoretical allegiances. . . . Nevertheless, it is the scientific method . . . that has often been responsible for increasing human understanding of the natural and social world. Despite its flaws, it remains the best means of delivering us from the errors of intuitive beliefs and intuitive methods for testing those beliefs. (p. 33)

CREATIVITY IN RESEARCH SYNTHESIS

Early in this text, I mentioned that one objection to the use of scientific guidelines for research synthesis is that this system stifles creativity. Critics who raise this issue think the rules for conducting and reporting primary research are a "straitjacket" on innovative thinking. I cannot disagree more. Rigorous criteria will not produce syntheses that are mechanical and uncreative. Your expertise and intuition will be challenged to capitalize on or create opportunities to obtain, evaluate, and analyze information unique to your problem area. I hope the syntheses examples have demonstrated the diversity and complexity of issues that confront those who adopt the scientific method. These challenges are created, not solved, by the rules of science.

CONCLUSION

I began this book with the supposition that research synthesis was a data-gathering exercise that needed to be evaluated against scientific criteria. Because of the growth in empirical research and the increased access to information, the conclusions of research syntheses will become less trustworthy unless we systematize the process and make it more rigorous. I hope that the concepts and techniques presented here have convinced you that it is feasible and desirable for social scientists to require rigorous syntheses. Such rules bring with them greater potential for creating consensus among scholars and for focusing discussion on specific and testable areas of disagreement when conflict does exist. Because of the increasing role that research syntheses play in our definition of knowledge, these adjustments in procedures are inevitable if social scientists hope to retain their claim to objectivity as well as their credibility with those who turn to scientists to help solve social problems and increase our understanding of the social world.

References

American Psychological Association. (2001). *Publication manual* (5th ed.). Washington, DC: Author.

American Psychological Association's Presidential Task Force on Evidence-Based Practice. (2006). Evidence-based practice in psychology. *American Psychologist, 61*, 271–283.

APA Publications and Communications Board Working Group on Journal Article Reporting Standards. (2008). Reporting standards for research in psychology: Why do we need them? What might they be? *American Psychologist, 63*, 839–851.

Anderson, K. B., Cooper, H., & Okamura, L. (1997). Individual differences and attitudes toward rape: A meta-analytic review. *Personality and Social Psychology Bulletin, 23*, 295–315.

Atkinson, D. R., Furlong, M. J., & Wampold, B. E. (1982). Statistical significance, reviewer evaluations, and the scientific process: Is there a (statistically) significant relationship? *Journal of Counseling Psychology, 29*, 189–194.

Barber, T. X. (1978). Expecting expectancy effects: Biased data analyses and failure to exclude alternative interpretations in experimenter expectancy research. *The Behavioral and Brain Sciences, 3*, 388–390.

Barnett, V., & Lewis, T. (1984). *Outliers in statistical data* (2nd ed.). New York: Wiley.

Becker, B. J. (2005, November). *Synthesizing slopes in meta-analysis.* Paper presented at the meeting on Research Synthesis and Meta-Analysis: State of the Art and Future Directions, Durham, NC.

Becker, B. J. (2009). Model-based meta-analysis. In H. Cooper, L. V. Hedges, & J. C. Valentine (Eds.), *The handbook of research synthesis and meta-analysis* (2nd ed., pp. 377–395). New York: Russell Sage Foundation.

Becker, B. J., & Wu, M. (2007). The synthesis of regression slopes in meta-analysis. *Statistical Science, 22*, 414–429.

Begg, C. B., & Berlin, J. A. (1988). Publication bias: A problem in interpreting medical research. *Journal of the Royal Statistical Society, Series A, 151*, 419–463.

Begg, C. B., & Mazumdar, M. (1994). Operating characteristics of a rank correlation test for publication bias. *Biometrics, 50*, 1088–1101.

Bem, D. J. (1967). Self-perception: An alternative interpretation of cognitive dissonance phenomena. *Psychological Review, 74*, 183–200.

Berlin, J. A., & Ghersi, D. (2005). Preventing publication bias: Registers and prospective meta-analysis. In H. R. Rothstein, A. J. Sutton, & M. Borenstein (Eds.), *Publication bias in meta-analysis: Prevention, assessment and adjustments* (pp. 35–48). West Sussex, England: John Wiley & Sons.

Borenstein, M. (2009). Effect sizes for studies with continuous data. In H. Cooper, L. V. Hedges, & J. C. Valentine (Eds.), *The handbook of research synthesis and meta-analysis* (2nd ed., pp. 221–352). New York: Russell Sage Foundation.

Borenstein, M., Hedges, L.V., Higgins J., & Rothstein, H. (2005). *Comprehensive meta-analysis, version 2.* Englewood, NJ: Biostat.

Borman, G. D., & Grigg, J. A. (2009). The visual and narrative interpretation of research synthesis. In H. Cooper, L. V. Hedges, & J. C. Valentine (Eds.), *The handbook of research synthesis and meta-analysis,*(2nd ed., pp. 497–519). New York: Russell Sage Foundation.

Boruch, R. F. (1997). *Randomized experiments for planning and evaluation.* Thousand Oaks, CA: Sage.

Bourque, L. B., & Clark, V. A. (1992). *Processing data.* Newbury Park, CA: Sage.

Bracht, G. H., & Glass, G. V. (1968). The external validity of experiments. *American Educational Research Journal, 5,* 437–474.

Bradley, J. V. (1981). Pernicious publication practices. *Bulletin of Psychonomic Society, 18,* 31–34.

Brown, S. P. (1996). A meta-analysis and review of organizational research on job involvement. *Psychological Bulletin, 120,* 235–255.

Bushman, B. J., & Wang, M. C. (1996). A procedure for combining sample standardized mean differences and vote counts to estimate the population standardized mean difference in fixed effects models. *Psychological Methods, 1,* 66–80.

Bushman, B. J., & Wang, M. C. (2009). Vote counting procedures in meta-analysis. In H. Cooper, L. V. Hedges, & J. C. Valentine (Eds.), *The handbook of research synthesis and meta-analysis* (2nd ed., pp. 207–220). New York: Russell Sage Foundation.

Campbell Collaboration. (2008). *Campbell Collaboration: What helps? What harms? Based on what evidence?* Retrieved February 13, 2008, from http://www.campbell collaboration.org/

Campbell, D. T. (1969). Reforms as experiments. *American Psychologist, 24,* 409–429.

Campbell, D. T., & Stanley, J. C. (1963). *Experimental and quasi-experimental designs for research.* Chicago: Rand McNally.

Carlson, M., & Miller, N. (1987). Explanation of the relation between negative mood and helping. *Psychological Bulletin, 102,* 91–108.

Chalmers, I., Hedges, L. V., & Cooper, H. (2002). A brief history of research synthesis. *Evaluation & the Health Professions, 25,* 12–37.

Coalition for Evidence–Based Policy. (2008). *Coalition for Evidence-Based Policy.* Retrieved February 13, 2008, from http://prod.ceg.rd.net/Programs/ProgramDetail .cfm?ItemNumber=9711&navItemNumber=9447

Cochrane Collaboration. (2008). *The Cochrane Collaboration: Reliable source of evidence in health care.* Retrieved February 13, 2008, from http://www.cochrane.org/ index.htm

Cohen, J. (1988). *Statistical power analysis for the behavior sciences* (2nd ed.). New York: Academic Press.

Cohen, J. (1994). The earth is round (p < .05). *American Psychologist, 49,* 997–1003.

Conn, V. S., Valentine, J. C., & Cooper, H. (2002). Interventions to increase physical activity among aging adults: A meta-analysis. *Annals of Behavior Medicine, 24,* 190–200.

Cook, D. J., Sackett, D. L., & Spitzer, W. O. (1995). Methodologic guidelines for systematic reviews of randomized control trails in health care from the Potsdam consultation on meta-analysis. *Journal of Clinical Epidemiology, 48,* 167–171.

Cook, T. D., & Campbell, D. T. (1979). *Quasi-experimentation.* Chicago: Rand McNally.

Cook, T. D., Cooper, H., Cordray, D. S., Hartmann, H., Hedges, L. V., Light, R. J., et al. (1992). *Meta-analysis for explanation: A casebook.* New York: Russell Sage Foundation.

Cooper, H. (1982). Scientific guidelines for conducting integrative research reviews. *Review of Educational Research, 52,* 291–302.

Cooper, H. (1984). *The integrative research review: A systematic approach.* Newbury Park, CA: Sage.

Cooper, H. (1986). On the social psychology of using research reviews: The case of desegregation and black achievement. In R. Feldman (Ed.), *The social psychology of education* (pp. 341–364). Cambridge, England: Cambridge University Press.

Cooper, H. (1988). Organizing knowledge syntheses: A taxonomy of literature reviews. *Knowledge in Society, 1,* 104–126

Cooper, H. (1989). *Homework.* New York: Longman.

Cooper, H. (2006). Research questions and research designs. In P. A. Alexander, P. H. Winne, & G. Phye (Eds.), *Handbook of research in educational psychology* (2nd ed., pp. 849–877). Mahwah, NJ: Lawrence Erlbaum.

Cooper, H. (2007a). *Evaluating and interpreting research syntheses in adult learning and literacy.* Boston: National College Transition Network, New England Literacy Resource Center/World Education.

Cooper, H. (2007b). *The battle over homework: Common ground for administrators, teachers, and parents* (3rd ed.). Thousand Oaks, CA: Corwin Press.

Cooper, H. (2009). The search for meaningful ways to express the effects of interventions. *Child Development Perspectives, 2,* 181-186.

Cooper, H., Charlton, K., Valentine, J. C., & Muhlenbruck, L. (2000). *Making the most of summer school.* Malden, MA: Blackwell.

Cooper, H., DeNeve, K., & Charlton, K. (1997). Finding the missing science: The fate of studies submitted for review by a human subjects committee. *Psychological Methods, 2,* 447–452.

Cooper, H., Hedges, L. V., & Valentine J. C. (2009). *The handbook of research synthesis and meta-analysis* (2nd ed.). New York: Russell Sage Foundation.

Cooper, H., Jackson, K., Nye, B., & Lindsay, J. J. (2001). A model of homework's influence on the performance evaluations of elementary school students. *Journal of Experimental Education, 69,* 181–202.

Cooper, H., & Patall, E. A. (in press). The relative benefits of meta-analysis using individual participant data and aggregate data. *Psychological Methods.*

Cooper, H. M., Patall, E. A., & Lindsay, J. J. (2009). Research synthesis and meta-analysis. In L. Bickman and D. Rog (Eds.), *Applied social research methods handbook* (2nd ed., pp. 344–370). Thousand Oaks, CA: Sage.

Cooper, H., & Ribble, R. G. (1989). Influences on the outcome of literature searches for integrative research reviews. *Knowledge: Creation, Diffusion, Utilization, 10,* 179–201.

Cooper, H., Robinson, J. C., & Patall, E. A. (2006). Does homework improve academic achievement? A synthesis of research, 1987–2003. *Review of Educational Research, 76,* 1–62.

Cooper, H., & Rosenthal, R. (1980). Statistical versus traditional procedures for summarizing research findings. *Psychological Bulletin, 87,* 442–449.

Crane, D. (1969). Social structure in a group of scientists: A test of the "invisible college" hypothesis. *American Sociological Review, 34,* 335–352.

Cronbach, L. J., & Meehl, P. E., (1955). Construct validity in psychological tests. *Psychological Bulletin, 52,* 281–302.

Cuadra, C. A., & Katter, R. V. (1967). Opening the black box of relevance. *Journal of Documentation, 23,* 291–303.

Davidson, D. (1977). The effects of individual differences of cognitive style on judgments of document relevance. *Journal of the American Society for Information Science, 8,* 273–284.

Deci, E. L. (1980). *The psychology of self-determination.* Lexington, MA: Heath.

Dickerson, K. (2005). Publication bias: Recognizing the problem, understanding its origins and scope, and preventing harm. In H. R. Rothstein, A. J. Sutton, & M. Borenstein (Eds.). *Publication bias in meta-analysis: Prevention, assessment and adjustments* (pp. 11–33). West Sussex, England: John Wiley & Sons.

Duval, S. (2005). The trim-and-fill method. In H. R. Rothstein, A. J. Sutton, & M. Borenstein (Eds.), *Publication bias in meta-analysis: Prevention, assessment and adjustments* (pp. 127–144). Chichester, UK: John Wiley & Sons.

Duval, S., & Tweedie, R. (2000a). A nonparametric "trim and fill" method of accounting for publication bias in meta-analysis. *Journal of the American Statistical Association, 95,* 89–98.

Duval, S., & Tweedie, R. (2000b). Trim and fill: A simple funnel plot-based method of testing and adjusting for publication bias in meta-analysis. *Biometrics, 56,* 276–284.

Eddy, D. M., Hasselblad, V., & Schachter, R. (1992). *Meta-analysis by the confidence profile approach.* Boston: Academic Press.

Egger, M., Davey Smith, G., Schneider, M., & Minder, C. (1997). Bias in meta-analysis detected by a simple, graphical test. *British Medical Journal, 315,* 629–634.

Elmes, D. G., Kantowitz, B. H., & Roediger, H. L. (2005). *Research methods in psychology* (8th ed.). St. Paul, MN: West.

Eysenck, H. J. (1978). An exercise in mega-silliness. *American Psychologist, 33,* 517.

Feldman, K. A. (1971). Using the work of others: Some observations on reviewing and integrating. *Sociology of Education, 4,* 86–102.

Festinger, L., & Carlsmith, J. M. (1959). Cognitive consequences of forced compliance. *Journal of Abnormal and Social Psychology, 58,* 203–210.

Fisher, R. A. (1932). *Statistical methods for research workers.* London, England: Oliver & Boyd.

Fiske, D. W., & Fogg, L. (1990). But the reviewers are making different criticisms of my paper! *American Psychologist, 45,* 591–598.

Fleiss, J. L., & Berlin, J. A. (2009). Measures of effect size for categorical data. In H. Cooper, L.V. Hedges, & J. C. Valentine, *The handbook of research synthesis and meta-analysis* (2nd ed., pp. 237–253). New York: Russell Sage Foundation.

Fowler, F. J. (2002). *Survey research methods* (3rd ed.). Thousand Oaks, CA: Sage.

Garvey, W. D., & Griffith, B. C. (1971). Scientific communication: Its role in the conduct of research and creation of knowledge. *American Psychologist, 26,* 349–361.

Glass, G. V. (1976). Primary, secondary, and meta-analysis of research. *Educational Researcher, 5,* 3–8.

Glass, G. V. (1977). Integrating findings: The meta-analysis of research. In *Review of research in education, Vol. 5*. Itasca, IL: F. E. Peacock.

Glass, G. V., McGaw, B., & Smith, M. L. (1981). *Meta-analysis in social research*. Beverly Hills, CA: Sage.

Glass, G. V., & Smith, M. L. (1978). Reply to Eysenck. *American Psychologist, 33*, 517–518.

Glass, G. V., & Smith, M. L. (1979). Meta-analysis of research on the relationship of class size and achievement. *Educational Evaluation and Policy Analysis, 1*, 2–16.

Gleser, L. J., & Olkin, I. (2009). Stochastically dependent effect sizes. In H. Cooper, L. V. Hedges, & J. C. Valentine (Eds.), *The handbook of research synthesis and meta-analysis* (2nd ed., pp. 357–376). New York: Russell Sage Foundation.

Gottfredson, S. D. (1978). Evaluating psychological research reports. *American Psychologist, 33*, 920–934.

Graham, S. (1994). Motivation in African Americans. *Review of Educational Research, 64*, 55–117.

Greenberg, J., & Folger, R. (1988). *Controversial issues in social research methods*. New York: Springer-Verlag.

Greenwald, A. G. (1975). Consequences of prejudices against the null hypothesis. *Psychological Bulletin, 82*, 1–20.

Greenwald, R., Hedges, L. V., & Laine, R. (1996). The effects of school resources on student achievement. *Review of Educational Research, 66*, 411–416.

Grubbs, F. E. (1950). Sample criteria for testing outlying observations. *Journal of the American Statistical Association, 21*, 27–58.

Hall, L. D., & Romaniuk, B. (2008). *Gale directory of databases*. London: Gale Cengage.

Harris, M. J., & Rosenthal, R. (1985). Mediation of interpersonal expectancy effects: 31 meta-analyses. *Psychological Bulletin, 97*, 363–386.

Hartung, J., Knapp, G., & Sinha, B. K. (2008). *Statistical meta-analysis with applications*. Hoboken, NJ: Wiley.

Hedges, L. V. (1980). Unbiased estimation of effect size. *Evaluation in Education: An International Review Series, 4*, 25–27.

Hedges, L. V. (1982). Fitting categorical models to effect sizes from a series of experiments. *Journal of Educational Statistics, 7*(2), 119–137.

Hedges, L. V. (1994). Fixed effects models. In H. Cooper & L. V. Hedges (Eds.), *The handbook of research synthesis*. New York: Russell Sage Foundation.

Hedges, L. V., & Olkin, I. (1980). Vote-counting methods in research synthesis. *Psychological Bulletin, 88*, 359–369.

Hedges, L., & Olkin, I. (1985). *Statistical methods for meta-analysis*. Orlando: Academic Press.

Hedges, L. V. & Vevea, J. L. (1998). Fixed and random effects models in meta-analysis. *Psychological Methods, 3*, 486–504.

Hunt, M. (1997). *How science takes stock: The story of meta-analysis*. New York: Russell Sage Foundation.

Hunter, J. E., & Schmidt, F. L. (2004). *Methods of meta-analysis: Correcting error and bias in research findings*. Thousand Oaks, CA: Sage.

Hunter, J. E., Schmidt, F. L., & Hunter, R. (1979). Differential validity of employment tests by race: A comprehensive review and analysis. *Psychological Bulletin, 86*, 721–735.

Hunter, J. E., Schmidt, F. L., & Jackson, G. B. (1982). *Meta-analysis: Cumulating research findings across studies.* Beverly Hills, CA: Sage.

Jackson, G. B. (1980). Methods for integrative reviews. *Review of Educational Research, 50,* 438–460.

Johnson, B. T. (1993). DSTAT: Software for the meta-analytic synthesis of research [Book, update, and disc]. Hillsdale, NJ: Erlbaum.

Johnson, B. T., & Eagly, A. H. (2000). Quantitative synthesis of social psychological research. In H. T. Reis & C. M. Judd (Eds.), *Handbook of research methods in social and personality psychology* (pp. 496–528). New York: Cambridge University Press.

Jüni, P., Witshci, A., Bloch, R., & Egger, M. (1999). The hazards of scoring the quality of clinical trials for meta-analysis. *Journal of the American Medical Association, 282,* 1054–1060.

Justice, A. C., Berlin, J. A., Fletcher, S. W., & Fletcher, R. A. (1994). Do readers and peer reviewers agree on manuscript quality? *Journal of the American Medical Association, 272,* 117–119.

Kane, T. J. (2004). *The impact of after-school programs: Interpreting the results of four recent evaluations.* New York: William T. Grant Foundation.

Kazdin, A., Durac, J., & Agteros, T. (1979). Meta–meta analysis: A new method for evaluating therapy outcome. *Behavioral Research and Therapy, 17,* 397–399.

Kline, R. B. (1998). *Principles and practices of structural equation modeling.* New York: Guilford Press.

Kline, R. B. (2004). *Beyond significance testing: Reforming data analysis methods in behavioral research.* Washington, DC: American Psychological Association.

Levin, H. M. (2002). *Cost-effectiveness and educational policy.* Larchmont, NY: Eye on Education.

Light, R. J., & Pillemer, D. B. (1984). *Summing up: The science of reviewing research.* Cambridge, MA: Harvard University.

Light, R. J. & Smith, P. V. (1971). Accumulating evidence: Procedures for resolving contradictions among research studies. *Harvard Educational Review, 41,* 429–471.

Lipsey, M. W., & Wilson, D. B. (1993). The efficacy of psychological, educational, and behavioral treatment: Confirmation from meta-analysis. *American Psychologist, 48,* 1181–1209.

Lipsey, M. W., & Wilson, D. B. (2001). *Practical meta-analysis.* Thousand Oaks, CA: Sage.

Lord, C. G., Ross, L., & Lepper, M. R. (1979). Biased assimilation and attitude polarization: The effects of prior theories on subsequently considered evidence. *Journal of Personality and Social Psychology, 37,* 2098–2109.

Mahoney, M. J. (1977). Publication prejudices: An experimental study of confirmatory bias in the peer review system. *Cognitive Therapy and Research, 1,* 161–175.

Mann, T. (2005). *The Oxford guide to library research.* New York: Oxford University Press.

Mansfield, R. S., & Bussey, T. V. (1977). Meta-analysis of research: A rejoinder to Glass. *Educational Researcher, 6,* 3.

Marsh, H. W., & Ball, S. (1989). The peer review process used to evaluate manuscripts submitted to academic journals: Interjudgmental reliability. *Journal of Experimental Education, 57,* 151–170.

Matt, G. E., & Cook, T. D. (1994). Threats to the validity of research syntheses. In H. Cooper & L. V. Hedges (Eds.), *The handbook of research synthesis* (pp. 503–520). New York: Russell Sage Foundation.

Matt, G. E., & Cook, T. D. (2009). Threats to the validity of generalized inferences from research syntheses. In H. Cooper, L. V. Hedges, & J. C. Valentine (Eds.). *The handbook of research synthesis and meta–analysis* (pp. 537–560). New York: Russell Sage Foundation.

McGrath, J. B. (1992). Student and parental homework practices and the effect of English homework on student test scores. *Dissertation Abstracts International, 53*(10A), 3490. (UMI No. 9231359)

McPadden, K., & Rothstein, H. R. (2006, August). *Finding the missing papers: The fate of best paper proceedings.* Paper presented at AOM Conferences, Academy of Management Annual Meeting, Atlanta, GA.

Miller, N., Lee, J. Y., & Carlson, M. (1991). The validity of inferential judgments when used in theory-testing meta-analysis. *Personality and Social Psychology Bulletin, 17*, 335–343.

Moher, D., Cook, D. J., Eastwood, S., Olkin, I., Rennie, D., & Stroup, D., for the QUOROM group. (1999). Improving the quality of reporting of meta-analysis of randomized controlled trials: The QUOROM statement. *Lancet, 354*, 1896–1900.

Moher, D., Tetzlaff, J., Liberati, A., Altman, D. G., & the PRISMA Group. (2008). *Preferred reporting items for systematic reviews and meta-analysis: the PRISMA statement.* (Manuscript under review).

Mullen, B. (1989). *Advanced BASIC meta-analysis.* Hillsdale, NJ: Lawrence Erlbaum.

New shorter Oxford English dictionary. (1993). Oxford, England: Clarendon Press.

Noblit, G. W., & Hare, R. D. (1988). *Meta-ethnography: Synthesizing qualitative studies.* Newbury Park, CA: Sage.

Noether, G. (1971). *Introduction to statistics: A fresh approach.* Boston: Houghton Mifflin.

Nunnally, J. (1960). The place of statistics in psychology. *Education and Psychological Measurement, 20*, 641–650.

Olkin, I. (1990). History and goals. In K. Wachter & M. Straf (Eds.), *The future of meta-analysis.* New York: Russell Sage Foundation.

Orwin, R. G., & Vevea, J. L. (2009). Evaluating coding decisions. In H. Cooper, L. V. Hedges, & J. C. Valentine, *The handbook of research synthesis and meta-analysis* (2nd ed., pp. 177–203). New York: Russell Sage Foundation.

Overton, R. C. (1998). A comparison of fixed-effects and mixed (random-effects) models for meta–analysis tests of moderator variable effects. *Psychological Methods, 3*, 354–379.

Patall, E. A., Cooper, H., & Robinson, J. C. (2008). The effects of choice on intrinsic motivation and related outcomes: A meta-analysis of research findings. *Psychological Bulletin, 134*(2), 270–300.

Paterson, B. L., Thorne, S. E., Canam, C., & Jillings, C. (2001). *Meta-study of qualitative health research.* Thousand Oaks, CA: Sage.

Pearson, K. (1904). Report on certain enteric fever inoculation statistics. *British Medical Journal, 3*, 1243–1246.

Peek, P., & Pomerantz, J. (1998) Electronic scholarly journal publishing. In M. E. Williams (Ed.), *Annual review of information science and technology* (pp. 321–356). Medford, NJ: Information Today.

Peters, D. P., & Ceci, S. J. (1982). Peer-review practices of psychological journals: The fate of published articles, submitted again. *The Behavioral and Brain Sciences, 5*, 187255.

Pigott, T. D. (2009). Methods for handling missing data in research synthesis. In H. Cooper, L.V. Hedges, & J. C. Valentine (Eds.), *The handbook of research synthesis and meta-analysis* (2nd ed., pp. 399–416). New York: Russell Sage Foundation.

Pope, C., Mays, N., & Popay, J. (2007). *Synthesizing qualitative and quantitative health evidence: A guide to methods.* Berkshire, England: Open University Press.

Popper, K. (2002). *The logic of scientific discovery* (Routledge Classics). London, England: Routledge.

Price, D. (1965). Networks of scientific papers. *Science, 149,* 510–515.

Promising Practices Network (PPN). (2007). *How programs are considered.* Retrieved March 25, 2007, from http://www.promisingpractices.net/criteria.asp

Randolph, J. J., & Shawn, R. (2005). Using the binomial effect size display (BESD) to present the magnitude of effect sizes to the evaluation audiences. *Practical Assessment, Research & Evaluation, 10*(14), 1–7.

Raudenbush, S. W. (2009). Random effects models. In H. Cooper, L. V. Hedges, & J. C. Valentine (Eds.), *The handbook of research synthesis and meta-analysis* (2nd ed., pp. 295–315). New York: Russell Sage Foundation.

Reed, J. G., & Baxter, P. M. (2003). *Library use: A handbook for psychology* (3rd ed.). Washington, DC: American Psychological Association.

Reed, J. G., & Baxter, P. M. (2009). Using reference databases. In H. Cooper, L. V. Hedges, & J. C. Valentine (Eds.), *The handbook of research synthesis and meta-analysis.* New York: Russell Sage Foundation.

Roberts, H., & Petticrew, M. (2006). *Systematic reviews in the social sciences: A practical guide.* Oxford, UK: Blackwell Publishing.

Rosenthal, R. (1978). How often are our numbers wrong? *American Psychologist, 33,* 1005–1008.

Rosenthal, R. (1979a). The "file drawer problem" and tolerance for null results. *Psychological Bulletin, 86,* 638–641.

Rosenthal, R. (1982). Valid interpetation of quantitative research results. *New Directions for Methodology of Social and Behavioral Science, 12,* 59–75.

Rosenthal, R. (1984). *Meta-analytic procedures for social research.* Newbury Park, CA: Sage.

Rosenthal, R. (1990). How are we doing in soft psychology? *American Psychologist, 45,* 775–777.

Rosenthal, R., & Rubin, D. B. (1978). Interpersonal expectancy effects: The first 345 studies. *Behavioral and Brain Sciences, 3,* 377–386.

Rosenthal, R., & Rubin, D. (1982). A simple, general purpose display of magnitude of experimental effect. *Journal of Educational Psychology, 74,* 166–169.

Ross, L., & Lepper, M. R. (1980). The perseverance of beliefs: Empirical and normative considerations. *New Directions for Methodology of Social and Behavioral Science, 4,* 17–36.

SAS. (1992). *SAS* (Version 6) [Computer software]. Cary, NC: SAS Institute.

Scarr, S., & Weber, B. L. R. (1978). The reliability of reviews for the *American Psychologist. American Psychologist, 33,* 935.

Schram, C. M. (1989). *An examination of differential-photocopying.* Paper presented at the annual meeting of the American Educational Research Association, San Francisco.

Shadish, W. R., Cook, T. D., & Campbell, D. T. (2002). *Experimental and quasi-experimental designs for generalized causal inference.* Boston: Houghton Mifflin.

Shadish, W. R., & Haddock, K. (2009). Combining estimates of effect sizes. In H. Cooper, L. V. Hedges, & J. C. Valentine (Eds.), *The handbook of research synthesis and meta-analysis* (2nd ed., pp. 257–277). New York: Russell Sage Foundation.

Shadish, W. R., & Rindskopf, D. M. (2007). Methods for evidence-based practice: Quantitative synthesis of single-subject designs. *New Directions for Evaluation, 113,* 95–109.

Smith, M. L., & Glass, G. V. (1977). Meta-analysis of psychotherapy outcome studies. *American Psychologist, 32,* 752–760.

SPSS. (1990). *SPSS* [Computer software]. Chicago: SPSS.

Stock, W. A., Okun, M. A., Haring, M. J., Miller, W., & Kinney, C. (1982). Rigor and data synthesis: A case study of reliability in meta-analysis. *Educational Researcher, 11*(6), 10–14.

Stroup, D. F., Berlin, J. A., Morton, S. C., Olkin, I., Williamson, G. D., Rennie, D., et al. (2000). Meta-analysis of observational studies in epidemiology. *Journal of the American Medical Association, 283,* 2008–2012.

Sutton, A. J., Abrams, K. R., Jones, D. R., Sheldon, T. A., & Song, F. (2000) *Methods for meta-analysis in medical research.* Chichester, England: John Wiley & Sons.

Taveggia, T.C. (1974). Resolving research controversy through empirical cumulation. *Sociological Methods and Research, 2,* 395–407.

Valentine, J. C., & Cooper, H. (2008). A systematic and transparent approach for assessing the methodological quality of intervention effectiveness research: The study design and implementation assessment device (Study DIAD). *Psychological Methods, 13,* 130–149.

Wachter, K. W., & Straf, M. L. (Eds.). (1990). *The future of meta-analysis.* New York: Russell Sage Foundation.

Wang, M. C., & Bushman, B. J. (1999). *A step-by-step approach to using the SAS system for meta-analysis.* Cary NC: SAS Institute.

Webb, E. J., Campbell, D. T., Schwartz, R. D., Sechrest, L., & Grove, J. B. (1981). *Nonreactive measures in the social sciences.* Boston: Houghton Mifflin.

What Works Clearinghouse (2007). *Review process: Standards.* Retrieved February 26, 2007, from http://ies.ed.gov/ncee/wwc/references/standards/

Wilson, D. B. (2009). Systematic coding for research synthesis. In H. Cooper, L. V. Hedges, & J. C. Valentine, *The handbook of research synthesis and meta-analysis* (2nd ed., pp. 159–176). New York: Russell Sage Foundation.

Xhignesse, L. V., & Osgood, C. (1967). Bibliographical citation characteristics of the psychological journal network in 1950 and 1960. *American Psychologist, 22,* 779–791.

Xu, J., & Corno, L. (1998). Case studies of families doing third grade homework. *Teachers College Record, 100,* 402–436.

Younger, M., & Warrington, M. (1996). Differential achievement of girls and boys at GCSE: Some observations from the perspective of one school. *British Journal of Sociology of Education, 17*(3), 299–313.

Author Index

Subject Index